TEACHING PRIDE FORWARD

Building LGBTQ+ Allyship in English Language Teaching

EDITED BY

Ethan Trinh, Kate Mastruserio Reynolds, and James Coda

bookstore.tesol.org

TESOL International Association
1925 Ballenger Avenue, Ste. 550
Alexandria, VA 22314 USA
www.tesol.org

Associate Director of Publications: Tomiko Breland
Copy Editor: Sarah J. Duffy
Reviewers: Jill Hakemian, Rabia Hos, Irina Levy
Cover and Interior Design: Citrine Sky Design
Head of Education and Events: Sarah Sahr

Recommended citation:
Trinh, E., Reynolds, K. M., & Coda, J. (2024). *Teaching pride forward: Building LGBTQ+ allyship in English language teaching.* TESOL Press.

ISBN 978-1-953745-20-0
ISBN (ebook) 978-1-953745-21-7
Library of Congress Control Number 2024931460

Table of Contents

Part 3: The Americas

Part 4: Moving Forward

Preface

Ethan Trinh, Kate Mastruserio Reynolds, and James Coda

The opening chapters are emotionally challenging to write. We all believe that we, as human beings, are born free and equal and deserve respect, dignity, and rights. Before we begin, we feel it is important to note that this book is not an effort to indoctrinate anyone or push Western values on other cultures; rather, this book is a scholarly exploration of how allies of LGBTQ+ (lesbian, gay, bisexual, transgender, and queer, among others) community members advocate for equal rights of humans, no matter what their sexual orientation or their gender identity is. Reading the chapters of this book and working with different authors around the world reaffirm to us, the editors, that building allyship in and beyond the teaching, research, and activism spaces is undeniably complex, never-ending, always changing, always partial, and always emotional, and thus requires a lot of patience, mutual understanding, respect, communication, and—the most important factor—love for each and every individual who engages in this heavy work.

Let us play with the word *allyship* a bit. Let us break down the words *ally* and *ship* metaphorically. The word *ship* standing separately describes a large watercraft that contains cargo and passengers to travel the ocean and carries us to shore no matter what problems will be in the way. Let us use a metaphor here. Imagine allies are the passengers on this ship and our ideologies, cultural backgrounds, upbringing, and so on are the suitcases we bring with us. The diversity of different suitcases is one of the factors to make the ship unique, fabulous, and multidimensional. On this ship, we as allies are traveling together to overcome the issues of homophobia, transphobia, racism, colorism, and linguistic oppression, among others. We do not travel alone. We travel together. As we travel together on this ship, we need to come to learn with each other, set our community's ground rules of communication, and share our knowledge and understanding in order to overcome the barriers and arrive safely. Therefore, before launching and "sailing this ship," we the editors want to invite all of you the passengers to open your hearts and minds, read the book, and engage with us compassionately. Be ready for some uncomfortable moments; it is **okay** to have these moments because they are the moments of unlearning to relearn. We hope that you will read and listen to the voices of this book with compassion so that you can start the queering/querying process with the editors and the authors sailing forward.

Teaching Pride Forward in Building Global LGBTQ+ Allyship in English Language Teaching: A Queer Introduction

Ethan Trinh, Kate Mastruserio Reynolds, and James Coda

Allyship

> "All human beings are born free and equal in dignity and rights."
>
> *United Nations,* Universal Declaration of Human Rights, *1948, 2019*

The essence of what an ally is and does is multifaceted. An ally in the world of English language teaching (ELT) may support and advocate for multilingual learners of English or peers from the LGBTQ+ community. Those peers may be other educators working in the same school/university or in the profession. As Brown and Ostrove (2013) stated, "Allies can be distinguished from individuals who are motivated simply to express minimal or no prejudice toward nondominant people. Allies are people willing to take action, either interpersonally or in larger social settings, and move beyond self-regulation of prejudice" (p. 2212). Allies are different from friends in that allies act effectively and productively on behalf of LGBTQ+ friends, colleagues, or peers (Becker et al., 2013), and it depends on what the ally says and does.

Confronting inequalities and communicating messaging with others are obviously important advocacy strategies (Selvanathan et al., 2020) when handled deftly. One can imagine two contrasting examples. In the first instance, an ally may observe a supervisor speaking derogatorily behind the back of an LGBTQ+ colleague and pull the supervisor aside to privately and gently share that this practice is inequitable and humiliating for the peer. In this case, the ally is productive and supportive, using their words to address inequity. Imagine another situation in which the ally is aggressive, angry, or divisive in their handling of the situation. If the ally does not treat the situation with finesse and respect for the supervisor, the LGBTQ+ peer may experience more, not less, prejudice and discrimination. We can connect these examples to the notion of *performative allyship,*[1] which is a concept that suggests the actions and language used by the ally in demonstrating their physical or symbolic solidarity with their student, peer, or friend can be positive or negative. Preparing allies, then, becomes vitally important!

---

1. The term *perfomative allyship* does not critique the level of commitment on the part of the ally or imply that allyship is only a surface-level performance.

Much of the literature on allyship, or *prosocial behavior*, focuses on the motivation of the ally. Allyship has a range of motivations. If these motivations are placed on a continuum, one end would have altruist motivations and the other end would have unconscious bias or prejudice. Unconscious bias or prejudice is included because the ally may be motivated to help because the recipient is perceived as not being able to act on their own (van Leeuwen & Zagefka, 2017). We thus must be careful in our support of the LGBTQ+ community so that we will act for altruistic reasons and constantly interrogate ourselves about motivations and thinking toward individuals in the community.

As an ally, we might feel motivated for the right reasons, but we need to be careful, too, that the community member wants the support of an ally. According to Selvanathan et al. (2020), individuals who are marginalized prefer their advantaged group allies to empower them and let them lead social change movements. Allies may take the reins and inadvertently tread on the feet of the individual for whom they are advocating. As such, individuals from marginalized groups would prefer allies to participate in efforts that explicitly challenge inequality and express anger through direct action (e.g., confronting discrimination, showing up to protests organized by the marginalized group) because it promotes feelings of empowerment (Selvanathan et al., 2020, p. 1350). Additionally, these strategies communicate support to the individual. Finally, individuals from marginalized groups hope allies will provide autonomy-oriented (and avoid dependency-oriented) help (e.g., desiring allies to show up to protests organized by marginalized groups, but remain in the background), again because it promotes feelings of empowerment (Selvanathan et al., 2020, p. 1351). Droogendyk et al. (2016) suggested allies take on the role of an accomplice or sidekick rather than seeing themselves as a hero or champion of a movement. In sum, allies occupy an important role in promoting the perception that participation in the social movement is socially and morally acceptable, which in turn creates more allies (Selvanathan et al., 2020, p. 1354).

Queer Allyship in English Language Teaching

In ELT, the insights of queer theory and pedagogies have been taken up in research, curriculum, materials, and pedagogy and have been referred to as queer inquiry and thinking (Nelson, 1999, 2020). Scholastic and pedagogical employment of queer theory and pedagogies in classrooms has not only centered on practicality (Paiz, 2020), inclusivity (Reynolds, 2015), and textbook materials (Pakuła et al., 2015; Trinh & Tinker Sachs, 2023), but also taken into consideration love (Moore, 2020; Trinh, 2020), emotions and feelings (Trinh, 2021, 2022a, 2022b), and the notion of deconstruction (Rhodes & Coda, 2017) to embrace, de-re-construct, and negotiate identities in the teaching and learning process (Pakuła, 2021). As ELT is an international undertaking, the differing cultures and belief systems influencing communities throughout the world must be considered when engaging in discussions of critical queer theory and pedagogy. Moreover, Vasey (2022) encouraged Western LGBTQ+ communities' acknowledgment of non-Western conceptions of gender, identities, and traditions. As such, intersectionality, or the understanding of the mutually inflecting axes of oppression (Crenshaw, 1989), is paramount when considering the entanglement of queerness, pedagogy, ELT, and allyship.

Thus far, we have briefly described terms such as queer inquiry and thinking as well as intersectionality, but what is queer allyship in ELT? To begin, Trinh (in press) provides an account of queer allyship in ELT, which they call ACTS, and "describes allies who work together to challenge common heteronormative and cisgender assumptions of oneself to think queer and provoke actions in relational systems of support." Similar to Moser and Coda's (in press) discussion of allies in world language education, Trinh's notion of allyship in ELT integrates queer theory's notion of deconstruction to encourage allies to trouble the normative regimes of which we all are a part. Connecting this to second language education, whether an educator teaches social language or academic language (Cummins, 1979, 1981, 2008), students interact on topics that are explored from various perspectives and can be productive sites for ensuring that allyship is cultivated. For example, language educators may choose reading or listening passages on a current event, such as the passage of LGBTQ+ rights laws in a country, as the topic for discussion to bring LGBTQ topics to the forefront. In tandem with the insights of queer pedagogy, such a discussion can provide a venue for language learning while teaching pride forward, advocating for and supporting LGBTQ+ students in the classroom and in the communities (e.g., professional organizations; community services; diversity, equity, inclusion, and access training). As such, it is essential that language educators have access to and incorporate instructional practices aligned with queer pedagogy in their own educational contexts.

As we take seriously the understanding that educators must develop culturally congruent and responsive practices to engage with LGBTQ+ individuals in their classrooms, we are aware of the norms that may affect such efforts, such as those related to religion. Samuels (2018), for example, illuminated participants' reluctance to embrace LGBTQ+ individuals due to religious beliefs. In cisheteronormative and conservative contexts as well as those in which parental rights bills have surfaced, educators may experience constraints in their practice related to inclusion or discussion of LGBTQ+ issues (Coda, 2023). Nevertheless, as ELT educators, we are called on to cultivate a critical language education (Kubota, 2023; Kubota & Miller, 2017) that questions our normative assumptions and ensures that all students' linguistic, cultural, sexual, gender, racial, ethnic, and other identities are represented in the classroom and that cisheteronormativity is problematized through our allyship efforts.

In K–20 school systems, many influences from outside of the classroom affect the experiences of individuals from the LGBTQ+ community. Similar to the experience of the child excluded from the game on the playground, educators may also exclude individuals or simply misunderstand pro-LGBTQ+ perspectives and ways of engagement. This is particularly true if the educator in question was born and raised in a culture that did not have open and constructive discussions of inclusivity and support for LGBTQ+ community members. In a global context, ELT educators travel and work with peers from different educational and cultural systems of belief. Some ELT educators may not have learned about culturally congruent or responsive instruction (Au & Kawakami, 1994; Gay, 2002, 2018), for example. Thus, it is imperative that we as educators recognize our role in creating an environment of respectful and critical engagement to support colleagues and students while being mindful that some ELT peers may be learning as we interact.

A corollary of respective engagement and support for colleagues in schools occurs in professional organizations; however, professional organizations, such as TESOL International

Association and its affiliates, differ from the school environment in key ways: time spent together, focus on professional development/learning/goals, and expectations for professionalism. As a significant example, consider this question: How do our personal beliefs about LGBTQ+ individuals influence our willingness to engage with individuals on professional projects? Many individuals in TESOL enter the organization after conducting missionary work. If those individuals' religious beliefs do not accept or validate LGBTQ+ individuals, how likely are they to network, collaborate on a project, or write a letter of recommendation for the Nominating Committee or Board of Directors? Consider which colleagues would stand with you, especially if it might mean they would experience backlash. As members of the ELT community of practice, we need to be thoughtful and reflective about our commitment to inclusivity, equity, diversity, and access. We need to enact allyship.

In this edited volume, we expand on Trinh's (2022b) suggestion that practitioners, theorists, and researchers "first become the thinkers of how to 'mess' and play with fixed knowledge, turn them upside down, and ask, What else can I do differently to benefit the students?" (p. 221). In their work, Trinh offered the three queer considerations and invited us to explore different ways of queering educational spaces in and outside of classrooms: acknowledging students' identities, adding the discourse of difference, and dropping knowledge through communities-based projects. Throughout the volume, the contributors have taken up these three considerations as well as others related to queer allyship to connect with building queer allyship in different educational systems, spaces, times, societies, cultures, and belief systems and to welcome global queer perspectives on how to suggest different queer considerations in ELT.

Introducing the Chapters

In this section, inspired by queer conversations (Gómez Portillo et al., 2022; McKenzie et al., this volume; Trinh & Behizadeh, 2023), we the editors share what each chapter is about, what each of us loved most about the chapter, and our favorite quote. We want to show a connection between the chapters and the editors; we are becoming one together rather than the editors-authors. We want to feel with each chapter, which reflects the purpose of writing it: weaving rationale and emotion to think queer (Trinh & Tinker Sachs, 2023). Further, since the chapters are contributed by authors around the world, we organized the chapters by region so that we can follow how queer allyship has been conducted across cultures, schooling, societies, and politics.

The Pacific Islands

In Chapter 1, "Problematising Intersectionality, Allyship, and Queer Pedagogy in TESOL Down Under: A Trio-ethnographic Approach," McKenzie, Chen, and Veliz demonstrate reflections, thinking, inquiry, and brutal honesty to support each other's understanding, which makes this chapter so emotional and exciting to read. Ethan particularly loved this sentence: "We recognized that only through disrupting and complicating our non/misunderstandings of and approaches to LGBTQIA+-inclusive TESOL education could we reach the core of the problem and serve as an ally." Reading this chapter has given Ethan love, hope, and reaffirmation and the authenticity of feeling in the conversation, especially in tackling sensitive topics. A question arose after reading the chapter: How could we use this approach in teaching, research, and activism with students, teachers, and administrators to promote brutal honesty and critical reflections to build allyship in and beyond school?

In Chapter 2, "Raising Awareness of Filipino English as a Second Language Preservice Teachers to Queer Literature: Toward Inclusivity and Allyship," Mendoza, Cabingan, and Cunanan show the objectives, learning targets, and can-do's were an excellent way to frame the chapter. James loved how, as a teacher educator, he was able to read about other teacher educators' experiences in relation to cultivating allyship with their students. This chapter encouraged James to continually be reflective in his practice in relation to cultivating queer allyship and provided considerations for deepening his practice in queer allyship.

In Chapter 3, "LGB English as a Foreign Language Teachers in Taiwan: LGBTQ+ Sensemaking in the Workplace," Ku recognizes the paradox of pro-LGBTQ+ legislation and conservative workplace settings and the challenges of working therein. Kate loved the statement, "LGBTQ-friendly teachers are often put in difficult positions, facing pressure from parents, colleagues, school authorities, and conservative organizations to not only avoid addressing LGBTQ+ topics, which are often deemed as 'controversial' and 'unsafe,' but also give access to educational materials and guest speakers sourced by conservative groups," because it illustrates the complexity of serving as an ally in any context that has a strong conservative influence, even the United States. Kate also loved that in two participants' bilingual schools, where they hired a lot of internationals, they felt comfortable being themselves because differences were accepted. It made her rethink her practices about taking a stronger, more vocal pro-LGBTQ+ stance on her syllabi in order to counter the cultural situation in the context that she resides in.

The Mediterranean

In Chapter 4, "Creating Queer Allyship in the English Language Teaching Classroom Through Critical Pedagogies With Young Migrants and Refugees in Greece," Fakalou utilizes the theoretical work of Butler (1990) and queer linguistics to make a connection to migration and displacement because this could encourage reflection toward queer allyship in various contexts. James loved that the chapter brings together the insights of queer linguistics, queer pedagogies, and critical pedagogies in relation to queer allyship. As such, this chapter encouraged James to consider how allyship can be cultivated globally and spurred his thinking in regard to contexts in which he has resided.

In Chapter 5, "Queer Inclusion and Allyship in the Turkish English Language Teaching Sphere," Coleman introduces us to the notion of allyship as a process, which is powerful as it underscores that allyship is not something that one does once or performs only in a specific context, but rather is something that is always becoming as it is never finished. James loved how Coleman incorporates intersectionality and allyship as both concepts are even more productive when utilized together to examine training related to diversity, equity, and inclusion as well as heteronormativity in Coleman's context. Moreover, the understanding that allyship is not fixed and is a process reminded James that as a gay man and an ally of the LGBTQIA+ community, the work that he does is always a process.

In Chapter 6, "Lived Experiences of English as a Foreign Language Teachers and Their (LGBTQ+) Students in Türkiye: Building Queer Allyship Even When You Do Not Have the Means," Güney shows the comparison between EFL and German classes in terms of how accepting they were of the LGBTQ+ community and how German texts represented different families, discussed love and parenthood, and the comparison to the idealized nature of EFL textbooks, which contribute to the queering of the classroom. Kate loved how the teachers created safe spaces and stepped in to protect students in their classrooms using inclusive language in a spontaneous manner. While reading this, she was in awe of the bravery of these students and teachers. It made her think about her own discourse of difference. It is about not only saying, "I'm pro-LGBTQ+," but also protecting students, giving them options, and adding material into the book when texts treat marriage or family in a heteronormative way.

The Americas

In Chapter 7, "It Is Not Weird Pedagogy, It Is Queer! Unpacking Assumptions, Beliefs, and Attitudes Toward LGBTQ+ in an English Language Classroom in Chile," Veliz shares an honest description of the discourse of difference and shows a complicatedness of discussing LGBTQ+ topics in the classroom that provoked the notion of allyship in students in a Chilean English language classroom. Ethan loved how "the complex, dynamic, and multifaceted ways in which students navigated their positionality and allyship moved in their conversations." This chapter can help teacher educators consider including queer topics in discussions to help students think queer with the materials and to teach to the tension (Trinh & Tinker Sachs, 2023) while ensuring that students' emotions and feelings are taken care of, as they were in a tense conversation.

In Chapter 8, "Translation Outside Binaries: Queer Pedagogy, English Language Teaching, and First Language>Second Language Translation," Velázquez-Lora employs critical queer theory in her approach to translation, questioning binaries and normative translation protocols of who is allowed to translate which texts. Kate particularly loved to see the role of allies as Velazquez-Lora discussed their translator preparation classes: "Working with texts that talk about identities different from cis hetero identities might provide opportunities for students to question such prejudices and stereotypes, leading them to become allies. This allyship might spread not only to their task as translators but also in their day-to-day lives as students and in their roles in society." This chapter provides a new lens for viewing ELT work, critical queer theory, and allyship.

In Chapter 9, "Educating English Language Teachers on LGBTQIA+S Language Variation and Play for Allyship in Language Courses," Schaefer and Warhol structure the chapter as a lesson plan and connect it with applied linguistics and other activities to make the theories applicable to language learners and teachers. James is positive that this chapter will be very well received by readers for its practicability. This chapter gave him the connection of both theories and practices and how we can build this bridge to advocate allyship in teaching. Also, it is a reminder for us that we need to understand the theories behind every activity in designing lesson plans, which need to be grounded in theory and research.

In Chapter 10, "Fostering Gender and Sexual Diversity in TESOL Educator Classrooms: A Teacher Educator's Allyship Through Classroom Interaction," Ethan loved how Seibert demonstrates queer inquiry and allyship through the teacher educator's discourse with students. In the context of anti-LGBTQ+ activity in and beyond the U.S. context, it is vitally important to promote this conversation between preservice teachers and teacher educators, especially in ELT, to unmask queer identities in professional spaces (Trinh & Behizadeh, 2023). Not only does this chapter provide readers with how-to, but the author as a researcher shows perseverance in his work to build allyship with the participants of his study.

In Chapter 11, "Cultivating Critical Love in Professional Organizations: A Queering Approach for English Language Teaching Leaders," Trinh, de Oliveira, and Andrade propose a critical love approach for ELT leaders in professional organizations. What Kate loved about this chapter is that the authors changed her perception by illustrating the fact that terms such as LGBTQ+ are in fact abusive and ostracizing. In and of themselves, these terms reinforce ideas that somehow various sexual identities fall outside of the norm and thus fall into counterproductive and inequitable binary ways of thinking. All humans are socialized through language (Schieffelin & Ochs, 1986; Ward, 2022). When we recognize that language plays an essential role in our thinking about the world around us, we can take steps to rewrite our discursive practices.

In essence, we the editors want to emphasize that the love and bravery exhibited by authors and participants in these chapters are inspirational. We hope that you, our readers, will use these ideas to further diversity, equity, inclusion, and accessibility for and with LGBTQ+ community members in our field and in the world.

Authors

Ethan Trinh, PhD, is an associate director of the Atlanta Global Studies Center. As a Vietnamese queer immigrant, Ethan enjoys thinking with emotions, gender, and language and explores how to embrace queerness as healing and meditative teaching and research practices.

Kate Mastruserio Reynolds, EdD, is a professor of TESOL/literacy at Central Washington University and a licensed K–12 educator who has taught teachers in several countries and multilingual learners of English in public school districts at elementary schools, middle schools, and universities in various contexts. In 2022, she was inducted onto TESOL International Association's Board of Directors (2022–2025).

James Coda, PhD, is assistant professor of ESL and world language education at the University of Tennessee Knoxville. His research interests include LGBTQIA+ issues in language teaching and learning, queer theories and pedagogies, and identity.

References

Au, K. H., & Kawakami, A. J. (1994). Cultural congruence in instruction. In E. R. Hollins, J. E. King, & W. Hayman (Eds.), *Teaching diverse populations: Formulating a knowledge base* (pp. 5–23). State University of New York Press.

Becker, J. C., Wright, S. C., Lubensky, M. E., & Zhou, S. (2013). Friend or ally: Whether cross-group contact undermines collective action depends on what advantaged group members say (or don't say). *Personality and Social Psychology Bulletin, 39*(4), 442–455. https://doi.org/10.1177/0146167213477155

Brown, K. T., & Ostrove, J. M. (2013). What does it mean to be an ally? The perception of allies from the perspective of people of color. *Journal of Applied Social Psychology, 43*(11), 2211–2222. https://doi.org/10.1111/jasp.12172

Butler, J. (1990). *Gender trouble. Feminism and the subversion of identity*. Routledge.

Coda, J. (2023). Learning the rules and then disrupting them: LGBQ Spanish language teachers' resistance to heteronormativity. *Teaching and Teacher Education, 122*, Article 103980. https://doi.org/10.1016/j.tate.2022.103980

Crenshaw, K. (1989). Demarginalizing the intersection of race and sex: A Black feminist critique of antidiscrimination doctrine, feminist theory and antiracist politics. *University of Chicago Legal Forum, 1989*(1), 139–167.

Cummins, J. (1979). Cognitive/academic language proficiency, linguistic interdependence, the optimum age question and some other matters. *Working Papers on Bilingualism, 19*, 121–129.

Cummins, J. (1981). The role of primary language development in promoting educational success for language minority students. In California State Department of Education (Ed.), *Schooling and Language Minority Students: A Theoretical Framework*. Evaluation, Dissemination and Assessment Center. California State University.

Cummins J. (2008). BICS and CALP: Empirical and theoretical status of the distinction. In B. Street & N. H. Hornberger (Eds.), *Encyclopedia of Language and Education: Volume 2. Literacy* (2nd ed., pp. 71–83). Springer Science + Business Media.

Droogendyk, L., Wright, S. C., Lubensky, M., & Louis, W. R. (2016). Acting in solidarity: Cross-group contact between disadvantaged group members and advantaged group allies. *Journal of Social Issues, 72*(2), 315–334. https://doi.org/10.1111/josi.12168

Gay, G. (2002). Preparing for culturally responsive teaching. *Journal of Teacher Education, 53*(2), 106–116. https://doi.org/10.1177/0022487102053002003

Gay, G. (2018). *Culturally responsive teaching: Theory, research, and practice* (3rd ed.). Teachers College Press.

Gómez Portillo, M. J., Trinh, E. T., & Pentón Herrera, L. J. (2022). Spilling the tea: Stories of confronting and addressing racism in ESOL classrooms. In G. Martínez-Alba, L. J. Pentón Herrera, & A. Hersi (Eds.), *Antiracist teacher education: Counternarratives and storytelling* (pp. 43–53). Rowman & Littlefield.

Kubota, R. (2023). Linking research to transforming the real world: Critical language studies for the next 20 years. *Critical Inquiry in Language Studies, 20*(1), 4–19, https://doi.org/10.1080/15427587.2022.2159826

Kubota, R., & Miller, E. R. (2017). Re-examining and re-envisioning criticality in language studies: Theories and praxis. *Critical Inquiry in Language Studies, 14*(2), 129–157. https://doi.org/10.1080/15427587.2017.1290500

Moore, A. (2020). Queer inquiry: A loving critique. *TESOL Quarterly, 54*(4), 1122–1130. https://doi.org/10.1002/tesq.597

Moser, K., & Coda, J. (in press). Inclusive language teaching: ALLY in the WL classroom. *The Language Educator.*

Nelson, C. D. (1999). Sexual identities in ESL: Queer theory and classroom inquiry. *TESOL Quarterly, 3*(33), 371–391. https://doi.org/10.2307/3587670

Nelson, C. D. (2020). Queer thinking about language learning: Current research and future directions. In K. Hall & R. Barrett (Eds.), *The Oxford handbook of language and sexuality.* Oxford University Press.

Paiz, J. (2020). *Queering the English language classroom: A practical guide for teachers.* Equinox.

Pakuła, Ł. (2021). *Linguistic perspectives on sexuality in education: Representations, constructions and negotiations.* Springer International.

Pakuła, Ł., Pawelczyk, J., & Sunderland, J. (2015). *Gender and sexuality in English language education: Focus on Poland.* Lancaster University.

Reynolds, K. M. (2015). *Approaches to inclusive English classrooms: A teacher's handbook for content based instruction.* Multilingual Matters.

Rhodes, C., & Coda, J. (2017). It's not in the curriculum: Adult English language teachers and LGBQ topics. *Adult Learning, 28*(3), 99–106. https://doi.org/10.1177/1045159517712483

Samuels, A. J. (2018). Exploring culturally responsive pedagogy: Teachers' perspectives on fostering equitable and inclusive classrooms. *SRATE Journal, 27*(1), 22–30.

Schieffelin, B. B., & Ochs, E. (Eds.). (1986). *Language socialization across cultures.* Cambridge University Press.

Selvanathan, H. P., Lickel, B., & Dasgupta, N. (2020). An integrative framework on the impact of allies: How identity-based needs influence intergroup solidarity and social movements. *European Journal of Social Psychology, 50*(6), 1344–1361. https://doi.org/10.1002/ejsp.2697

Trinh, E. (2020). "Still you resist": An autohistoria-teoria of a Vietnamese queer teacher to meditate, teach, and love in the Coatlicue state. *International Journal of Qualitative Studies in Education, 33*(6), 621–633. https://doi.org/10.1080/09518398.2020.1747662

Trinh, E. (2021). What does social justice look like in the United States? Critical reflections of an English language classroom in a field trip. *Multicultural Perspectives, 23*(2), 108–113. https://doi.org/10.1080/15210960.2021.1914046

Trinh, E. (2022a). Crossing the split in nepantla: (Un)successful attempts to dismantle a TESOL teacher candidate in after-queer research. *Journal of Homosexuality, 69*(12), 2027–2048. https://doi.org/10.1080/00918369.2021.1987749

Trinh, E. (2022b). Supporting queer SLIFE youth: Initial queer considerations. In L. J. Pentón Herrera (Ed.), *English and students with limited or interrupted formal education: Global perspectives on teacher preparation and classroom practices* (pp. 209–225). Springer International. https://doi.org/10.1007/978-3-030-86963-2_12

Trinh, E. (in press). Queer allyship in TESOL: We need to ACTS now! *TESOL Journal.*

Trinh, E., & Behizadeh, N. (2023). Unmasking queer bodies to humanize teacher education: A diffractive collaborative autohistoria-teoria. *Teaching and Teacher Education, 131*, Article 104189. https://doi.org/10.1016/j.tate.2023.104189

Trinh, E., & Tinker Sachs, G. (2023). Thinking queer with Vietnamese EFL textbooks. *Critical Inquiry in Language Studies*. https://doi.org/10.1080/15427587.2023.2190524

van Leeuwen, E., & Zagefka, H. (2017). *Intergroup helping*. Springer. https://doi.org/10.1007/978-3-319-53026-0

Vasey, P. (2022, May 11). Stop imposing Western LGBTQ+ identities on non-Western cultures. It's gender colonialism. *Newsweek*. https://www.newsweek.com/stop-imposing-western-lgbtq-identities-non-western-cultures-its-gender-colonialism-opinion-1705785

Ward, S. (2022). Language socialization. *Oxford Research Encyclopedia of Anthropology*. https://oxfordre.com/anthropology/view/10.1093/acrefore/9780190854584.001.0001/acrefore-9780190854584-e-585

PART 1

THE PACIFIC ISLANDS

Problematising Intersectionality, Allyship, and Queer Pedagogy in TESOL Down Under: A Trio-ethnographic Approach

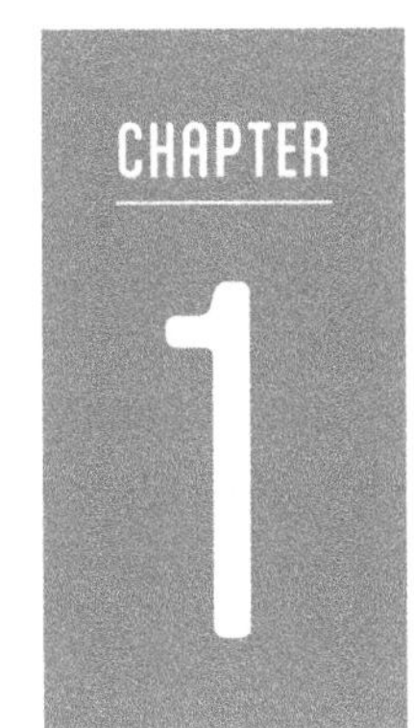

Bri McKenzie, Julian Chen, and Leonardo Veliz

Background

A note to our readers: What you are about to read is the result of three-way, organic conversations on queering Australian English for speakers of other languages (ESOL) classrooms undertaken by three practitioner researchers working in Australian higher education. Bri, Julian, and Leonardo embody various gender identities (cisgender, nonbinary), have different ethnicities (White, Asian, Latino), use a variety of pronouns (she/her, they/them, he/him), and come from diverse disciplinary backgrounds (history, social science, applied linguistics, TESOL). Together, we explore and unpack how our teaching is shaping, and shaped by, our intersectional identities and lived experiences with an awareness of the great need for LGBTQIA+-inclusive education in Australia.

Autoethnography embodies the nature of storytelling in that it "use[s] personal experience ('auto') to describe and interpret ('graphy') cultural texts, experiences, beliefs, and practices ('ethno')" (Adams et al., 2017, p. 1). Through critical dialoguing with one's inner self, social-emotional intricacies of identity, struggle, and vulnerability—shaped by wider sociocultural and political factors on personal and professional levels—can be revealed layer by layer (Adams et al., 2022; Wheeler et al., 2023). Autoethnography as a research method enables researchers to dive deep into their own experiences using critical and reiterative reflections to (re) investigate sociopolitical, cultural, epistemological,

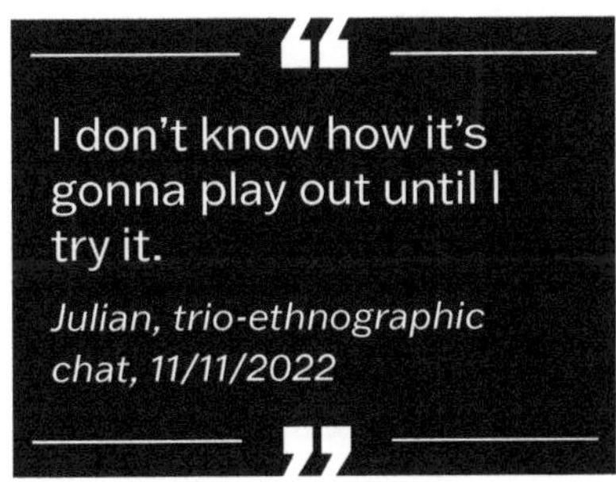

or pedagogical issues (Chen & Sato, 2023; Ellis et al., 2011). Seeing ourselves as not only research "tools," but also "sites for investigation" (Rogers-Shaw et al., 2021, p. 397), we amplify autoethnography in tripartite collaboration to further interrogate and relearn queering TESOL pedagogies "in a move toward envisioning a better tomorrow" (Adams et al., 2022, p. 1).

Through critical trio-ethnographic dialoguing, we endeavor to be brutally honest about our understandings, experiences, and concerns with queer pedagogical practices in language education in Australia and beyond. Despite some hard conversations that reveal the "dark sides" of our own teaching practices, the process of exploring our teaching behaviors is integral to helping us better understand who we really are as (queer) educators and allies. Utilizing our shared understandings of critical and queer pedagogies (Mayo & Rodriguez, 2019; Pinar, 1998; Seal, 2019), we problematize the paucity of LGBTQIA+-inclusive education currently available in Australia and seek new strategies to build empathy, respect, and inclusion for LGBTQIA+ people in ESOL classrooms whilst raising awareness of intersectionality and allyship.

We invite you to enter our world with an open mind and encourage you to share our curiosity, criticality, and creativity as we reflect on our own positioning and evaluate our own (in)experience with LGBTQIA+-inclusive education in TESOL. In sharing our stories, reflections, and proposed lesson episodes, we hope to inspire colleagues in the Australian context to trial queer TESOL learning activities and to deepen their understanding of LGBTQIA+ inclusivity.

Our Positionality and Trajectory

Before demonstrating how we joined forces in three-way dialoguing remotely but collectively (see Trio-ethnography section later in the chapter), we feel it is vital to first share with readers our own positionality that intersects gender identities, ethnicities, pronouns, and experiences with queering TESOL pedagogies. We utilized OneDrive to co-share and document our own story and agreed to be totally honest with our reflections, regardless of what dark and shameful feelings it might unearth, before sharing it with each other and inviting feedback using the commenting feature. Only through this unpretentious, critical reflection were we able to look deeper into ourselves and our trajectory of enacting inclusive education in TESOL with a queer lens.

Julian's Story: A Queer Academic of Color in TESOL/Applied Linguistics

It's scary to be vulnerable in a public space like this. Queer identity is something that I have never dodged, but I never wear my rainbow flag deliberately. Not that I try to hide it or water it down, but I was ignorant of the legitimacy of pronouns and championing them to express who I really was as a queer academic. My identity as a queer academic started to emerge from hibernation during the pandemic year of 2020. I embraced this unprecedented crisis that had pushed me to corner my "identity limbo" and Westernized teaching pedagogy.

This deep soul searching, mirrored in my autoethnography, enabled me to reveal my true queer self unapologetically.

I harnessed this (un)relearned knowledge of my queer identity by starting to use they/them as my pronouns as a queer academic. Truthfully, I am a bit ashamed of myself for not being conscious (or even capable) enough to celebrate and incorporate inclusive pedagogy and queering curriculum in my teaching throughout my academic training. Admittedly, I was taught and programmed into the Eurocentric school of thought and standardized approach to lesson planning. Back then, the TESOL focus was (and still is) centered around the four language skills, second language acquisition, and language teaching methods. Despite some key concepts introduced, such as understanding learners' culturally and linguistically diverse backgrounds, the field did not focus on LGBTQIA+-inclusive issues, much less intersectionality and allyship.

Let's face it—queer pedagogy is not a conventional subject that sits comfortably with all teachers and students. Even when some more progressive teachers are queer identified or allies, they are also seeking resources or best practices to be better equipped in educating their students about this topic. I am in the latter camp, frankly, and this trio-ethnographic dialoguing with Bri and Leo propels me to interrogate my current teaching status quo in queer pedagogy while deepening my understandings and integrating concepts from queering pedagogy, allyship, and intersectionality into my curriculum and teaching. My goal is to incorporate queering pedagogies in my teaching and research and share our co-designed queering lessons with impacted stakeholders in TESOL and beyond. This excites me!

Bri's Story: A Straight, White, Cisgender Ally of LGBTQIA+ People Working in Social Sciences

In my higher education history classrooms, my approach to learning and teaching was always intuitive and very rarely directly informed by evidence-based pedagogy. It is only in retrospect that I have applied a theoretical and evidence-based lens to what I do. Critical pedagogical approaches to learning and teaching that problematize power structures, require teacher and student self-reflexivity, and insist on constant questioning of curricula development and delivery do not feel at odds with how I would intuitively teach. But as I came to explore my learning and teaching approaches more, I recognized that in my intuition, I drew on the philosophy and wisdom of Freire, Giroux, Mezirow, and hooks. Education for social justice, increasing awareness of my own positioning and privilege, respect for the lived experiences of my students, and the opportunity to be part of transformative change as a facilitator were what drove me to begin queering my history teaching in 2017.

I come from a family tradition of living outside the mainstream. With grandparents who were active in the Australian Communist Party and a draft dodger for a dad, I couldn't help but be a bit different. I grew up with very left-wing opinions and was a vocal feminist in high school who never shaved my legs, defended the queer kids, and spoke up about the rights of Aboriginal and Torres Strait Islander people. Despite being straight, cisgender, and White, I still feel that I understand outsider status, yet I recognize that my privilege gives me "the luxury to 'opt-in' to struggles for liberation" (Potvin, 2016, p.10).

I also recognize that my queering efforts have very rarely been intersectional enough. My students have usually been White. I think I have many assumptions about students who are learning English as a second language. I wonder if there are too many cultural barriers and think, how could I ever really approach LGBTQIA+ topics safely without causing offence or stepping on a cultural or religious land mine?

Leo's Story: TESOL/Applied Linguist of Color, Dissident of Normativity/ies and Strong Ally of LGBTQIA+ Communities

I grew up with a narrow view of our diverse world and with a limited understanding of what it means to tolerate, accept, and integrate the other into my world and my worldview. The specific sociocultural values were grounded in binaries: heaven and hell, believers and unbelievers, sinners and saints, rich and poor, male and female, homosexual and heterosexual, good and evil, and so on. I was stuck in a dualistic world that was constantly affirmed by strict rules imposed by parents who nurtured a male-dominated environment. My home environment would constantly validate heteronormative beliefs through discursive practices that reinforced such binaries that, at the same time, eliminated the slightest possibility of sympathy, acceptance, or respect for difference. No one (in my family) was really sympathetic with anything that would differ from our narrow life perspective. What some people would call "being different" was a real issue to me (us). Having been psychologically and physically bullied during my primary school years, I became increasingly intolerant of difference because I kept thinking that I was bullied because I was perceived as different purely on religious grounds. I was not tolerant of anything or anyone that would not conform to my narrow parameters of reality.

What also troubled me when I was young was a selfish sense of religiosity that made me shortsighted of the real world. Rather than having a tolerant heart for diversity, my narrow understanding of the religious values and beliefs that I upheld often positioned me as a judge, one who was constantly making uninformed judgmental remarks about anyone that didn't fit within the hierarchies of gender and sexuality of my heteronormative framework. I am glad nothing lasts forever and that I have experienced massive transformation that afforded me with a wider life perspective and inclusive lenses through which I see the world, and that empower me to consider myself a dissident of normativity/ies and a strong ally of LGBTQIA+ communities. As such, my endeavors as a teacher and academic revolve around creating more liberating and inclusive learning classrooms where students of different genders, races, languages, and sociocultural backgrounds feel safe, respected, included, and cared for.

LGBTQIA+ Allyship, Inclusion, and Inquiry in TESOL Education

In initiating our trio-ethnographic inquiry into queering English language teaching (ELT), we understood that there was a long history of exploration of the issues in the European and U.S. contexts (Pennycook, 1999, 2001, 2007), with scholarship dating from the 1980s. In contrast, we discovered very little from Australian practitioners, leaving aside notable exceptions such as the work of Cynthia Nelson (1999, 2002, 2006) and Anthony Liddicoat (2009). Australia is one of the most multicultural societies in the world; we regularly welcome students from overseas to study in our universities, and ever-growing numbers of our primary and secondary students are multilingual and come from diverse cultural backgrounds. Yet, traditionally, Australian education systems at all levels have struggled to adapt to non-Western approaches to learning and teaching, and efforts to queer learning and teaching have at times met with stern resistance from politicians and social commentators (Cumming-Potvin, 2022, p. 18).

Given our context and the ongoing dispossession and marginalization of Aboriginal and Torres Strait Islander people in our own country of Australia, we recognized the importance of "decoloniality" as it applied to our educational practice. Much of the intellectual work under the broad term of decoloniality, as used in and applied to education, lies at the intersection of LGBTQIA+ and allyship. For us, we adopt decoloniality that refers to "long-standing patterns of power that emerged as a result of colonialism, but that define culture, labour, intersubjective relations and knowledge production" (Maldonado-Torres, 2007, p. 243). Decoloniality is not a means to reject all the well-established forms of modernity, but a method to unveil ways in which dominant matrices of power disadvantage and silence certain groups in society who constantly suffer the consequences of marginalization, segregation, and inequality. In addition to unveiling forms of oppression against marginalized and minoritized peoples, such as LGBTQIA+ communities, a decolonial stance in education embraces a level of restoration, reinvigoration, and reparation of the positionality, voices, and lived experiences of queer students and teachers alike. For us, queer pedagogy, with its primary focus on and strong impetus for disrupting constructed binaries (Morris, 1998; Pointek, 2006), makes a significant contribution to amplifying the voices and lived experiences of our LGBTQIA+ students.

The disruption of mainstream binaries (e.g., male/female, White/Color), and the questioning of one single privileged reality, lies at the heart of poststructuralism and postmodernism (Fox, 2014). Poststructuralists/-modernists aim to decenter and destabilize existing assumptions or stereotypes that have been perpetuated by the imbalanced, dominant power (Çalkıvik, 2020). Sharing the same values and core ethos of poststructuralism/-modernism, queer theory unapologetically calls out heteronormativity and cisnormativity; it confronts traditional understandings of gender and sexuality that present limited understandings of what it means to be "normal" (Nelson, 2002; Reynolds, 2010). Queer theorists and activists actively challenge the dominant ideology that not only marginalizes and suppresses gender expressions outside of the binary (male/female), but demonizes the LGBTQIA+ community broadly while perpetuating gender inequity (Cumming-Potvin, 2022). Through a decolonial lens and a posture of resistance, we believe queer theory helps us critically frame our stance on queer pedagogical approaches with a rainbow spirit of allyship and inclusion in TESOL education.

LGBTQIA+ Allyship in the Classroom

Research has consistently demonstrated the importance of teacher allyship with LGBTQIA+ students, with scholarship establishing links between the allyship of facilitators and better outcomes for queer learners (Potvin, 2016; Shelton, 2019). Though notions of what constitutes allyship (and indeed the term itself) are contested (Cummings-Potvin, 2022), we take our lead from Reynolds (2010), who argued that the role of allies is to disrupt privilege, power, and normativity. In this context, and using queer theory, Reynolds highlighted the way allyship is performative and the identity of ally is not static but fluid and, by nature, intersectional (p. 13). Relevant to our trio-ethnographic approach, Reynolds also argued that allyship is a collective action and not dependent on the behavior of individuals. We are also led by Potvin's (2016) ideas on teacher allyship, which highlight the importance of LGBTQIA+ allies sharing their failures, mistakes, and challenges and recognizing that the ally identity is never static. Trinh (in press) has noted that "queer allyship" works to co-construct and cocreate "a space of togetherness" where we learn about ourselves and others with the intent to challenge normativity and the status quo. This is the essence of the work we have undertaken in our trio-dialoguing. Each of us enacts our ally identities differently, and we recognized early in our conversations that our allyship evolved within the context of our own positionality and the intersections of privilege and disadvantage that we each embody and enact.

Shifting From LGBTQIA+ Inclusion to Inquiry

Many recent studies have explored the ways TESOL practitioners enact queer pedagogical approaches in various contexts (Banegas, 2021; Bollas, 2021; Buyserie & Ramírez, 2021; Gray, 2021). In our view(s), such approaches are needed in language classrooms because, as Ó'Móchain (2006) highlighted, "dominant heteronormative discourses work as and through language to confer heterosexuality with normal, natural, taken-for-granted status" (p. 55). We suggest that the same is true for the ways in which language reinforces notions of binary gender. In reflecting on our own experiences, the resources and materials used in TESOL classrooms have traditionally been heavily influenced by normative representations of gender and sexuality and, as such, promote heteronormative and cisnormative ways of being and knowing to ESL students (Trinh & Tinker Sachs, 2003; Widodo & Elyas, 2020). This is problematic on multiple levels. As Bollas (2021) suggests, if gender and sexually diverse students of ESL cannot see themselves represented in materials and resources, this can negatively impact their ability to use English in ways that are relevant to them, while at the same time establishing the "ideal" English speaker as cisgender and heterosexual (p. 133). If exclusionary resource materials, coupled with classroom discourses, reinforce gender binaries and tacitly support classroom hierarchies between the students and teacher, ESOL classrooms become sites for replicating heteronormative and cisnormative approaches to language and culture (Bollas, 2021). There is a great need for queer allyship to challenge heteronormative and cisnormative teaching and learning approaches, both within and beyond English language classrooms (Trinh, in press). As allies of our LGBTQIA+ students, we seek ways to work against these normative approaches to learning and teaching, to develop our own queer practices, and to share and learn from each other through trio-ethnographic dialoguing.

We learned that TESOL practitioners elsewhere have worked hard to develop curricula that are more representative of gender and sexually diverse identities (see, e.g., Liddicoat, 2009; Nelson, 1999; Seburn, 2019). In some cases, this has been done by increasing the representation of homosexuality and gender diversity in hitherto unrepresentative materials (Bollas, 2021). But as Bollas pointed out, such approaches can be understood as homonormative, because the underlying structures of hetero- and cisnormative societies remain in place. The alternative is what Bollas called a "diversity approach" where notions of normalcy are rejected in favor of critical pedagogical approaches designed to deconstruct and problematize "normalcy." We take the lead of Nelson (1999), who has argued for the use of queer theoretical frameworks in ELT because they "shift the focus from inclusion to inquiry" (p. 371). Such an approach has unique value to ELT educators because it is necessarily focused on language and can assist learners to see others through the lens of diversity, not difference (Bollas, 2021, 138). At the same time, queer pedagogies recognize the ways binaries help to develop both dominant and subordinate identities within specific social and cultural contexts, thus shaping ways of living, being, and knowing for individual subjects (Nelson, 1999). In classroom contexts in which culture is central to curricula and language itself, queering approaches can enable TESOL educators to resist and interrogate normative practices (Buyserie & Ramírez, 2021).

Trio-ethnography: Our Tripartite Dialoguing and Critical Inquiry

We came to our trio-ethnographic approach through our preexisting professional and friendship connections. Julian served as the liaison to bring Leonardo and Bri together to form a trio of passionate allies and practitioners. Each of us engaged in our own personal reflective processes while seeking an outlet for further queer exploration and scholarship of learning and teaching. Our rationale for using trio-ethnography as a research inquiry approach is simple but also profound. Queering English language education in Australia and creating LGBTQIA+-inclusive content and materials were initially beyond our own teaching repertoires and practices. Truthfully, queering approaches in the TESOL context disrupted our teaching comfort zones. Yet, throughout our inquiry, we came to terms with our internal fear that at times overshadowed our strong and persistent LGBTQIA+ allyship. We sought to be authentic, vulnerable, and willing to re(un)learn our approaches to queering to transform our teaching practices. We recognized that only through disrupting and complicating our non/misunderstandings of and approaches to LGBTQIA+-inclusive TESOL education could we reach the core of the problem and serve as allies.

To achieve this goal, we engaged in a series of critical conversations synchronously (via Microsoft Teams) and asynchronously (reflective narratives via OneDrive) over a 4-week period in late 2022. These conversations allowed us to jointly interrogate our intersectional identities and experiences with queering pedagogies in TESOL (see Figure 1). Through this process, we sought to push each other to dive deeper into the possibilities of challenging the status quo of "inclusive education" and reflect on how queering language education can liberate or challenge our existing practices, ourselves as teachers, and our English language learners. We found that our (hard) conversations often highlighted the way fear played a part in our former teaching practices, which were often shaped by Eurocentric binaries (nonnative vs. native English speaking, White vs. Color) that dictated (language) curriculum design and pedagogy. In keeping our conversations queer, we were aware we needed to move beyond these binaries and welcome the messiness of non-normative learning and teaching practices (Trinh, in press).

An example occurred in our first trio-ethnographic conversation, when Bri shared her own fears of "going too far or not going far enough" in the context of LGBTQIA+ allyship in social science classrooms. As shown in Table 1, both Leo and Julian responded around the theme of fear while highlighting ways to uplift understanding by drawing upon their life experiences and previous teaching practices. Reflecting on this conversation later, Bri was able to explore her own Eurocentric assumptions while reexamining the different reasons that caused us all to experience fear in queering our teaching.

Figure 1. Screenshots of a regular trio-ethnographic chat via Microsoft Teams (top) and three-way reflective dialoguing via OneDrive (bottom).

Table 1. Trio-ethnographic Dialogue Around the Theme of Fear, Followed by Bri's Subsequent Reflective Annotation

Trio-ethnographic chatlog in real time	Bri's reflection ad hoc
Bri: I probably avoided things. I'm thinking about a potential conflict where I might bring up [LGBTQIA+-affirmative] content in a way that I usually would, but I'm a bit worried about offending the religious sensibilities potentially, and then that bringing up conflict, like, for example, a student saying, "Well, actually, you know, I don't think this conversation is appropriate. And I actually feel really uncomfortable having this conversation." I'm unsure about my own ability to appropriately facilitate that dynamic because I don't think I have enough knowledge or background in the lived experiences of people who have English as a second language, people who are non-White.... So, I think for me that this kind of intersection of queer pedagogy and TESOL...brings up a lot of fear.	This is about me as a person. I don't like conflict with students because, at core, I think they need to like me to learn from me. If they don't like me, they will shut down or not attend class, so there is no point, in my mind, bringing up certain things with certain students if it will cause offence.
Julian: But do you think it also happens in your mainstream classroom where some of your students might come from different multicultural backgrounds? Although they were born here, it doesn't mean they don't have a cultural heritage. Australia is such a multicultural country where a lot of students were born here but their parents might be migrants... So, our students could be domestic students, international students, or second language learners, and we all have to deal with different sociocultural and religious aspects carefully and with respect. So, holding the space for anyone in need, particularly those who come from culturally and linguistically diverse backgrounds, is vital. That's just my interpretation of how you were describing your fears.	Here Julian highlights an inconsistency with my view above about international students by showing that all students bring cultural baggage. This highlights the way my approach as expressed above was quite Western and failed to recognize that all students have culture (not just the non-White students).

Leo: I think one of the key elements, common to all three [of us], is that element of fear. So, when you started talking about that, yeah, I could relate to that very, very well. Because for me queering the curriculum has also been very problematic in terms of that perceived fear of opposing the dominant ideas and the dominant ideologies and the dominant beliefs, not only in the classroom but in the wider community where I might be teaching, whether it is in Australia, overseas, or in a different context. It's probably that fear of not wanting to be what others expect you to be, that fear of feeling like a fish out of water in a particular context. But at the same time, I'm always very mindful of making sure that everyone in my class is included and I tried to do my best pedagogically, methodologically, personally, individually with each of the students in the class, but also with great care and being very cautious about not going too far and trying to make sure that everyone feels safe and respected.	This is a very interesting part of the conversation from my view because Leo experiences fear too, but for different reasons to me. I was not concerned about opposing dominant ideologies because my upbringing was all about opposing dominant ideologies. But I don't like conflict, I want to avoid it at all costs, so I just didn't engage in certain conversations with certain students out of fear.

Another example of the impact of our dialoguing became evident when Julian started to explore how queering pedagogy was enacted in one of their academic writing classes, even though they were not aware of the concept of queering pedagogy at that time. Julian was able to replay the learning episode to both Bri and Leo, paving the way for a codesigned LGBTQIA+-inclusive lesson later in their trio-ethnographic journey:

> **Julian:** Teaching back in the old days, you know, when I was teaching academic writing in Taiwan, for one of the assignments I would ask them to compose a standard academic essay. I didn't want to just ask them to write about the same old essay topic because it's as boring to the students as it is to me. So, I used authentic material, which was a newsflash at that time, where two male penguins in a New York Zoo fell in love and cast no eye on other female penguins but only each other. I used this real-life news as the essay topic, prompting them to use critical thinking to address questions like: 'So what are your views about the two gay penguins? Do you think gay people should be accepted and respected in society? Shall we legalize same-sex marriage in Taiwan?" So that was my initial incorporation of a queer topic in teaching. So yeah, I think my fear would be not knowing much about how to design queering curriculum particularly touching upon intersectionality...but I think it's a good start because we try to be honest about our conflicts.

Through this trio-ethnographic conversation, we have questioned, challenged, and confronted our own positionality based upon our life stories and lived experiences, and on the complexities driven by the underlying dominant Eurocentric ideologies and diverse genders and cisnormative discourses that need to be disrupted to create meaningful pathways for the inclusion of diverse sexuality and gender identities in classrooms. The next section unfolds our critical conversations on the codesign of a lesson episode that could be enacted by English language teachers with the purpose of both queering the ELT curriculum and creating inclusive learning environments.

A Codesigned Lesson Episode Through Trio-ethnographic Inquiry

Bri's Suggested Experiment With Miriam Margolyes

Bri: Despite our diverse contexts and experiences as teacher educators, we all use autoethnographic and reflective writing exercises with our students to connect with them personally, enhance a sense of belonging, and facilitate reflection on learning. I also suggest that such exercises are inherently queer in the way they can lead to uncertainty, require vulnerability, and necessitate self-reflexive understandings about "knowing" (Buyserie & Ramirez, 2021). To situate this lesson episode in the Aussie context and with an eye to the importance of intersectionality, I propose an autoethnographic and reflective activity for Australian TESOL students, using a video excerpt from the program *Almost Australian* (season 1, episode 2), hosted by Miriam Margolyes (ABC TV & iview, 2020; www.youtube.com/watch?v=Fc-WPnNH55c). The video acts as an accessible way for students to learn about Aboriginal and Torres Strait Islander people who live at the intersection of queer identity in Australia. The responses of Margolyes—an English actor and presenter—as she meets the Sistergirls of the Tiwi Islands, reflect common assumptions about trans* identities, thus providing a point of connection for students who are less comfortable with LGBTQIA+ topics. But as the video progresses, we see Margolyes learning about Australian identity, queerness, and Aboriginality in a way that might offer a path forward for students to not only develop their understanding of Australian culture and society, but enhance their empathy with and understanding of transgender people.

We could begin such an exercise by asking students to respond to a set of questions after viewing the short video. Accessible modes of sharing could include students blogging, vlogging, or drawing their reflections on the questions.

Julian: I really like this lesson episode as I also finished watching *Almost Australian* and found Miriam's candor and no holding back to push boundaries a breeze of fresh air! Whilst Bri's suggested material is relevant and suitable for developing into a queering TESOL lesson Down Under, I also wonder how we can scaffold student language development and foster content knowledge at the same time. As a TESOL educator, I think it's crucial to also address the language skill aspect. In the back of my mind, I can come up with a few activities but would like to hear what Bri and Leo think first, especially for mainstream teachers without a TESOL background but keen to introduce this content to both locals and English language learners.

Leo: I love Miriam's sociopolitical work as an activist, and I have watched her episodes on *Almost Australian* numerous times. I agree with Bri that students could be asked to respond to or reflect on a set of questions aimed at unpacking their own views and understandings of gender diversity in various social and cultural environments. This reminds me of a strong homophobic remark I once heard from someone who belonged to a closed-knit religious community that went something like (translated from Spanish into English), "Homosexuality in animals is an anomaly. Homosexuality in Indigenous communities is uncivilized ignorance." Every time I watch the episode on the Sistergirls, I am prompted to think of any activity, in either TESOL contexts or mainstream classrooms, which explores our multiple identities. This is something I do all the time. I would normally start by discussing "what's in a name?" I would ask students to think and discuss how different they feel if they are called by their first or middle names. This would be more particularly relevant to those students who come from non-English backgrounds that choose to replace, for instance, their Asian names with an Anglo name to avoid potential episodes of linguistic or racial discrimination. Very much linked to this idea of identity, we could also try what I call "the 10 I am(s)." This would start off as a short individual writing task whereby students would write 10 statements that would speak to the various roles/identities they have in society, such as "I am a father," "I am a friend," "I am a heterosexual," "I am an international student," and so on. While it may be unlikely to see bold statements that reveal openly students' sexual identities, it is an opportunity to delve into those racialized identities that are less salient in students' stories or discourse.

Bri: I am thinking in a very linear and structured way here, but would students watch the video after "the 10 I am(s)"? I think that would make most sense, as it occurs to me that the activity you describe, Leo, is excellent for starting off those conversations about what identity is, and we could look to (potentially) exploring ways that identity is performative too, if we wanted to queer it up.

Julian: "Queer it up," eh, nice one! I am more of a visual person and have evidenced the effect of using graphic organizers or visuals to support language learning, particularly for low-proficiency learners. Whilst it is useful to tap into learner identity as a discussion topic and lesson activity, I also think it's pivotal to guide them through navigating the third space in queer identity and gender diversity, whilst holding the space for them. For me, I'd use one or two key segments of that episode as a springboard for them to watch again and jot down their thoughts in a worksheet (or graphic organizer if you like) that circles "identity" in the center with related underlying themes around it (e.g., gender diversity, sexual orientation, pronouns). They can work either individually or in pairs/groups to write down their understandings or even questions in relation to those themes after watching the segments. After that, they can share and compare/contrast their sample work with their partners. It's a simple activity but can encourage production of the four skills (listening to discussion, speaking about one's own views, reading peers' samples, and writing down their initial interpretations), critical thinking, and new knowledge (co)construction. The teacher can bring each group back to the class and use the whiteboard to generate ideas and views among the groups, opening another round of conversation on this topic. The teacher can also address students' questions about unknown vocabulary (e.g., queer, trans, binary) or key phrases (e.g., gender diversity) or push them to come up with their own definitions.

Leo: If this activity was to be enacted in a TESOL context, and depending on students' command of English, it could be an opportunity to extend their explorations of identity across time through the use of grammatical tenses (past and present), future time, and progressive aspect. Students would be encouraged to reflect on what they were, what they are, what they have been, and what they will be. One would expect things like: "I was engaged in a heterosexual relationship for many years. I am an LGBTQIA+ supporter now." "I have been an ally of gender diversity for some time now. I will be a strong advocate for minority groups in the future."

Concurring with Paiz (2019) on the "need of continued engagement and active expansion" (p. 272) of LGBTQIA+-inclusive approaches in the ELT classroom, as teacher educators, whose souls intersect in an allyship site for our students, we also feel that intentional changes can be made, and conditions created, to queer our ELT practice. This, however, takes courage, openness, and vulnerability to mitigate our own privileged positions in the classroom and embrace the multiple identities of our students.

Our Final Trio-dialoguing

Having codeveloped a (queer) classroom episode through our ongoing trio-dialogues, we share our final reflections on the experience of our queer inquiry and the future of our queer allyship:

Leo: It's not been easy to open our souls and queer our own identities. Although it's been an elusive process of repositioning ourselves as both queer educators and enthusiastic advocates of inclusive ELT education, it's been reassuring to validate our strong allyship of LGBTQIA+ peoples through our critical dialoguing. Through our own self-discovery process, as we unpacked our (often) silenced positionalities, we agreed on the need for creating safe and welcoming classroom spaces (Trinh, 2022) where all English language learners feel respected, integrated, and included. As we dialogued about our pursuits for creating inclusive ELT classrooms, we became critically aware not only of our positionings as academics and TESOL practitioners but also of our pedagogical practices and the modifications and adjustments needed to exercise more socially just pedagogies. What's more, as an ally teacher and teacher educator, I've developed a heightened awareness of how compelled I feel to be not only more respectful, self-reflective, and willing to live in humility (Potvin, 2016), but also a catalyst for the creation of safe spaces for queering the ELT classroom.

Bri: At first with this process, I felt like a fish out of water. I feel confident with queering curricula, but what does that mean in the context of culturally diverse ESL classrooms? To learn from Leo and Julian that they also suffered insecurities and doubts, particularly when they were so experienced as TESOL practitioners, made my journey easier. To base our practice in the spirit of queer inquiry (Nelson, 1999) brings great freedom from the original doubts and fears I had about how my LGBTQIA+-inclusive approach would land with culturally diverse students. As we seek to interrogate, challenge, and problematise binaries and normalcy, we can develop an appreciation for human diversity (Bollas, 2021) and this can only ever be a positive thing for learners in the ELT classroom.

Julian: It's never too late, is it? Advocating for gender diversity and inclusive education and fighting against bullying and discrimination against LGBTQIA+ students should be everyone's duty, not just queer-identified students and teachers. Cisgender and straight students and teachers can also join forces and become allies for our rainbow community, as demonstrated in Bri's and Leo's allyship. Queering curricula such as introducing the concept of pronouns and incorporating authentic materials such as gay penguins or reported homo-/transphobic bullying in local schools can stimulate discussion around the heated issues. These meaningful and difficult conversations, though too "out there" for some, can foster the development of oral communication skills, critical thinking, rich vocabulary, and knowledge about social justice, inclusion, and empathy. Only when topics and materials like these are woven into language education can LGBTQIA+-responsive allyship be established and promoted. Our three-way dialoguing and critical reflection have pushed me out of my teaching comfort zone as much as empowered me to queer TESOL education unapologetically from now on. I feel liberated.

Food for Thought

Through our "critical talks and actions" (Trinh, in press) in our trio-dialoguing, we have sought to challenge ourselves, to learn about our practice and develop queer allyship between us and beyond. In doing so, and in better recognizing our own positionality, we encountered our own fears and internal resistance to queering curricula and were forced to confront the limitations of our past practices.

The implications of our work together include the potential for further development of trio-ethnography as a method for fostering LGBTQIA+ allyship within student cohorts. By creating safe environments where small groups of students can explore their own fears and challenges together, with appropriate support and scaffolding from facilitators, there is scope for this technique to enhance both individual and collective allyship (Cumming-Potvin, 2022). Specifically, promoting and celebrating queer thinking in class not only validates students' gender and sexuality diversities, but further stimulates their criticality in approaching content materials beyond face value, thus unlocking creativity in language use and class discussion. This liberates them from being receptive in traditional language instruction that focuses mainly on the language aspects (Nelson, 2002, 2006, 2007).

As we trio-dialogued the possible avenues for queering our TESOL pedagogies, we not only concurred that "educational institutions have too often been sites of exclusions and indeed discrimination for same-sex attracted youth" (Rhodes, 2009, p. 44), but also dissented from heteronormative discourses in education while searching for meaningful opportunities for "gay-friendly" (Nelson, 1999, 2007) pedagogies in our TESOL contexts. This led us to deep moments of reflection about how we confronted oppression and marginalization in our own lives and the ways in which we can develop more social justice–oriented practices as allies. Trinh (in press) explored the ways queer allyship "is always in the making, in contestation, and in inquiry," and it is in this spirit that we codeveloped a teaching episode uniquely designed for queering the Australian TESOL classroom. The lesson episode is a clear reflection of our openness and vulnerability but, most importantly, of our earnest pursuits for "the practice of allyship" (Sharma, 2019).

Authors

Dr. Bri McKenzie (she/her) is a professional learning designer, historian and LGBTQIA+ inclusive education consultant at Curtin University, Australia.

Dr. Julian Chen (they/them) is an associate professor of applied linguistics/TESOL and course coordinator of Asian languages at Curtin University, Australia.

Dr. Leonardo Veliz (he/him) is an associate professor in language and literacy in the School of Education at the University of New England, Australia.

References

ABC TV & iview. (2020, May 26). *Miriam Margolyes meets the sistergirls of the Tiwi Islands* [video]. YouTube. https://youtu.be/Fc-WPnNH55c?si=JWXlY3Lf8R9koAzp

Adams, T. E., Jones, S. H., & Ellis, C. (2017). Autoethnography. In J. Matthes, C. S. Davis, & R. F. Potter (Eds.), *The international encyclopedia of communication research methods* (pp. 1–17). John Wiley & Sons.

Adams, T. E., Jones, S. H., & Ellis, C. (2022). Introduction: Making sense and taking action: Creating a caring community of autoethnographers. In T. E. Adams, S. H. Jones, & C. Ellis (Eds.), *Handbook of autoethnography* (2nd ed., pp. 1–19). Routledge.

Banegas, D. L. (2021). Comprehensive sexual education and English language teaching: An endeavour from southern Argentina. *Innovation in Language Learning and Teaching, 15*(3), 210–17. https://doi.org/10.1080/17501229.2020.1737704

Bollas, A. (2021). A critical discussion of inclusive approaches to sexualities in ELT. *ELT Journal, 75*(2), 133–141. https://doi.org/10.1093/elt/ccaa075

Buyserie, B., & Ramírez, R. (2021). Enacting a queer pedagogy in the composition classroom. *ELT Journal, 75*(2), 193–202. https://doi.org/10.1093/elt/ccaa072

Çalkıvik, A. (2020). Poststructuralism and postmodernism in international relations. In *Oxford research encyclopedia of international studies*. https://doi.org/10.1093/acrefore/9780190846626.013.102

Chen, J., & Sato, E. (2023). Reimagining crisis teaching through autoethnography: A case of an online Japanese course. *Innovation in Language Learning and Teaching, 17*(1), 157–167. https://doi.org/10.1080/17501229.2021.1973011

Cumming-Potvin, W. (2022). *LGBTQI+ allies in education, advocacy, activism, and participatory collaborative research.* Taylor and Francis. https://doi.org/10.4324/9780429455025

Ellis, C., Adams, T. E., & Bochner, A. P. (2011). Autoethnography: An overview. *Historical Social Research, 36*(4), 273–290.

Fox, N. J. (2014). Post-structuralism and postmodernism. In W. C. Cockerham, R. Dingwall, & S. R. Quah (Eds.), *The Wiley Blackwell encyclopedia of health, illness, behavior and society* (pp. 1855–1860). Wiley.

Gray, J. (2021). Addressing LGBTQ erasure through literature in the ELT classroom. *ELT Journal, 75*(2), 142–151. https://doi.org/10.1093/elt/ccaa079

Liddicoat, A. (2009). Sexual identity as linguistic failure: Trajectories of interaction in the heteronormative language classroom. *Journal of Language, Identity, and Education, 8*(2–3), 191–202. https://doi.org/10.1080/15348450902848825

Maldonado-Torres, N. (2007). On the coloniality of being: Contributions to the development of a concept. *Cultural Studies, 21*(2–3), 240–270. https://doi.org/10.1080/09502380601162548

Mayo, C., & Rodriguez, N. M. (Eds.). (2019). *Queer pedagogies: Theory, praxis, politics* (Vol. 11). Springer Cham. https://doi.org/10.1007/978-3-030-27066-7

Morris, M. (1998). Unresting the curriculum: Queer projects, queer imaginings. In W. F. Pinar (Ed.), *Queer theory in education* (pp. 275–286). Routledge.

Nelson, C. (1999). Sexual identities in ESL: Queer theory and classroom inquiry. *TESOL Quarterly, 33*(3), 371–391. https://doi.org/10.2307/3587670

Nelson, C. (2002). Why queer theory is useful in teaching: A perspective from English as a second language teaching. *Journal of Gay and Lesbian Social Services, 14*(2), 43–53. https://doi.org/10.1300/J041v14n02_04

Nelson, C. (2006). Queer inquiry in language education. *Journal of Language, Identity and Education, 5*(1), 1–9. https://doi.org/10.1207/s15327701jlie0501_1

Nelson, C. (2007). Queer thinking about language teaching: An overview of published work. In H. Decke-Cornill & L. Volkmann (Eds.), *Gender studies and foreign language teaching* (pp. 63–76). Guter Narr.

Ó'Móchain, R. (2006). Discussing gender and sexuality in a context-appropriate way: Queer narratives in an EFL college classroom in Japan. *Journal of Language, Identity, and Education, 5*(1), 51–66. https://doi.org/10.1207/s15327701jlie0501_4

Paiz, J. M. (2019). Queering practice: LGBTQ+ diversity and inclusion in English language teaching. *Journal of Language, Identity and Education, 18*(4), 266–275. https://doi.org/10.1080/15348458.2019.1629933

Pennycook, A. (1999). Critical approaches to TESOL. *TESOL Quarterly, 33*(3), 329–348. https://doi.org/10.2307/3587668

Pennycook, A. (2001). *Critical applied linguistics.* Lawrence Erlbaum.

Pennycook, A. (2007). ELT and colonialism. In J. Cummins & C. Davison (Eds.), *International handbook of English language teaching* (pp. 13–24). Springer.

Pinar, W. F. (Ed.). (1998). *Queer theory in education.* Routledge. https://doi.org/10.4324/9781410603760

Pointek, T. (2006). *Queering gay and lesbian studies.* University of Illinois Press.

Potvin, L. (2016). Radical heterosexuality: Straight teacher activism in schools. *Confero, 4*(1), 9–36. https://doi.org/10.3384/confero.2001-4562.160614

Reynolds, V. (2010). Fluid and imperfect ally positioning: Some gifts of queer theory. *Context, 111*, 13–17.

Rhodes, D. (2009). Out of the silence: Bridging the queer divide in Australian secondary English classrooms. *English in Australia, 44*(2), 43–52.

Rogers-Shaw, C., Carr-Chellman, D., & Choi, J. (2021). A trioethnography of organic mentoring in the doctoral process. *Mentoring & Tutoring: Partnership in Learning, 29*(4), 389–411. https://doi.org/10.1080/13611267.2021.1952394

Seal, M. (2019). Educating the pedagogical practitioner: The liminal spaces of a queer and critical pedagogy. In *The interruption of heteronormativity in higher education* (pp. 255–270). Palgrave Macmillan. https://doi.org/10.1007/978-3-030-19089-7_13

Seburn, T. (2019, July 31). This post will make you gay (or your mats anyway). *FourC*. http://fourc.ca/lgbtqia2-coursebook/

Sharma, A. (2019). Allyship and social justice: Men as allies in challenging men's violence and discrimination against women. In D. Baines, B. Bennett, S. Goodwin, & M. Rawsthorne (Eds.), *Working across difference: Social work, social policy and social justice* (pp. 103–119). Red Globe Press.

Shelton, S. A. (2019). "When I do 'bad stuff,' I make the most difference": Exploring doubt, demoralization, and contradictions in LGBTQIA+ ally work. *International Journal of Qualitative Studies in Education, 32*(6), 591–605. https://doi.org/10.1080/09518398.2019.1609117

Trinh, E. T. (2022). Supporting queer SLIFE youth: Initial queer considerations. In L. J. Pentón Herrera (Ed.), *English and students with limited or interrupted formal education: Global perspectives on teacher preparation and classroom practices* (pp. 209–255). Springer International. https://doi.org/10.1007/978-3-030-86963-2_12

Trinh, E. T. (in press). Queer allyship in TESOL: We need to ACTS now! *TESOL Journal.*

Trinh, E. T., & Tinker Sachs, G. (2023). Thinking queer with Vietnamese EFL textbooks. *Critical Inquiry in Language Studies*. https://doi.org/10.1080/15427587.2023.2190524

Wheeler, E. M., Schwartz, A., & Ramos Pellicia, M. (2023). Language, identity, and racialization: A trio-ethnography of Spanish linguists. *International Review of Qualitative Research, 16*(2), 110–127. https://doi.org/10.1177/19408447221097632

Widodo, H. P., & Elyas, T. (2020). Introduction to gender in language education. *Sexuality & Culture, 24*(4), 1019–1027. https://doi.org/10.1007/s12119-020-09753-1

Raising Awareness of Filipino English as a Second Language Preservice Teachers to Queer Literature: Toward Inclusivity and Allyship

Jess V. Mendoza, Alice A. Cabingan, and Robelyn P. Cunanan

Objectives

- Introduce the importance of queer literature in education.
- Analyze how forms of heteronormativity are embedded in instructional materials.
- Engage in self-reflection in relation to personal attitudes, beliefs, and behaviors regarding queer literature and the LGBTQIA+ community.

Learning Targets

- Articulate the importance of integrating queer literature into education, explaining how it promotes diversity, allyship, inclusion, and representation in the classroom.
- Identify instances of heteronormativity embedded in instructional materials, and critically analyze their impact on the perpetuation of stereotypes and excluding LGBTQIA+ perspectives.
- Demonstrate an increased awareness of personal biases and a commitment to personal growth and development in fostering inclusivity and queer allyship.

Can Do's

- Can advocate for the inclusion of queer literature in the curriculum.
- Can identify forms of heteronormativity in various educational resources and analyze their consequences in the perpetuation of stereotypes, marginalization, and limited representation.
- Can demonstrate an increased awareness of personal biases and actively seek opportunities to challenge and expand their understanding of queer literature and LGBTQIA+ issues.

Success Criteria

- Raised awareness of queer literature.
- Problematized traditional views on gender.
- Fostered queer allyship among ESL preservice teachers.

Positionality

We acknowledge the significance of our positionality in raising awareness among Filipino ESL preservice teachers about queer literature, and we recognize areas for improvement in our approach. Our individual and collective experiences, viewpoints, and identities shape our teaching methods and our dedication to queer allyship within the educational landscape.

In Jess's journey as a student and a teacher, he gained experiential knowledge and understanding of the cultural nuances, challenges, and opportunities within the Filipino educational system. It was his story of introducing queer literature that was shared in this chapter. As coauthors and reflective partners, Alice and Robelyn also contributed their unique perspectives and lived experiences to enrich the conversation. Alice's background in literature teaching provided valuable insights that illuminated our reflections on practice, while Robelyn's expertise in teacher training and curriculum development aided in understanding how to effectively incorporate queer literature into the curriculum.

As allies, our positionality as educators and advocates for social justice compels us to challenge traditional norms and foster queer allyship within the Filipino teacher education context. To achieve this, we believe in the power of queer literature. We also admit that our work is an ongoing and evolving process. We are aware that our own privileges and biases may have influenced the teaching practices narrated and reflections shared in this chapter. Nevertheless, we strived to cultivate a collaborative learning environment where all voices and experiences were valued, which guided the direction and content of this work.

Our positionality as Jess, Alice, and Robelyn has shaped our commitment and practice of raising awareness among 43 Filipino ESL preservice teachers about queer literature, as detailed in the chapter. We firmly believe that education and continual reflection can foster empathy and queer allyship, which are crucial for creating inclusive and accepting classrooms. We are dedicated to ongoing growth and improvement as we work toward creating a more inclusive educational landscape.

Classroom Setting

The work of Moore (2020) serves as a great introduction to the concept of heteronormativity, an oppressive ideology that subjects people to binary poles of sexes, promoting heterosexuality as the normal mode of sexual orientation. Moore's work sparks curiosity about gender issues in language teaching, which leads one back to the works of Bonny Norton Pierce, Joshua Paiz, and Cynthia Nelson, among others. For instance, Nelson's (2009) research on how sexual identities intersect with English language education provides valuable insights into the necessary changes in classroom practices to address sexual diversity. Norton Pierce's (1995) concepts of identity and investment are now used as frameworks for exploring the impact of sexual orientation on language learning. Joshua Paiz's (2020) book, on a more contemporary note, provides research-grounded, practical strategies on how to establish queer-inclusive classrooms and challenge normative views of language and gender. These concepts highlight how the classroom can both perpetuate and challenge this oppressive ideology.

As students enter the classroom, they bring with them cultural values shaped by their interactions and influenced by broader social and cultural practices. These values can manifest in various forms, ranging from acts of politeness and kindness to the promotion of oppressive ideologies like heteronormativity. It is important to note that heteronormativity is intricately woven into one's cultural fabric (van der Toorn et al., 2020), and religion, being an integral component of culture, has the potential to contribute to the perpetuation of these negative ideologies.

In the Philippines, Roman Catholics make up 78.8% of the population (Philippine Statistics Authority, 2023), and the Roman Catholic Church wields a strong influence on the LGBTQIA+ members in the country, particularly regarding discrimination and political rights (United Nations Development Programme & U.S. Agency for International Development, 2014). The Roman Catholic Church has historically dismissed sexual diversity (Joaquin, 2014), which may have contributed to the nonpassage of the Sexual Orientation and Gender Identity Expression Equality bill in the Philippines, which was designed to protect people from acts of discrimination based on their sexual orientation, gender identity, or expression. The Roman Catholic Church was also said to be not supportive of LGBTQIA+ people in the country, and the conservative moral ideologies it imposes have influenced educational policies (Tang & Poudel, 2018). Negative attitudes toward gays and lesbians are widespread among Filipinos, correlated with values tied to intergroup beliefs (Bernardo, 2013), posing challenges for Filipino teachers who wish to integrate queer perspectives into their teaching. Some students also have reservations when dealing with LGBTQIA+ concepts because of their firm morality standards influenced by their family and religious backgrounds along with the Philippine educational system's rarely uncontested heteronormative culture (Tarrayo & Salonga, 2022). Nevertheless, despite the ingrained Catholic culture in the country, many Filipinos remain tolerant of same-sex relations. This can be seen in the Indigenous culture of the ancient Filipinos. Before the Spanish colonization of the Philippines and the widespread dissemination of Christianity, Filipinos used to have *asog*, a male shaman who used to wear skirts, was treated as a woman, and married and had sexual relations with men (Salazar, 2022). Taking a more contemporary perspective, it is evident that younger generations of Filipinos have embraced the concept of sexual diversity. According to a survey conducted by the Pew Research Center (Poushter & Kent, 2020), a significant majority of Filipino respondents believed in the acceptance of homosexuality. Furthermore, the study found that younger Filipino adults exhibited a more progressive and open-minded attitude toward accepting homosexuality compared to their older counterparts.

With these insights, we recognize our role in contributing to the growing movement to amplify the voices of the LGBTQIA+ community in classrooms. Indeed, Moore's (2020) practical taxonomy of representational heteronormativity has prompted us to reflect on the heteronormative aspects of our practices. This helped us take on Moore's challenge—to weaken the hold of heteronormativity in English language teaching (ELT) by first developing a critical understanding of it. To accomplish this, we undertook the task of raising awareness among 43 Filipino ESL preservice teachers about queer literature, aiming to instill the principles of queer allyship, which involves the collaborative efforts of allies who actively challenge the prevailing heteronormative assumptions of themselves and encourage individuals to think queer. By nurturing this collaboration, we strive to bring about transformative changes in support systems and inspire actions that promote and uplift the LGBTQIA+ community (Trinh, in press).

The class was conducted online during the second semester of the 2021–2022 academic year. In the Philippines, "Contemporary, Popular, and Emergent Literature" is a specialization course for preservice ESL teachers, and it is a great avenue to introduce queer literature and queer pedagogy. For clarity, we define queer literature as encompassing all literary works that highlight themes, experiences, and identities related to the LGBTQIA+ community. Additionally, we refer to queer pedagogy as the techniques, strategies, or approaches that challenge and disrupt heteronormative assumptions and practices embedded in queer literature, with the verb *queer* indicating the act of questioning and problematizing these assumptions and practices.

Throughout this course, students engage in discussions about various emerging genres of literature that reflect the realities of contemporary society. It requires extensive reading that is useful in encouraging students to understand and evaluate critical issues in contemporary and popular literature. This will help them be critical of their pedagogical decisions when they officially become teachers. In addition, as literature reflects society, the realities mirrored in literary texts can help preservice teachers be socially aware and be advocates of changes that are needed in order to create a progressive world.

Before the start of the semester, we purposefully asked students to list the popular literary works that they would like to discuss in class. With the rise of the *boys' love* series in the country, it is not surprising that students suggested including works tackling this theme, like the Thai romantic comedy series *2Gether* or the Chinese animated series *Heaven Official's Blessing*. The class then decided to include the animated short film *In a Heartbeat* by David and Bravo (2017), which received positive reactions from the preservice teachers. This led to our discussion of issues in queer literature. To systematically facilitate the teaching–learning process, we divided the course content into three lesson activities: Setting Up and Looking Back, Firming Up, and Moving Forward.

This queering practice might not apply to everyone due to cultural and curricular differences. Religious beliefs and political ideologies of preservice teachers may also affect implementation. Factors such as age, generation, sexual orientation, and gender identity may also influence preservice teachers' motivation and engagement in class discussions. Openness to the topic is a big factor in achieving the goal. Fortunately, the 43 Filipino ESL preservice teachers in our study were very open to the idea of queer literature. Their welcoming attitude toward this topic greatly helped in introducing and fostering queer allyship.

Methods

In this chapter, we share how we attempted to foster queer allyship among preservice teachers. We used a qualitative data analysis approach with a reflective and interpretive lens. We intended to analyze the preservice teachers' reflections and activities to gain insights and inform our own reflections. The archived online classroom, which contained copies of the students' reflections and answers, served as the primary source of data. To guide us, we borrowed concepts and methods of interpretative phenomenological analysis (Smith et al., 2009), which focuses on exploring, describing, interpreting, and situating meanings derived from other people's experiences and understandings.

As a preliminary step, we provided an online informed consent form to 43 preservice teachers. It outlined the purpose of using their reflections and answers to the activities and how confidentiality would be ensured. They were informed that pseudonyms or codes would be used to ensure anonymity. The consent form also had explicit statements that there would be no direct benefits or compensation involved. After consent was secured, we then proceeded with the analysis.

We first familiarized ourselves with the students' reflections and activities. We had multiple readings of the data to develop a comprehensive understanding of the content. As we engaged with the data, we took notes, identified key ideas, and made preliminary observations. Once we were acquainted with the data, our focus shifted to a qualitative data analysis approach.

Rather than strictly adhering to a predefined thematic structure, we opted for an exploratory approach. We delved into the documents to generate insights into students' perspectives and experiences. This iterative and interpretive method allowed us to continuously reflect on the students' reflections and activities, informing our own thoughts and practices in the context of teaching.

It is important to note that we did not explicitly generate themes; however, the qualitative data analysis and reflective approach provided a thorough examination of students' reflections and activities. This, in turn, contributed to a deeper understanding of the topic and enriched our reflections.

Queering the Contemporary, Popular, and Emergent Literature Class

Setting Up and Looking Back

To queer or to question heteronormative assumptions of oneself, the Setting Up activity was first facilitated. Its purpose was to stimulate the preservice teachers' background knowledge of queer literature. This activity took place before the start of the semester, when they were asked to share movies or TV series that explicitly portrayed LGBTQIA+ members and to suggest LGBQIA+-themed literature (also known as queer literature) that they would like to include in the syllabus and discuss in class. In the end, the students chose the animated short film *In a Heartbeat*, which is about a schoolboy who has a same-gender crush and is outed in school.

During the time when queer literature had to be discussed, the Looking Back activity was facilitated, in which the preservice teachers had to reflect on their experiences in the classroom. We posted this question in the online classroom: "Back when you were in elementary and high school, do you remember any LGBTQIA+-themed text or article that you read and discussed during your English classes?" Everyone was encouraged to have a healthy discussion by replying to their classmates' answers on the discussion board. As expected in a country with a predominantly Christian population, none of the 43 preservice teachers remembered any instance when they specifically discussed queer literature. It is an indication of the absence of queer lives' representations in instructional materials and schools in general. This also resonates with the "politico-socio-cultural-educational-capitalist" restrictions faced by Vietnamese EFL textbooks (Trinh & Tinker Sachs, 2023); thus, people should think more queerly to challenge the normative and regulatory practices.

Ideally, the stories and experiences of LGBTQIA+ people should be included in educational settings, but not all may welcome this idea because of cultural, religious, and political beliefs. Additionally, discussing LGBTQIA+ topics may increase the risk of bullying and other adverse effects on the lives of LGBTQIA+ students. This was evident in a notable exchange between a bisexual (L) and straight (G) preservice teacher (PST), capturing the challenges and complexities surrounding LGBTQIA+ inclusion in education:

> **PST L:** I [cannot] remember any. None of it was used and discussed during our English classes in elementary and high school.
>
> **PST G:** Did you wish that they had done it at that time?
>
> **PST L:** As a kid, probably no.... I [have] always been afraid of anything that might subject me to [bullying] because I had more than enough and discussing LGBT-themed text/article in the class would just make me the subject, particularly on this topic. [It] would only [give] the bullies [the opportunity] to give [me] unsolicited and insensitive comments.... However, now that I learned how literature can be an eye-opener to the realities of life and society, I think it would [not] hurt to risk being subjected to offensive comments,... They will say what they [want to] say anyway. At least I [know] now that an effort to eradicate gender stereotypes and to become more inclusive is [implemented] by the teacher or institution when they include these themes.

It is understandable that some students who identify as members of the LGBTQIA+ community may not be receptive to the idea of incorporating these texts into the curriculum. Some reasons behind this reluctance are fear of getting bullied, vulnerability, and marginalization. The potential for unwanted attention an LGBTQIA+ child might receive can trigger anxiety and can eventually be the reason for demotivation and reduced learning. This is why some queer theorists have concerns about including queer texts, even positive representations of the LGBTQIA+ community such as the valorization of the idea of coming out, because they may further divide those who are in and out of the closet (Talburt, 2007).

Bullying in the form of homophobic and transphobic remarks may lower one's self-esteem and confidence, leading to nonparticipation in class. Furthermore, it can contribute to issues such as absenteeism, high dropout rates, suicide, and other forms of self-harm (UNESCO Office Bangkok & Regional Bureau for Education in Asia and the Pacific, 2018). In a poignant exchange, a preservice teacher shared how bullying caused a student to transfer to another school and how her cousin suffered from the negative impacts of bullying on mental health due to rejection:

> **PST B:** I can still clearly remember one of my former teachers making fun of my gay classmate and calling him in public *"bakla"* [gay] and some of my classmates shouting *"'Pag bakla, salot!"* [If you're gay, you're a plague!] Seeing him transfer school because of that bullying incident pains me.... I have an older cousin. We're very close, and I can still remember how she had a hard time convincing herself not to like girls. She always [told] me that she's not well, she didn't feel normal... and thought she's sick for liking girls. She told me not to be like her because our relatives might reject our existence. And she was right. Her mother got her a boyfriend, and they didn't work out. Now, she's in London with her girlfriend. And now I thank these experiences with them because they became a reason for me to get to know them, know their world, and not be ignorant. It's like a lesson I didn't learn in school, but I chose to learn by myself.
>
> **PST T:** With that, we can see how important it is to include such text or literature to educate and raise awareness among students at an early age because different stories help shape the students' minds to develop, mature, and be open to gender diversity.

Capturing again the words of preservice teachers L and T, their discussion illustrates that efforts to include queer literature in the K–12 curriculum are one step toward inclusion. It is also through the use of instructional materials that teachers can ensure that no one is left out of classroom experiences (Paiz, 2015). As preservice teacher B pointed out, she was grateful for those experiences because she was able to learn more about the community. Therefore, if these experiences are reflected in the literary texts, they serve as valuable resources to enhance students' critical thinking and raise awareness about gender diversity. In addition, incorporating queer materials provides teachers and students with an opportunity to develop social justice thinking that may transform their and others' actions in the community. This suggests that queer literature can benefit not only members of the community but all students as well. As long as there are people willing to accept the existence of the LGBTQIA+ community, there is hope for genuine acceptance and acknowledgment.

In summary, the original intention of the Setting Up and Looking Back preliminary activities was to help ESL preservice teachers realize the pervasiveness of heteronormativity by recognizing that there is a negligible or limited representation of the LGBTQIA+ community in curricular materials (Curaming & Curaming, 2020; Manalo, 2018; Paiz, 2015; Rhodes & Coda, 2017; Trinh & Tinker Sachs, 2023). Heteronormativity is predicated on the notion that heterosexuality is the accepted norm (Motschenbacher, 2010). By avoiding or silencing the existence of the LGBTQIA+ community in instructional materials, heteronormativity is perpetuated as the erasure could be interpreted as a hint that nonheterosexual relationships and related subjects are not suitable for the classroom. This erasure, referred to as heteronormative erasure by Moore (2020), reinforces traditional views. Nevertheless, these activities opened discussions about the experiences of LGBTQIA+ people and the power of stories to raise awareness about their community. This encourages us to think queer. Particularly, the Looking Back activity allowed preservice teachers to share their own values and clarify their stance toward the LGBTQIA+ community by reflecting on their own experiences and the experiences of others. For preservice teachers, it is a good moment to problematize traditional views on gender. By doing so, educators reinforce the belief that the LGBTQIA+ community is normal, is supported by the community, and needs allies. To foster queer allyship among preservice teachers, it is crucial for them to reflect on these topics and connect their personal experiences to gain a deeper understanding of the complexity of these issues. Again, queer allyship is about allies who collaboratively work to challenge heteronormative assumptions of themselves and incite actions of support. Just like Setting Up and Looking Back, providing similar opportunities for reflection is important to ensure that students have time to reflect on what heteronormative assumptions they have so that they can engage in necessary actions to challenge them.

Firming Up

After having realized that the absence of queer literature is a result of heteronormativity, the preservice teachers took proactive steps to understand various forms of heteronormative beliefs and behaviors. As an extension of self-reflection, preservice teachers must think queer in order to enkindle queer allyship. To think queer here means to examine how normative beliefs can be "challenged, unfixed, unlearned, inquired, and placed into new learnings and understandings" (Trinh & Tinker Sachs, 2023, p. 20). However, one must know the enemy before the battle.

To strengthen their knowledge of heteronormativity as it relates to queer literature, the preservice teachers engaged in the Firming Up activity. During this learning session, they were introduced to Moore's (2020) taxonomy of representational heteronormativity, which serves as both a framework for designing instructional materials and a model for identifying different forms of heteronormativity (see Table 1). The taxonomy outlines five types of heteronormative representations: explicit heterosexism, heteronormative erasure, heteronormative marginalization, heteronormative mainstreaming, and queer inclusion. By familiarizing themselves with this framework, preservice teachers can make informed decisions in their pedagogy and effectively address heteronormativity in their instructional materials.

Table 1. Moore's Taxonomy of Representational Heteronormativity	
Type of heteronormativity	**Meaning**
Explicit heterosexism	There is clear preference toward heterosexuality; other sexual identities are belittled and seen as abnormal.
Heteronormative erasure	Only heterosexual relations are shown; no reference to other sexual identities is included.
Heteronormative marginalization	Nonheterosexual relations are portrayed in stereotypical, controversial, and rare themes.
Heteronormative mainstreaming	There are positive depictions of nonheterosexual relationships, but they are contingent upon the characters conforming to traditional (Western) heterosexual relationships.
Queer inclusion	There are diverse types of relationships that do not necessarily conform to Western heteronormative norms; social and political interests and concerns beyond their sexual orientation are included.

In explicit heterosexism, there are direct statements in the text that devalue being part of the LGBTQIA+ community. It perpetuates the notion that heterosexuality, or sexual, romantic relations between opposite sexes, is the only normal sexuality. Meanwhile, heteronormative erasure undermines the existence of LGBTQIA+ people; hence, there is no LGBTQIA+ character or topic in the material. Heteronormative marginalization is a form of heteronormativity where the LGBTQIA+ community is included but in the context of essentialized and controversial themes like HIV, AIDS, and social discrimination. In contrast, heteronormative mainstreaming includes positive representations of LGBTQIA+ people, but they tend to copy or imitate heterosexual relationships by getting married, being in a monogamous relationship, and having children. Lastly, queer inclusion shows more nuanced representations where the social and political rights of LGBTQIA+ people are tackled and visual or narrative renditions of sexuality, desire, and affection that defy traditional or stereotypical relations are included. In all, this taxonomy, aside from being a framework for creating nonheteronormative instructional material, may also be used as a reflexive tool to interrogate one's own practices.

After an hour of online discussion of this framework, the preservice teachers were given the task of analyzing two ESL textbooks used by some private schools in the Philippines. The objective was to engage them in analyzing literary texts, specifically looking for forms of heteronormativity, while fostering queer allyship and developing critical thinking skills through the exchange of ideas. To explore potential similarities and differences in heteronormativity between local and global contexts, the class was randomly divided into eight groups. Four groups were assigned to analyze a Grade 7 textbook, while the other four groups analyzed a Grade 10 textbook. In the Philippines, Grade 7 English textbooks are focused on Philippine literature, while Grade 10 English textbooks are centered around world literature. Each book consisted of four units, and every group was randomly assigned to focus on one unit. To guide their analysis, the students were provided with a matrix where they recorded the title of the literary text, identified the form of heteronormativity present, and wrote a brief explanation justifying their categorization. Throughout this process, the preservice teachers were encouraged to critically reflect on the texts and their underlying heteronormative elements.

As a culminating activity, each group was tasked with writing a reflection based on the outcomes of their analysis. The purpose of these reflections was to deepen their understanding of heteronormativity, prompt critical self-reflection, and promote a greater sense of queer allyship among the preservice teachers. With this structured approach, the activity sought to create a meaningful learning experience, enabling preservice teachers to develop the necessary skills to identify and challenge heteronormative representations in literature, ultimately fostering inclusivity and allyship in their future teaching practice.

After their analysis, they discovered that two forms of heteronormative representation were present: heteronormative erasure and heteronormative marginalization. In the Grade 7 textbook, one group noted an instance of heteronormative marginalization in a literary text while the rest of the literary texts in the units represented heteronormative erasure. Likewise, the Grade 10 textbook had heteronormative erasure as there were no LGBTQIA+ characters mentioned in any of the literary texts. The heteronormative marginalization was noted to be present, especially in the Philippine short story "My Brother's Peculiar Chicken" by Alejandro R. Roces. In the story, two brothers argue about whether the peculiar chicken is a hen or a rooster. One brother argues that it has no comb or wattles, which is why it is a hen, while the other brother argues that the chicken has such great skills in fighting, so it is a rooster. It became clear that this story was a form of heteronormative marginalization when the mother says, "That chicken is a *binabae* [gay]. It is a rooster that looks like a hen." Because of its feminine appearance, the chicken is judged to be a gay rooster. In addition, the brothers seek help from the villagers to decide whether the chicken is a hen or a rooster. The chief of the village comments, "It does not look like any hen I have ever seen." Another villager, an expert in poultry raising, also says, "I have never run across a chicken like this before." In these cases, queerness is only mentioned during a taboo argument and is framed as something controversial and rare. Thus, it can be considered a form of heteronormative marginalization based on Moore's (2020) taxonomy since the story includes nonstraight representations but in essentialized, controversial, and rare frames. At the end of the story, the chicken lays an egg, which proves that it is indeed a hen.

With this status of the two textbooks, it is no wonder that heteronormativity has been pervasive in classrooms because the texts reflect what is happening in society. Families, religious institutions, culture, and media have all reinforced this ideology, resulting in its prevalence. However, the classroom as a reflection of the larger society can also be the place where people disrupt the heteronormative hegemony, as demonstrated by the Firming Up activity, which proves that Moore's (2020) taxonomy is a valuable tool for understanding heteronormativity in instructional materials and problematizing sexual orientation and gender identity representations in ESL textbooks.

This activity also affirmed the preservice teachers' initial realizations during the Looking Back activity, when they reflected on the absence of LGBTQIA+-themed texts in their elementary and secondary education. Similar findings were identified by Manalo (2018) in four textbooks used by some Filipino learners, which lacked explicit representation of gender variance. The presence of the same form of heteronormativity was also noted in two sets of EFL textbooks used in Spanish high schools, emphasizing the dominance of traditional family relationships and heterosexual love (Ruiz-Cecilia et al., 2021). In a heavily Christian country like the Philippines, the erasure of the LGBTQIA+ community in textbooks is not surprising. As Curaming and Curaming (2020) previously noted, textbook authors may be constrained by their heteronormative sphere, avoiding the risk of offending the conservative market, including publishing houses, administrators, educators, and students. This assertion is supported by Trinh and Tinker Sachs (2023), who emphasized the restrictions imposed by politico-socio-cultural-educational-capitalist systems.

In all, this Firming Up activity is needed in fostering queer allyship since it is not only about being aware of heteronormative assumptions of oneself but also about thinking queer and provoking actions to create safe spaces where preservice teachers can talk about LGBTQIA+ experiences and inclusion. They must be equipped with this kind of pedagogical and content knowledge so as to be strategic in troubling gender issues in the classroom. With this, they can also better challenge heteronormativity as they revisit their questioning techniques, strategies, and lesson plans, which are necessary to create spaces for everyone (Coda, 2018). By having a principled way of looking at things, preservice teachers will be guided on how to best solve the problem. It is also important that they not only become knowledgeable of the various theories, but also be given time to test out the principles that they have learned.

Moving Forward

If the Looking Back activity is intended to activate the schema and the Firming Up activity facilitates acquiring specific knowledge about heteronormativity and its forms, Moving Forward is meant to encourage reflection on what one can do about the problem. The main objective of this third activity is to encourage preservice teachers to think of what they can do once they officially become educators. Specifically, the intention is to help students develop the belief that queer literature and queer pedagogy are powerful tools to advance the causes of the LGBTQIA+ community and to establish equity in the community for all marginalized peoples. The aim is to push the idea that queer literature must be included in instructional materials together with carefully crafted activities in order to help ease, if not solve, the issue of lack of representation in the classroom. From a broader perspective, queer allyship is being nurtured by provoking a sense of communal responsibility to support LGBTQIA+ people through the inclusion of queer literature.

To realize the intentions, we posted this question on the class's discussion board: "Do you think you should include and discuss LGBTQIA+-themed texts when you officially become teachers?" Thankfully, the 43 preservice teachers shared the view that they would be likely to discuss queer literature, as captured by the following exchange:

> **PST Q:** Yes, I believe LGBT-themed texts should be included because we value diversity. In school, especially in society, we should also embrace the people who are part of this LGBT community. Through teaching this kind of theme, we can teach students to respect and accept individual differences. Many people have negative stereotypes about LGBT people, and as a teacher who teaches moral values [aside from facts], I can help everyone understand and learn more about their situation. We can understand where they're coming from and learn new and useful information from them.
>
> **PST I:** I agree with [PST Q]. In schools, we are open to diversity, and thus teaching them to also value it through LGBT-themed text is a great and creative way!
>
> **PST B:** Yes, including and discussing LGBT-themed texts when I am officially a teacher is a great opportunity to open the minds of young students... because as a teacher, I can play a big role in advocating fair treatment when it comes to gender identity of an individual.

This reflection activity is a good way to conclude the discussion about queer literature and its power to advocate inclusivity and allyship in the classroom. It is also a good approach to develop and produce preservice teachers who are active advocates of LGBTQIA+ inclusion. Evident in their answers is the preservice teachers' desire to emphasize the values of respect, acceptance, and diversity in their classes when they officially become teachers. It gives us hope that there will be more inclusive classrooms in the future, although these preservice teachers already have some concerns:

> **PST A:** From what I observed on how LGBT-themed texts were introduced to us, I realized that it is possible... so I see nothing wrong with trying to introduce them in our future classes. I admit when we watched the video, it [felt] so new to me, maybe since I'm not that exposed to that kind of topics even back then, so I really think I have a long way to go to discover, learn, and appreciate more with regards to these themes and topics. We may not be able to totally end discrimination, but still, we teachers can have the power to help the future generation and that is to know and understand the words RESPECT and ACCEPTANCE... whatever their gender identity is and whoever they are.... I think we teachers can help our world a bit better if we will start inculcating in our students' minds how to be respectful and open towards the changes and how truly diverse our world is.

Preservice teacher A is just one of many future teachers who are willing to accept the individuality of students. They are the generation that prioritizes and embraces diversity, so they can really sympathize and empathize with LGBTQIA+ people. They also show their willingness to improve themselves so that they can create safe spaces in their classroom, though they might feel unsure because they feel they lack knowledge and training on how to do so. In addition, because of their lack of experience and unfamiliarity with queer literature, some of these preservice teachers lack confidence in how they will teach it. Consequently, preservice teachers must be trained on how to queer their classrooms and on how to manage negative situations brought about by applying this critical pedagogy. This has also been the concern of many in-service teachers both in the Philippines and abroad. Some teachers in New York City claimed that they have not received any formal training in queer pedagogy or in the creation of queer-inclusive curricula (McLaughlin Cahill, 2019). Filipino teachers, on the other hand, shared that they have difficulties related to time, effort, knowledge, and skills in integrating gender in ELT, as well as the lack of institutional programs and training on gender integration. Furthermore, long-standing and pervasive religious beliefs and conservative ideals are obstacles that must be overcome (Tarrayo et al., 2021). With this, preservice teachers must be made aware of various queer texts that they can use when they teach and must be further taught how to apply critical pedagogies in teaching, for example, queer pedagogy.

Lastly, it is not a matter of whether LGBTQIA+ texts should be included today, but rather a matter of offering students a wide variety of literature that represent the range of human experience. As a preservice teacher said:

> I would love to include and discuss LGBTQ-themed texts.... We often say that literature is the story of humans' lives. It expresses the history of society. Also, it is a form of human expression. So, I find it contradicting when others prohibit or limit the LGBTQ's access to literature. Literature is for everyone, regardless of how they identify their selves [*sic*]. Inclusivity should be given to LGBTQ, even in literature.

This quote emphasizes the need to represent the LGBTQIA+ community in educators' choices of literature because it creates a culture of inclusivity and acceptance that is much needed in society. Queer texts also highlight the diversity that is a defining feature of the world today.

Hearkening to Moore's (2021) plea to stop debating and erasing queer lives in ELT, we will continue raising awareness of the existence of popular and emerging queer literature. To weaken heteronormativity's foothold in ELT is to develop a critical understanding of it. With the positive attitudes of the 43 preservice teachers in our study toward queer literature, it gives us hope to see in the future at least 43 inclusive classrooms where everyone is listened to and represented. Their answers to the reflective question in the Moving Forward activity make us believe that a sense of queer allyship was enkindled in the preservice teachers. Their intention to include queer literature in their future classes is a good start to expand the knowledge about queer literature and its existence as valuable reading material and as a powerful tool to support and advocate for inclusivity and allyship.

Reflection on Practice

Leni Robredo, a former vice president of the Philippines, once said, *"Ang namulat, hindi na muling pipikit,"* which means that once someone has been enlightened about what is happening, the person will not turn a blind eye anymore. The purpose of the activities in this chapter is to awaken the minds of preservice teachers toward queer literature in order to nurture queer allyship. Once they are made aware of it and the lives of the LGBTQIA+ community reflected in it, it is hoped they will become allies and advocates to help the LGBTQIA+ community further their causes. In pursuing this goal, we learned a few things.

First, the Setting Up and Looking Back activities prove that PSTs lack knowledge of and experience with queer literature. They have encountered LGBTQIA+-themed texts outside the classroom, but these were not discussed in class. In that case, the inclusion of queer literature in the curriculum must be considered. If schools really want to make learning authentic, the interests of the new breed of students must be given importance. Consequently, preservice teachers must be made familiar with these texts. Queer literature can be as powerful as classical texts in teaching values and can help raise awareness of the lives of LGBTQIA+ people, which is the first step in cultivating the culture of allyship.

Second, the experience in implementing the Firming Up activity has made us realize that we must also explain to preservice teachers how gender identity and sexual orientation play critical roles in the teaching and learning process. This has to be thoroughly discussed and must include examples. Initially, we just wanted them to know more about the forms of heteronormativity so that they would understand what they should and should not do when they create materials, decide on their teaching strategies, and interact with students. However, during the discussion, we realized that we must emphasize how gender identity and sexual orientation are important considerations to create a more inclusive and supportive learning environment for all students, because awareness about this can help preservice teachers realize the potential biases and prejudices that may exist in themselves, the curriculum, or the classroom environment. It will allow them to question and challenge personal assumptions about what is considered "normal" or "typical."

It must also be emphasized that some LGBTQIA+ students will eventually assert their identity if they are continuously not listened to. In a democratic country like the Philippines, they will exercise their freedom of speech, as one preservice teacher shared:

> **PST G:** As far as I can remember, the students themselves were the ones to initiate such kinds of themes, on small programs, but there were no LGBTQIA+-themed texts initiated by the school.

This quote proves that some people, if they are unheard, will find ways to express their individuality. In fact, the younger generations are more open-minded; they are willing to learn about the community, and they value the uniqueness of a person. If schools truly want to create an inclusive environment, stakeholders must approach the younger generations from the perspectives they hold by considering their values, beliefs, and attitudes. However, it must also be emphasized that other people will not accept this kind of thinking. Some people will find ways to stop these initiatives. These individuals also need help in order to be enlightened on why queer literature and queer pedagogy are important.

Third, the Moving Forward activity encouraged preservice teachers to express their willingness to discuss queer literature and to be trained on how to effectively queer their classrooms and their schools. This is a big issue in the Philippines. We feel the exigency to be further trained. This initiative was implemented only through our own efforts. There is a lack of a clear national framework on how to implement queer pedagogy. There are only micro-efforts by teachers, but there is no concrete, contextualized model used in the country. Queering the English language classroom by including queer texts is easy enough, but providing carefully planned activities to counter heteronormative actions and dealing with the consequences need considerable effort. Without proper training, the effort may not come to fruition. This calls for stakeholders to convene and collaborate to make a contextualized model of queer pedagogy. The lack of training of teachers indicates that there is also a lack of queer activities that may help the LGBTQIA+ community in the achievement of their ideals.

In general, to foster queer allyship among ESL preservice teachers, they were introduced to queer literature and the power that this genre holds. As literature is a mirror of life, it is a helpful medium for people to learn about LGBTQIA+ people and the different issues the community is battling with every day. It is by having a clear grasp of what is happening that preservice teachers can effectively plan how they can establish inclusive classrooms once they officially become teachers. Now that the 43 Filipino preservice educators in our study have been made aware of some of the problems of using queer literature in the classroom and the power it holds, we fervently hope that they spread the knowledge of this genre and try to include it in their own practices so that many people will be encouraged to be queer allies.

Action Items

There are still many things to do before we can truly create inclusive classrooms and foster queer allyship, but we can take simple steps to achieve our dream. First, we can educate ourselves and engage in self-reflection. Queer allyship needs people to be aware of their own heteronormative assumptions, and because of our lack of knowledge, we may not realize that we ourselves are being heteronormative. What we believe to be normal because it has long been part of our cultural and religious systems may actually be silently promoting heteronormativity and other forms of prejudice. Thus, it is important to contemplate and assess our own practices and beliefs.

Second, we must act on our realizations. Being aware is not enough; we have to act. Queer allyship calls for the collective effort of allies to disrupt and problematize heteronormative assumptions, and we can do this by thinking queer. It does not necessarily limit us to the LGBTQIA+ community but rather pushes us to rethink the normative practices and existing power dynamics. We can increase LGBTQIA+ representation in our classrooms by incorporating queer literature and using queer strategies. In the same light, Filipino preservice teachers must be further trained for a truly diverse world. We first need to develop a national framework on queer pedagogy through conversations with various stakeholders and scholars. Though this is important, it is also essential that we address the potential complexities around those instances, through honest dialogues with people, colleagues, and students about their views and beliefs related to heteronormativity, especially when social and cultural values have been framed by the Catholic Church. If respect and acceptance are what we want for the LGBTQIA+ community, we have to also give them to people who have different values and beliefs than ours.

Third, we can foster queer allyship by establishing a network of people who care for everyone. Just like the flora and fauna, we must cocreate a community where everyone can feel safe and truly belong, regardless of their sexual orientation or gender identity. For teacher education, we can already start forming a network of allies by engaging them in discussions about LGBTQIA+ experiences, encouraging them to collaborate with local LGBTQIA+

organizations, and involving them in advocacy and policy development activities. Queer allyship involves working together to challenge common heteronormative assumptions and promote a supportive environment that embraces diverse identities. As allies, we can actively support LGBTQIA+ students, friends, relatives, and community members by advocating for their rights, amplifying their voices, and standing up against discrimination. By fostering queer allyship, we contribute to the creation of inclusive classrooms and communities where everyone's experiences and identities are respected and valued.

Finally, we must answer this question: After reading this chapter, what can I do to show my support to my LGBTQIA+ students, friends, relatives, and community members?

Authors

Jess V. Mendoza, an instructor and campus research coordinator at National University Lipa, specializes in linguistics, literary criticism, and stylistics. His current research delves into the intersection of gender in language and literature education, exploring the dynamics of identity and expression.

Alice A. Cabingan has a PhD in English language studies from the Lyceum of the Philippines University and serves as an assistant professor at the Batangas State University. She specializes in teaching Philippine literature in English, Philippine linguistics, and the teaching and assessment of macro skills. Her research focuses on the analysis of literary texts and enhancing reading proficiency.

Robelyn P. Cunanan has a PhD in Philippine studies with a specialization in language, culture, and media from De La Salle University serves as an assistant professor of Filipino in the College of Teacher Education at the Batangas State University. Her expertise extends to validating prototype syllabi for preservice teacher education programs, which are now widely adopted by universities across the Philippines.

References

Bernardo, A. B. I. (2013). Exploring social cognitive dimensions of sexual prejudice in Filipinos. *Philippine Journal of Psychology, 46*(2), 19–48.

Coda, J. (2018). Disrupting standard practice: Queering the world language classroom. *Dimension*, pp. 74–89.

Curaming, E. M., & Curaming, R. A. (2020). Gender (in)equality in English textbooks in the Philippines: A critical discourse analysis. *Sexuality and Culture, 24*(4), 1167–1188. https://doi.org/10.1007/s12119-020-09750-4

Joaquin, A. (2014). Carrying the cross: Being gay, Catholic, and Filipino. *Sociology and Anthropology Student Union Undergraduate Journal, 1*, 17–28.

Manalo, A. S. D. (2018). Gender representation and stereotypes in the K–12 English learner's materials. *International Journal of Scientific Research and Management, 6*(8), 558–567. https://doi.org/10.18535/ijsrm/v6i8.el02

McLaughlin Cahill, J. (2019). *Queering secondary English: Practitioner research examining culturally responsive pedagogy and YA queer book clubs* [Doctoral dissertation, Columbia University]. https://doi.org/10.7916/d8-47nh-ff92

Moore, A. R. (2020). Understanding heteronormativity in ELT textbooks: A practical taxonomy. *ELT Journal, 74*(2), 116–125. https://doi.org/10.1093/elt/ccz058

Moore, A. R. (2021). A plea to stop debating and erasing queer lives in ELT. *ELT Journal, 75*(3), 362–365. https://doi.org/10.1093/ELT/CCAB029

Motschenbacher, H. (2010). *Language, gender and sexual identity.* John Benjamins.

Nelson, C. D. (2009). Sexual identities in English language education: Classroom conversations. Routledge. https://doi.org/10.4324/9780203891544

Norton Peirce, B. (1995). Social identity, investment, and language learning. *TESOL Quarterly, 29*(1). https://doi.org/10.2307/3587803

Paiz, J. M. (2015). Over the monochrome rainbow: Heteronormativity in ESL reading texts and textbooks. *Journal of Language and Sexuality, 4*(1), 77–101. https://doi.org/10.1075/jls.4.1.03pai

Paiz, J. M. (2020). *Queering the English language classroom: A practical guide for teachers.* Equinox.

Philippine Statistics Authority. (2023). *Religious affiliation in the Philippines (2020 census of population and housing).* https://psa.gov.ph/content/religious-affiliation-philippines-2020-census-population-and-housing

Poushter, J., & Kent, N. (2020). *The global divide on homosexuality persists.* Pew Research Center. https://www.pewresearch.org/global/2020/06/25/global-divide-on-homosexuality-persists/

Rhodes, C. M., & Coda, J. (2017). It's not in the curriculum: Adult English language teachers and LGBQ topics. *Adult Learning, 28*(3), 99–106. https://doi.org/10.1177/1045159517712483

Ruiz-Cecilia, R., Guijarro-Ojeda, J. R., & Marín-Macías, C. (2021). Analysis of heteronormativity and gender roles in EFL textbooks. *Sustainability, 13*(1), 1–18. https://doi.org/10.3390/su13010220

Salazar, J. O. M. (2022, July 30). How "bakla" explains the struggle for queer identity in the Philippines. *Foreign Policy.* https://foreignpolicy.com/2022/07/30/bakla-queer-identity-philippines/

Smith, J. A., Flowers, P., & Larkin, M. (2009). *Interpretative phenomenological analysis: Theory, method and research.* SAGE.

Talburt, S. (2007). Queer theory. In B. Bank, S. Delamont, & C. Marshall (Eds.), *Gender and education: An encyclopedia* (Vol. I, pp. 63–70). Praeger.

Tang, X., & Poudel, A. N. (2018). Exploring challenges and problems faced by LGBT students in Philippines: A qualitative study. *Journal of Public Health Policy and Planning, 2*(3), 1–17.

Tarrayo, V. N., Potestades, R. R., & Ulla, M. B. (2021). Exploring the gender perspective in English language teaching (ELT): Voices from ELT practitioners in Philippine higher education institutions. *Sexuality and Culture, 25*, 1634–1652. https://doi.org/10.1007/s12119-021-09840-x

Tarrayo, V. N., & Salonga, A. O. (2022). Queering English language teaching: Insights from teachers in a Philippine state university. *Critical Inquiry in Language Studies.* https://doi.org/10.1080/15427587.2022.2112532

Trinh, E. (in press). Queer allyship in TESOL: We need to ACTS now! *TESOL Journal.*

Trinh, E., & Tinker Sachs, G. (2023). Thinking queer with Vietnamese EFL textbooks. *Critical Inquiry in Language Studies.* https://doi.org/10.1080/15427587.2023.2190524

UNESCO Office Bangkok & Regional Bureau for Education in Asia and the Pacific. (2018). *School-related violence and bullying on the basis of sexual orientation and gender identity or expression (SOGIE): Synthesis report on China, the Philippines, Thailand and Viet Nam.* https://unesdoc.unesco.org/ark:/48223/pf0000366434

United Nations Development Programme & U.S. Agency for International Development. (2014). *Being LGBT in Asia: The Philippine country report.* https://www.undp.org/sites/g/files/zskgke326/files/publications/Philippines%20Report_Final.pdf

van der Toorn, J., Pliskin, R., & Morgenroth, T. (2020). Not quite over the rainbow: The unrelenting and insidious nature of heteronormative ideology. *Current Opinion in Behavioral Sciences, 34,* 160–165. https://doi.org/10.1016/j.cobeha.2020.03.001

Additional Resources

David, B., & Bravo, E. (Directors). (2017). *In a heartbeat* [Film].

Li, H. (Director). (2020). *Heaven official's blessing* [TV series].

Thongjila, W. (Director). (2020). *2gether* [TV series].

LGB English as a Foreign Language Teachers in Taiwan: LGBTQ+ Sensemaking in the Workplace

Eric K. Ku

Setting

Taiwan has often been at the forefront of LGBTQ+[1] issues in Asia, largely due to being the first country in Asia to legalize same-sex marriage, in 2019 (Ku, 2020). In addition, some aspects of the workplace in Taiwanese society are more LGBTQ+-friendly considering the broader Asian context. In particular, Achyldurdyyeva et al. (2021) noted that one feature of the workplace environment in Taiwan that sets it apart from neighboring Asian countries is the introduction of sexual orientation–friendly legislation at the national level. For example, Taiwan has passed legislation that protects employees from discrimination in the workplace, which includes discrimination on the basis of gender and gender orientation (i.e., the Employment Service Act of 1992; Ministry of Labor, 2018), as well as legislation that more specifically addresses gender equality, gender discrimination, and sexual harassment in the workplace (i.e., the Act of Gender Equality in Employment; Ministry of Labor, 2022). These laws served as the first step toward companies setting their own policies that explicitly address inclusion and equality with regard to gender and sexual orientation.

Cultural Challenges

Despite having sexual orientation–friendly legislation in place, the workplace in Taiwanese society still proves to be a complex and, at times, hostile landscape for LGBTQ+ individuals to navigate. The effectiveness of national legislation in promoting sexual orientation–friendly

1. Throughout the chapter, the acronyms LGB and LGBTQ+ are used. LGB refers to the participants and scope of this study, since no transgender or other gender-diverse participants were included. LGBTQ+ refers to the broader literature covered by other scholars.

workplaces has been limited by other aspects of Taiwanese society. For example, LGBTQ+ individuals may be limited by or under the pressure of a generally conservative workplace culture established under institutionalized heteronormative views enforced by senior leadership or within their own families stemming from traditional Confucian values regarding gender norms and family role expectations (Achyldurdyyeva et al., 2021; Adamczyk et al., 2015). Thus, they may choose to hide their sexual orientation in the workplace due to fear of not fitting in, being discriminated against, or being excluded from career advancement (Achyldurdyyeva et al., 2021).

The broader problems regarding the workplace experiences of LGBTQ+ individuals were investigated in detail in the "2020 Workplace Equality Survey in Taiwan" conducted by the Taiwan Tongzhi Hotline Association (i.e., Taiwan's oldest and largest LGBTQ+ non-profit organization) with 2,121 respondents (Taiwan Tongzhi Hotline Association, 2020). The survey focused on the status of LGBTQ+ individuals in the workplace after the legalization of same-sex marriage in Taiwan, covering a wide range of job sectors (e.g., service, education, technology, food, construction, medicine, government, arts). Findings from the survey showed that coming out in the workplace was still not widespread; 55% of respondents had come out to a few of their coworkers, but less than 30% had come out to superiors. Over half of respondents thought that they might have a coworker who is in the closet, and 35% of respondents had pretended to be heterosexual in their interactions with coworkers or superiors. This is perhaps the result of a lack of LGBTQ+ support or allyship in the workplace culture in Taiwan, with nearly 40% of respondents having experienced a coworker make homophobic comments in their workplace and only 8% of respondents having LGBTQ+-friendly[2] coworkers or social groups at their workplace (Taiwan Tongzhi Hotline Association, 2020). Finally, when it comes to educational institutions as a workplace, the survey found education to be one of the job sectors in Taiwan with the biggest gap between the percentage of people who believe that coming out is important and the percentage of people who had actually come out.

The study described in this chapter examined the experiences of five Taiwanese elementary school EFL teachers who self-identified as LGB individuals. One might argue that, particularly in recent years, elementary school EFL teachers have been uniquely presented with challenges positioned at the intersection of language and gender in education.

On the one hand, since 2018, English education in Taiwan has been faced with the enormous task of transitioning Taiwan into a Mandarin-English bilingual society by 2030, as mandated by the Taiwanese government's new nationwide initiative "2030 Bilingual Nation." The primary focus of the policy has been the spread of English, or the "Englishification" of Taiwanese society, for the purposes of internationalization and increasing national competitiveness in the global economy. To achieve this, English has been designated as "a primary factor in the success of the Bilingual Nation policy" at the exclusion of other languages used in Taiwan, including Mandarin, Southern Min, Hakka, and indigenous languages (Ferrer &

2. In the context of this survey, the term *LGBTQ+-friendly* (in Mandarin Chinese: 同志友善) is used. In both English and Mandarin Chinese, the term *LGBTQ+-friendly* is slightly different from *ally* or *allyship*. While the former connotes a general acceptance and kindness toward LGBTQ+ people, the latter connotes a more intentional stance, identity, or effort toward supporting LGBTQ+ people.

Lin, 2021, p. 8). Though the intention of "English supremacy" (Chang, 2022, p. 137) is overtly expressed in the policy, the actual implementation has been much more ambiguous. For example, Graham and Yeh's (2023) study of teachers' implementation of bilingual education showed that teachers often had different understandings of how bilingual education was to be implemented (e.g., whether classes should be English-only or bilingual Mandarin-English), leading to confusion. Furthermore, though EFL teachers play a major role in the implementation of the 2030 Bilingual Nation policy, their actual role has also been ambiguous, with some EFL teachers teaching alone, some coteaching with native-English-speaking teachers, some coteaching with content teachers, and some coteaching with both (Graham & Yeh, 2023). In sum, since the introduction of the 2030 Bilingual Nation policy in 2018, EFL teachers have been thrust into the spotlight and expected to adapt to a rapidly changing English landscape.

At the same time, LGBTQ+ education and broader LGBTQ+ issues have become increasingly common and controversial topics in educational settings. In recent years, Taiwan's sociopolitical landscape around LGBTQ+ rights has been progressing rapidly, including the legalization of same-sex marriage in 2019 (Ku, 2020) and granting full adoption rights to same-sex couples in 2023 (Cheung, 2023). With advances in LGBTQ+ rights, the implementation of gender equality education (as mandated by the Gender Equality Education Act) has taken on even greater importance as well as controversy. The Gender Equity Education Act [性別平等教育法] was enacted in 2004 "to promote substantive gender equality, eliminate gender discrimination, uphold human dignity, and improve and establish education resources and environment of gender equality" (Ministry of Education, 2022, para. 1). For example, it mandated the establishment of gender equality education committees in schools, gender-neutral school admissions, and gender equality education in school curricula. Under this Act, LGBTQ+ education is categorized as part of gender equality education and often seen as one of the more sensitive, harder-to-implement parts of gender equality education (Chiang & You, 2022; Li, 2012). Teachers have noted that LGBTQ+ education in the classroom most often occurs when students ask questions about LGBTQ+ issues (Yang, 2020). In such situations, LGBTQ-friendly teachers are often put in difficult positions, facing pressure from parents, colleagues, school authorities, and conservative organizations to not only avoid addressing LGBTQ+ topics, which are often deemed as "controversial" and "unsafe," but also give access to educational materials and guest speakers sourced by conservative groups (Yang, 2020).

Therefore, currently in Taiwan English education and LGBTQ+ education are undergoing extensive, nationwide changes, and LGBTQ+ and LGBTQ+-friendly EFL teachers are positioned at the forefront to take on critical roles in the government's sociopolitical aspirations. Thus, this study focused on the experiences of LGB EFL elementary school teachers in Taiwan and explored how they navigate the relationship between their LGB and EFL teacher identities and their observations of the workplace (i.e., LGBTQ+ sensemaking) in terms of coming out and queer allyship.

Literature Review

Being an LGBTQ+ Teacher

Previous studies have shown that coming out, or disclosing or acknowledging one's sexual orientation, often involves not just a single event or a one-off declarative statement, but more likely ongoing "processes of living, expressing, and disclosing" sexual identities (Khayatt & Iskander, 2020, p. 6; Jhang, 2018). Studies have shown that one of the major challenges LGBTQ+ teachers face is feeling the need to "manage" their sexual identity in the workplace (Cui, 2022; Ferfolja 2009; Griffin, 1992; Llewellyn & Reynolds, 2021; Moore, 2019). Identity management can be carried out in various ways, such as "passing" as heterosexual, "covering" one's queer identity, or using achievements in their professional roles to shield themselves from possible discrimination (Griffin, 1992; Mizzi et al., 2021; Msibi, 2019).

Broadly speaking, identity management can serve as a way of navigating the complexities and "puzzlements" of teachers' sexual identities, or what Nelson (2004) refers to as "coming out conundrums." On the one hand, many LGBTQ+ teachers are confronted with the pressure to stay closeted, attempting to create a clear divide between their private and professional lives due to the dominant heteronormative expectations of teaching as a "moral profession" (Gray, 2013, p. 704). LGBTQ+ teachers may decide to stay closeted for a number of reasons, including fear of discrimination or losing their jobs (Coda, 2021; Cui, 2022, 2023; Llewellyn & Reynolds, 2021; Mayo, 2020; Mizzi et al., 2021). Though staying closeted can be interpreted as passive or lacking agency, studies have shown a more complex perspective of how closeted teachers have their own agency in maintaining their own safety while still allowing them to challenge heteronormativity (Brockenbrough, 2012; Cui, 2023; Msibi, 2019). For example, Cui (2023) showed how in the context of university classrooms in China, where repressive politics and classroom surveillance restrict academic freedom, queer teachers use the protection of the closet (e.g., positioning themselves as heterosexual) to give themselves space to safely teach queer topics in class. On the other hand, LGBTQ+ teachers also face pressure to come out in order to challenge stereotypes, counter the dominance of heteronormativity, achieve a more authentic teacher self for themselves, and provide a role model for their students (Lander, 2018; Llewellyn & Reynolds, 2021; Neary, 2013). Gray (2013) has described the simultaneous pressure to stay closeted and to come out as LGBTQ+ teachers' identities being "'bayoneted' from two sides" (p. 704).

Queer Allyship in Taiwan

Queer allyship involves "allies who work together to challenge common heteronormative assumptions of oneself to think queer and provoke actions in relational systems of support" (Trinh, in press). Ideally, queer allyship involves both thought and action: an ongoing effort to build a mutual understanding based on differences and diversities as well as actions that build community and affect social change in everyday lives (Trinh, in press).

So far, I have not been able to find any academic scholarship specifically addressing queer allyship in Taiwan. An important starting point is how allyship is referred to in Mandarin Chinese. In Taiwan, the Mandarin Chinese equivalent of the English term *ally* or *allyship* is often rooted in the commonly used term *tóngzhì* [同志], often written as *tongzhi* in English, an overarching term akin to *LGBTQ+* used in Taiwan and other Sinophone areas (Chen-Dedman, 2022; Wong, 2015). For example, the term *zhí tóngzhì* [直同志], which translates directly to "straight tongzhi," is used to refer to straight allies. This term has been used in a variety of formal contexts, such as the *Workplace Equality Guidebook* published by Taiwan Tongzhi Hotline Association (2019), *Resources for Sexual and Gender Diversity and Equality and LGBTQ+ Issues* webpage and brochure published by the Taipei City Government Gender Equality Education Committee (2019), and a number of Taiwanese university webpages dedicated to providing resources for the LGBTQ+ community (National Cheng Kung University Gender Equity Education Committee, 2022; National Pingtung University Student Counseling Center, 2005).

Another term used in Taiwan to specifically refer to straight allies is *LGBTSQQ*,[3] with the S standing for "tongzhi-friendly straight," a local variant of the English-based LGBTQ+ acronym. This term was first introduced by the Taiwan Adolescent Association on Sexualities [臺灣青少年性別文教會] in 2005 (Chao et al., 2008), and since then it has been adapted in various educational contexts, including the Ministry of Education publication *Understanding Tongzhi: A Manual of Educational Materials* [認識同志教育資源手冊] (Chao et al., 2008) and a number of Taiwanese university webpages offering LGBTQ+ resources (National Changhua University of Education 2010; National Kaohsiung University of Hospitality and Tourism 2011; National Taichung University of Education, 2007). Finally, the terms 異性戀盟友 [heterosexual allies] and 異性戀同盟 [heterosexual alliance] have also been used to refer to straight allies, but to a lesser extent, such as in Taipei City Office of Commerce's promotional materials for highlighting LGBTQ+-friendly businesses in Taipei (Taipei City Office of Commerce, 2023).

LGBTQ+ Sensemaking in the Workplace

The Taiwan Tongzhi Hotline Association (2019) *Workplace Equality Guidebook* reported from an online survey that "fake friendliness" [假友善] toward LGBTQ+ people was one of the major problems in workplaces for LGBTQ+ people in Taiwan. In this context, "fake friendliness" refers to the act of claiming support for the LGBTQ+ community at work when one actually does not. This is a good example of the way LGBTQ+ teachers may feel the need to assess queer allyship in the workplace, in the same way that LGBTQ+ teachers use identity management strategies to navigate their own sexual identity in the workplace. In fact, Minei et al. (2020) referred to this as "LGBTQ+ sensemaking," adapting Weick's (1995) term "sensemaking," or "the process that stems from an individual observing the workplace and drawing conclusions about the function and characteristics of the role and the people within that setting" (Minei et al., 2020, p. 2). Minei at al. considered LGBTQ+ sensemaking to be a mental burden because the difficulties of assessing allyship can be invisible and unrecognized. They found that LGBTQ+ employees used sensemaking based on three domains: demographics (i.e., region, religion, politics), industry (i.e., industry type, culture), and observed and experienced interactions.

3. LGBTSQQ stands for lesbian, gay, bisexual, transgender, tongzhi-friendly straight, queer, questioning.

LGBTQ+ sensemaking can also take place in classrooms. Moore (2019) detailed the strategies queer language learners engaged in to assess the queer-friendliness of teachers and classmates, such as paying attention to classmates' nationality, religion, and age, and making conclusions based on their prior knowledge of those indicators. As classmates spent more time working with each other on activities, some adjusted their judgments of their classmates, using their classroom interactions to update their perceptions of classmates' queer-friendliness. For teachers, LGBTQ+ sensemaking can often mean silencing a part of one's life as a safe strategy before knowing whom to trust (Gray, 2013; Rudoe, 2010). This can lead to teachers feeling burnt out from constantly assessing the environment and yearning for a workplace where they can simply be themselves (Gray, 2013).

Judging allyship based on these domains can become problematic and inaccurate as it may rely on stereotypes and overgeneralizations. Colleagues who are allies can alleviate some of that burden by proactively and directly signaling their support in workplace interactions (Minei et al., 2020) and teachers can explicitly communicate to students their commitment toward inclusivity and acknowledge their identities (Moore, 2019; Paiz, 2019; Trinh, 2022). However, what is expected from queer allyship is not always consistent. Forbes and Ueno (2020) have found that individuals can have different expectations of straight allies depending on how they conceptualize their own queerness. For example, LGBTQ+ individuals who do not see their LGBTQ+ identities as a major part of their life or aim for assimilation (i.e., we are all the same) do not expect allies to be deeply involved in the broader LGBTQ+ social movement. In fact, they may prefer straight allies to see past or ignore their queerness, which Smith and Shin (2014) call "queer blindfolding." On the other hand, LGBTQ+ individuals who are more heavily engaged with their LGBTQ+ identities and aim for differences to be celebrated have higher expectations of straight allies, such as voicing support and participating in political activism. Lastly, Forbes and Ueno also noticed that some expectations of straight allies consisted of a combination of the two perspectives. This suggests that, in the process of engaging in LGBTQ+ sensemaking at their workplace, LGBTQ+ language teachers may approach their surroundings and assess safety, inclusion, and acceptance with different expectations.

Methodology

This study involved five LGB participants who were all early career EFL elementary school teachers in Taiwan. Table 1 shows the participants' demographic information. Participants were asked to choose their own pseudonyms. I was an insider researcher (Llewellyn & Reynolds, 2021) in two ways: as an openly gay academic as well as the participants' former teacher. Each of the participants had once been my student during their undergraduate education in a preservice English teacher education program in Taiwan. When I taught in Taiwan as their university EFL teacher, I had come out to them as gay at some point during the semester, and each of them had privately come out to me, some in person while others through email. After they had graduated and moved on to their careers as elementary school English teachers, I kept in touch with them via social media.

Table 1. Participants' Demographic Information				
Pseudonym	**Gender identity**	**Sexual identity**	**Teaching experience**	**Teaching contexts**
An	Cismale	Gay	3 years	Elementary school
Betty	Cisfemale	Bisexual	5 years	Elementary school and cram school
Gin	Cismale	Gay	3 years	Elementary school and cram school
K	Cismale	Gay	4 years	Elementary school and cram school (part time)
Kou	Cisfemale	Lesbian	5 years	Elementary school

When this study was conducted, not only had the participants started their teaching careers, but I had left Taiwan and taken on a new teaching position in Japan. It was my hope that having known the participants on a personal level while also having established some distance by the time of the interview (as I was no longer their teacher) helped the participants feel safer and more comfortable during the sharing and retelling of their experiences.

Data collection consisted of the following tasks:

- a questionnaire (to collect background information on their sexual identity, teaching history, etc.)
- a semistructured interview (to elicit their experiences of navigating their LGB identities in the workplace; roughly 60–90 minutes each)
- an "LGBTQ+ language teacher portrait" task (asking participants to draw/color how being LGBTQ affects who you are as a teacher) inspired by Lau's (2016) and Martin's (2012) uses of language portraits

All data collection was conducted remotely through Google Forms, Zoom, and email, respectively. First, participants who conveyed initial interest in participating in the study were sent a Google Form questionnaire and informed consent documents. Then, those who agreed to participate in the study were asked to schedule a semistructured interview and provided with the prompt for the LGBTQ+ language teacher portrait (see Appendix). The completed LGBTQ+ language teacher portraits were collected from the participants before the interview date by email and discussed during the interview. The semistructured interviews were video- and audio-recorded through Zoom with informed consent from the participants. Interviews were conducted mainly in English with some occasional use of Mandarin Chinese. I fully transcribed all interviews for data analysis.

Data analysis was conducted using Braun and Clarke's (2006) thematic analysis consisting of six phases: (1) familiarizing oneself with the data, (2) generating initial codes, (3) organizing initial codes into themes, (4) refining themes, (5) defining and labeling themes, and (6) writing the results. Phases 1 and 2 were first conducted with each participant's data independently. After generating a set of initial codes for each of the participants, Phases 3 through 6 were conducted with all participants' data in mind.

Finally, my positionality as an insider researcher enabled me to see themes and patterns in the data that others may not have, particularly regarding the lived experience of having been an LGBTQ+ teacher in the Taiwanese context.

Findings

The findings are based on all five of the participants' experiences and are divided into two subsections: (1) LGB and EFL teacher identities and (2) LGBTQ+ sensemaking in terms of coming out and queer allyship. Throughout this section, I refer to the participants' LGBTQ+ language teacher portraits (Figures 1–5).

LGB and English as a Foreign Language Teacher Identities

Of the five participants, An, Gin, and Kou described their LGB identities as not relevant to or separate from being an EFL teacher. An and Gin attributed this to being elementary school teachers in particular, where their students were too young for their LGB identities to come up in their classes, which has been shown to be a common belief in school settings dominated by heteronormative assumptions (Khayatt, 1997; Rudoe, 2010). In contrast, they speculated that LGB identities may be more relevant to high school teachers, where students are more aware of LGBTQ+ issues and the workplace might also be more open-minded.

The separation of LGB and EFL teacher identities was also described through expressions of indifference, or an "I don't really think about it" kind of approach. Kou and Gin positioned their indifference as a kind of strength at the workplace, that being able to separate one's LGB identity from their job as an EFL teacher was related to one's work ethic. For example, Kou explained, "I just do what I ought to do at work. Don't really think about being lesbian when I'm at work." This sentiment was echoed in Kou's portrait (Figure 1), in which she colored her arms and feet brown. She explained that this represented the Chinese idiom "jiǎo tà shí dì" [腳踏實地], which literally translates as "to have one's feet firmly planted in the ground" and is often used to mean "realistic and down to earth." Kou felt that this described her approach to her job as an EFL teacher in which she aimed to be "grounded in her job responsibilities" and "did what she was required to do." In addition, Gin described that "ultimately [the younger generation] don't care about what other people do as long as it's not affecting us." For Gin, younger teachers having a general sense of apathy toward their colleagues was a sign of social progress, because perhaps it meant that being LGBTQ+ would not be seen as an issue. Gin echoed his indifference in his LGBTQ+ language teacher portrait (Figure 2), in which he pointed to his heart as recognizing the importance of his LGB identity, but he wrote that he "ultimately did not care as much." It is possible that Kou and Gin's approach of enacting indifference at the workplace comes from a position of privilege, specifically straight-passing privilege, in which they are not visibly marked as queer coded. Thus, their ability to claim indifference and maintain a separation of LGB and EFL identities likely excludes transgender and gender-diverse identities, in which indifference and separation may not be an option.

Figure 1. Kou's LGBTQ+ language teacher portrait.

Figure 2. Gin's LGBTQ+ language teacher portrait.

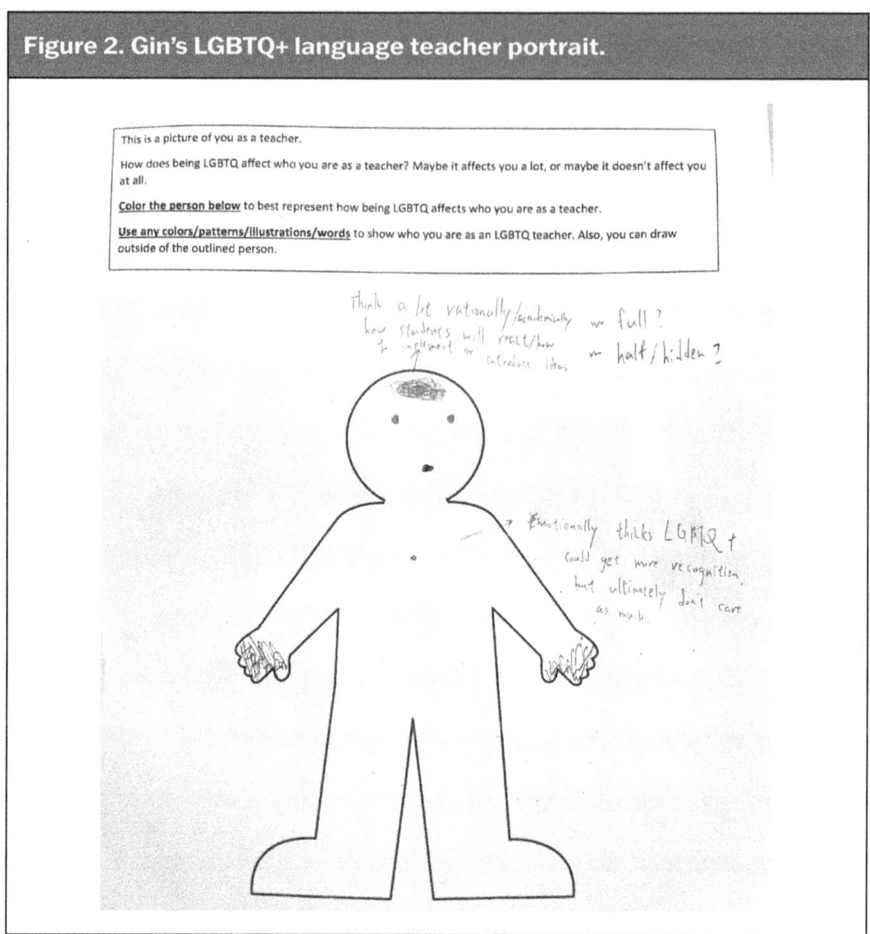

Interestingly, although An, Gin, and Kou at some point described their LGB and EFL identities as separate, other parts of their interview responses and portraits suggested that such a separation was not always so clear or consistent. For example, An explicitly said that he felt being LGB had nothing to do with his job as an EFL teacher. However, in his portrait (Figure 3), he drew himself wearing a chest harness underneath his teacher outfit as well as carrying a pair of high heels and an English textbook with a rainbow on it, which he described as objects from his personal life as an LGB individual. He explained, "This picture shows that the dual identities of teachers and LGBTQ can exist in harmony with each other without conflict." Furthermore, during his interview, An also described ways that being LGB influenced him as a teacher. He explained that although he never explicitly taught any LGBTQ+ topics in his classes, he did notice that being LGB made him more sensitive toward name-calling or bullying among his students and he did try to teach his students to be more accepting of differences. These different perspectives suggest greater nuance and possibly multiple layers in the relationship between An's LGB and EFL teacher identities rather than simply a strict separation.

Figure 3. An's LGBTQ+ language teacher portrait.

In contrast to An, Gin, and Kou, Betty and K expressed an integration of their LGB and EFL teacher identities. Betty described her LGB self as contributing to the EFL teacher she aspired to be and guided part of what she hoped she could teach her students. Betty's portrait (Figure 4) showed rainbow-colored stars and rays of light shining from her body. She explained that as a bisexual woman, she felt she could accept anyone, regardless of sexual identity, and wanted to share her positivity and love with the people around her. She also left her body in the portrait white because to her that represented purity, neutrality, and objectivity. This was related to her religious faith as a Christian, and she hoped she could see and treat people without bias or judgment, especially her students. K expressed similar ideas (Figure 5), describing his LGB identity as a source of positivity and acceptance for himself and his students. K explained that he wanted to boldly show his LGB identity through his bold fashion choices (e.g., dyed hair, leopard print shirts), allowing not only LGBTQ+ students but also students who feel like they are outcasts in general to feel accepted. Like Betty, K also felt that his LGB identity contributed to his EFL teacher identity by highlighting the importance of avoiding judging people based on stereotypes, a standard he held for himself and his students. Finally, it is important to note that Betty and K taught at the same school and thus were navigating the same workplace culture. This will be discussed further when it comes to queer allyship.

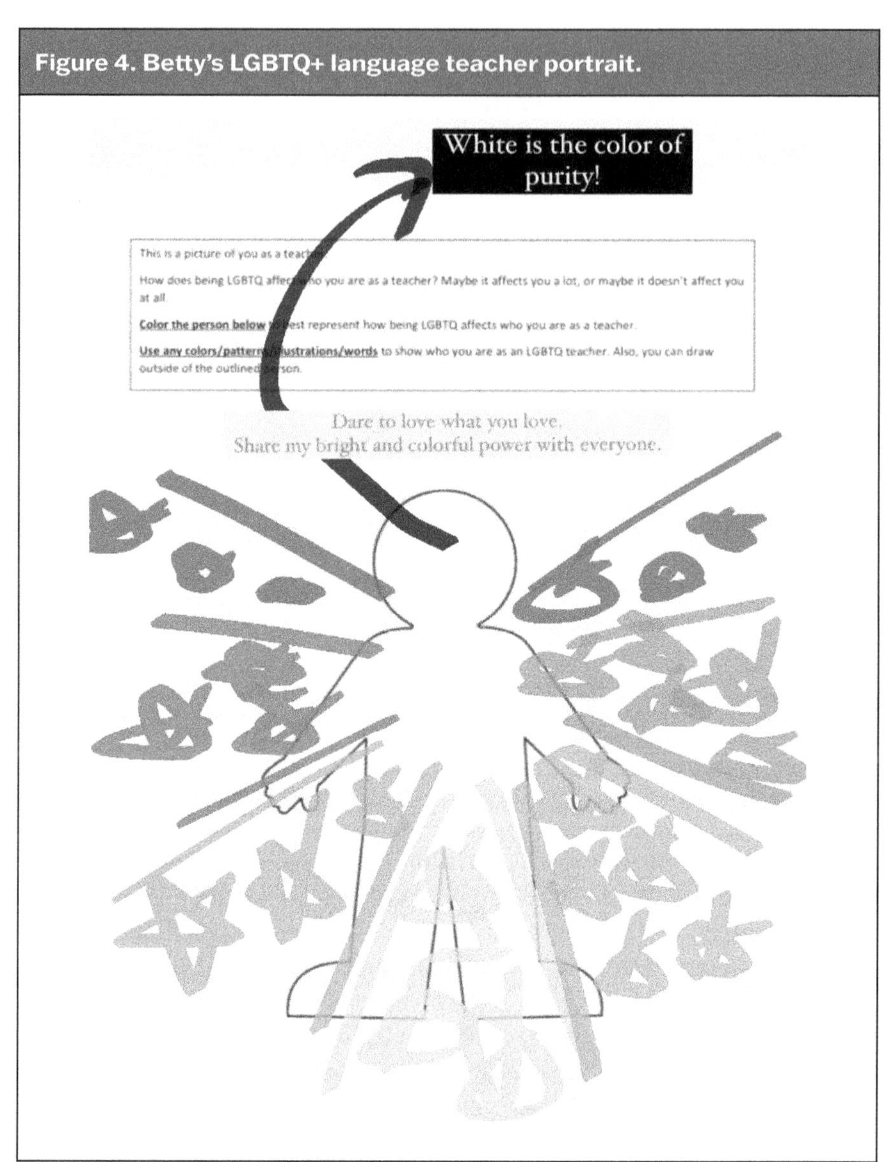

Figure 4. Betty's LGBTQ+ language teacher portrait.

Figure 5. K's LGBTQ+ language teacher portrait.

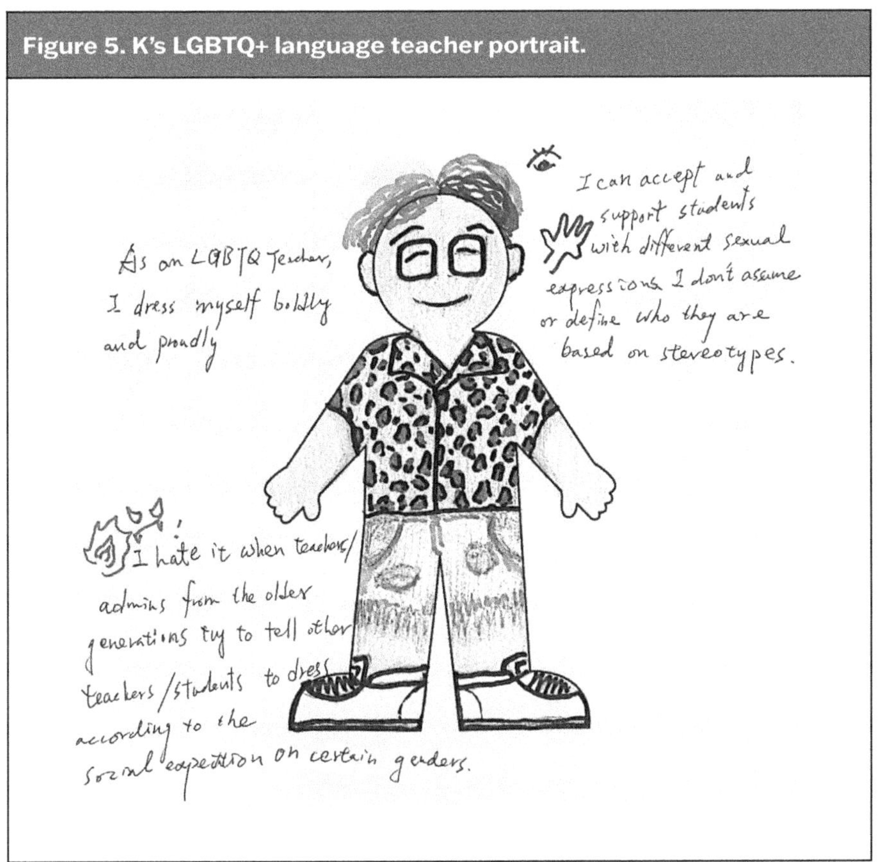

LGBTQ+ Sensemaking as English as a Foreign Language Teachers

Coming Out

For all five participants, coming out in the workplace as EFL elementary school teachers was a complex issue, depending on how they perceived the relationship between their LGB and EFL teacher identities and what they observed about the workplace culture through LGBTQ+ sensemaking.

An, Gin, and Kou described themselves as being mostly closeted at their workplace. An and Gin were out to only a few coworkers they were close with; otherwise, they did not proactively talk about being LGB or their relationship life with their coworkers. If their colleagues asked them about being LGB, An explained that he "wouldn't particularly hide it" and that "if they find out, it's fine, but it's not something I need to explicitly talk about." Similarly, Gin explained that if a colleague asked him about being LGB, he would "mostly try to hide it, to not explicitly say one or another. I would say yes or maybe." Both An and Gin seemed to approach the matter of coming out by responding with a strategic ambiguity (McKenna-Buchanan et al., 2015), using the gray areas of sexual identity as a kind of "protective positioning" (Llewellyn & Reynolds, 2021, p. 18). Unlike An and Gin, Kou was not out to any of her colleagues, only to some of her college friends and former colleagues. In fact, Kou described her workplace as being very conservative and feeling the need to lie about being lesbian in order to protect herself. This was apparent in her portrait (Figure 1), in which she drew a thin blue outline and small blue rays of light as representing the need to portray a stable and calm persona to her colleagues. Furthermore, she is surrounded by little stick figures showing mixed positions toward LGBTQ+ people and a gray shield protecting herself "carefully." An also drew a gray "net" that served to protect him. Such barriers are meant to convey the feeling of needing to protect themselves in their workplace, but they also suggest a distancing or separation between their EFL and LGB identities.

In contrast to An, Gin, and Kou, Betty and K were both openly LGB in their workplace. They both described their school as being very open-minded and accepting. As mentioned before, Betty and K taught at the same school, which was an English-Mandarin bilingual school. This meant that the school hired a large number of international teachers. K explained that with teachers coming from many different countries and cultures, the school administration had no choice but to be accepting of differences. Thus, K felt like he never had to explicitly come out, in the sense of saying "I am gay." Instead, he was able to "just talk normally" and be himself. One example illustrating this point was during Halloween at school, when K was able to dress up as a female Disney villain two years in a row. Similarly, Betty described the experience of not having to explicitly come out and instead coming out "naturally." She recalled having conversations with her coworkers about their romantic relationships and she felt safe "very naturally" talking about her relationships without saying directly that she was bisexual.

It is important to note that even though Betty and K had come out in their workplace and did not feel the need to hide their sexual identities, that did not mean they had come out to everyone. As part of LGBTQ+ sensemaking, both Betty and K made assessments as to when they wanted to come out and when they preferred not to. K mentioned that there was one coworker that he knew was homophobic, so he had warned other LGBTQ+ colleagues to be wary of that coworker. Betty described that with some people, it was not that she "shouldn't" come out to them, but more so that she simply "didn't want to" come out. Her description seemed to emphasize that it was not a matter of her ability or power to come out to her colleagues, but rather a matter of discernment and preference.

Queer Allyship

An and Kou did not know of any queer allies at their workplace. Kou (Figure 1) and An (Figure 3) were the participants who drew the gray barrier between them and their coworkers in their portraits, which they described as representing self-protection. An explained during his interview that since he felt his LGB identity was not relevant to his job as an EFL teacher, finding or having workplace allies was not an issue for him. Kou, on the other hand, recalled a key incident of LGBTQ+ sensemaking that confirmed suspicions she previously had that her workplace had no queer allies:

> There's a colleague that once asked me… one time we had a teacher field trip and I brought my girlfriend and the colleague asked, "Don't you think you might be mistaken as being lesbian?" That's what she asked me. So I knew she is a conservative

> person, so I said, "We're just roommates" to protect myself. And I pretended that I'm a straight girl to that colleague. So I knew, yeah, the school is conservative. I didn't want to talk about it any further. I think it's a way to protect us.

Kou's LGBTQ+ sensemaking allowed her to make a quick evaluation of the way her coworker worded the question about her being lesbian and assess the extent to which her colleagues may or may not be queer allies. For Kou, this was not only a momentary self-protection strategy but also a litmus test that helped her make broader generalizations about the level of queer allyship in her workplace culture.

Though Kou's example of LGBTQ+ sensemaking resulted in the perception of a lack of queer allyship at her workplace, LGBTQ+ sensemaking for Gin, Betty, and K had a different impact. For example, Gin recalled this key sensemaking incident from his workplace:

> I would say, from what I've observed, I'm not sure if this is a stereotype or what, but it is said that a lot of men who study education—in Chinese we say *wén kē* [文科, the liberal arts]—are gay. There's this stereotype. So there are a few older male teachers, so I think... I assume they are gay. One of them is very obvious, I think, because one of them is a *zhǔ zhǎng* [主掌, a person in charge], and when I go to his office, his computer wallpaper is a muscular man. Like, do you know *xiāo yà xuān* [蕭亞軒, Elva Hsiao]? You know, she is like a female singer that gays like. And she has a lot of muscular men in her music videos. So he has like a screenshot of that. So I thought, wow he really isn't hiding. I'm 80% sure he's not hiding.

Gin explained that, in the context of his conservative elementary school, his superior openly displaying computer wallpaper of muscular men seemed like an open expression of his queerness, giving Gin a feeling of hope that one day he may also be able to openly express his queerness while being an EFL elementary school teacher. In this case, Gin's conclusion was that his *zhǔ zhǎng* was probably gay and was expressing part of his gay identity through other meaning-making resources, such as his computer wallpaper. Though the actual sexual identity of his *zhǔ zhǎng* was not confirmed, in a way it did not matter. Gin was still able to gain a sense of allyship from the physical visibility of a male superior displaying gay-coded images.

K, who was openly out at his school, also described a key sensemaking incident that led to establishing a longstanding friendship with a workplace ally:

> [LGBT topics] are still a more reserved topic, I guess, at school, especially at elementary, even though I think it's necessary, because you can hear kids calling each other "gay" during break time. They will use the word *gay* as a kind of humiliation. Like, *nǐ gay ō* [你gay喔, oh, you're gay]. My homeroom teacher was actually a big supporter of the LGBT community actually, like he immediately stopped the kids from calling each other gay, like this is not a word you use to humiliate other people, and even if they are actually gay, you should respect them. It's not wrong to be gay. I was actually really touched. So we were good friends. We are still good friends now.

Like Kou, K's sensemaking incident also involved observing the use of language but with a positive result. What makes K's sensemaking incident unique from what any of the other participants reported was that his colleague took a proactive approach to affirming LGBTQ+ support and taught his students to do the same.

Despite the varying levels of queer allyship that the participants described, all of them described limitations in discussing or incorporating LGBTQ+ topics into their classes. All of the participants described their own versions of "subtle LGBTQ+ plugins" as the extent to which they could introduce LGBTQ+ topics in their classes as their own efforts to contest and disrupt the heteronormative ways that teaching and learning are expected to be conducted in their classrooms. An, for example, designed a lesson around a current event in Taiwan relating to boys wearing dresses at school but did not explicitly relate it to LGBTQ+ issues. Gin tried to challenge the idea of heterosexuality as a default by designing mathematics questions including same-sex couples. Kou had been in the position of an "ethical education manager" at her school and invited lecturers to talk to students about bullying, though without any mention of LGBTQ+ perspectives. Even Betty and K, who both described their workplace as open and accepting of the LGBTQ+ community, felt that they could not openly discuss LGBTQ+ topics in class. Betty displayed rainbow "decorations" in class, explaining that if anyone asked her about the decorations, she would just say they were simply rainbows; however, she avoided putting a rainbow flag because the flag was too explicitly LGBTQ+. K had read picture books with themes around gender equality and gender expression because gender stereotypes was one of the important topics covered in elementary health education classes. Furthermore, in a fourth-grade social studies lesson on the topic of discrimination, he experimented with putting a graphic representing marriage equality on a PowerPoint slide, wary that there were some parents who meticulously reviewed his class materials and had filed complaints after seeing something they deemed inappropriate or incorrect. K felt relieved that he did not receive any complaints after that lesson and hoped to continue to teach that lesson using the same PowerPoint slides. These efforts can be seen as each teacher's strategies for resisting and challenging the dominance of heteronormative workplace cultures in their schools.

Discussion/Implications

This study focused on two main questions: How do LGB EFL elementary school teachers in Taiwan perceive the relationship between their LGB and EFL teacher identities? How do they engage in LGBTQ+ sensemaking regarding coming out at the workplace and assessing queer allyship? In response to the first question, the participants perceived their LGB and EFL teacher identities in different ways, some seeing little connection between them and others seeing them as integrated parts of who they are. However, what seemed to be consistent among the five participants was that the way they perceived their LGB and EFL teacher identities influenced and was influenced by the extent to which they had come out in the workplace. In other words, those who described being LGB as an important part of being an EFL teacher seemed to have come out in their workplace to a greater extent and vice versa. It is impossible to know what came first—the perception that being LGB is relevant (or not) to being an EFL teacher or the decision to come out (or not) at their workplace. It is more likely that the two experiences were happening simultaneously in teachers' everyday lives and each had an impact on the other in a holistic, nonlinear way.

This is made even more apparent in the second question, which focuses on the ways the participants engaged in LGBTQ+ sensemaking in terms of coming out and assessing queer allyship. One can conceptualize LGBTQ+ sensemaking through a map-making metaphor—as LGB EFL teachers navigate their workplace, they are mapping out people, moments, and places of safety and queer allyship, and that map can be used to guide their own self-expression in the workplace. Thus, in a way, these are two sides of the same sensemaking coin; both are forms of sensing the performance and signaling of LGBTQ+ identities at the workplace, with the former directed toward the self and the latter directed toward others. This is not to say that the participants' assessments of queer allyship had a direct impact on their coming out. For example, Gin observed a coworker possibly being openly gay but did not necessarily feel safe coming out. One possible reason is that coming out in the workplace can involve many other factors (e.g., parental attitudes, teachers' own personal journeys with their sexual identities).

Another possible reason is that the examples of queer allyship described by the participants were not open declarations of support toward the participants directly (e.g., "I am here for you"), nor were they sustained expressions of support (e.g., a school policy that has a long-term effect). It is possible that more direct and sustained forms of queer allyship would have a stronger influence on the EFL teachers' self-expression at the workplace. For the participants, queer allyship (or the lack thereof) was recognized throughout the full range of everyday encounters in their elementary school EFL lives: in spoken and unspoken ways, in actions and inactions, in mostly the mundane as opposed to the grandiose, and in the interwoven relationships between students, colleagues, and parents. However, broadly speaking, the participants' stories often pointed to momentary superficial experiences of what queer allyship should (or could) be for EFL teachers (e.g., computer wallpaper, rainbow decorations). Though these small gestures represent the moments of queer allyship remembered by the participants, these seem like the beginnings for greater potential in deeper queer allyship that involves "work[ing] together to challenge common heteronormative assumptions of oneself" and "co-creat[ing] and co-construct[ing] a space of togetherness" (Trinh, in press).

Finally, it is also important to note that the participants described many different domains of activity from which they performed their job as EFL teachers, and thus their approach toward coming out and their observations of queer allyship varied in different domains. Using the map-making metaphor, one might think of these as different terrains or different ecologies in which they may shift their behaviors or emotions toward being LGB. Nelson (2004) presented this insightfully in describing it as a way of thinking about sexual identities transculturally or globally, meaning that sexual identities are not framed as "inner truths" or "objective facts" but rather that which emerges in specific localized contexts. Thus, we should be aware that EFL elementary teachers may change when they are interacting with students, coworkers, superiors, and parents; each of these presents different social contexts in which teachers' sensemaking of the self and others may result in different conclusions.

Actions: What Are the Next Steps?

As LGB EFL teachers engaged in LGBTQ+ sensemaking in the workplace, all of the participants of this study, whether or not they had come out, expressed degrees of fear and uncertainty when assessing the presence of queer allies at their workplace. This often involved a lot of observation, speculation, confusion, and even gossip among colleagues that went beyond individuals, establishing a workplace culture that left LGBTQ+ identities hidden or only spoken of in hushed voices. This kind of workplace culture is not conducive to building queer allyship. I conclude this chapter by offering some practical steps toward creating a more positive workplace culture for LGB EFL teachers, one that aligns with what Trinh (in press) calls a "space of togetherness" that can lead to greater efforts toward queer allyship. Some sources have already suggested that workplaces need to clearly indicate their support for LGBTQ+ issues and communities, such as sponsoring LGBTQ+-related activities and establishing policies that protect the rights of LGBTQ+ teachers (Taiwan Tongzhi Hotline Association, 2019, 2020). I think there is a need to take a step back from that and propose the idea of creating a more LGBTQ+-friendly workplace culture for teachers in Taiwan through "establishing LGBTQ+ presence."

In Taiwanese schools, it can be difficult for LGBTQ+ teachers to come out because no one wants to be the first or only one to come out. If LGBTQ+ teachers face a workplace culture that feels empty or devoid of any other LGBTQ+ individuals or queer allies, queer allyship cannot thrive. Therefore, establishing LGBTQ+ presence in the workplace is a crucial first step toward building queer allyship. Establishing LGBTQ+ presence means letting people at the workplace know that LGBTQ+ individuals and queer allies exist in that space. It does not mean publicly outing colleagues without their consent or gossiping about colleagues' sexual identities behind their backs. Establishing LGBTQ+ presence means signaling to all colleagues that, by default, anyone should assume that LGBTQ+ individuals and queer allies are present at the workplace, whoever they may be, whether they choose to come out or not, and that should be treated as the workplace norm. This is partially inspired by the experiences of two participants, Betty and K, who were EFL teachers at a bilingual school in Taiwan that hired many international teachers from various cultural backgrounds. At that school, diversity and difference in how teachers dressed and acted were treated as the norm, thus creating the environment for K, in particular, to express his sexual identity through his clothing and personality.

This can be accomplished by designing a space that establishes LGBTQ+ presence for teachers and students, such as providing gender-neutral bathrooms, encouraging a gender-neutral dress code, putting up posters relating to LGBTQ+ issues and events, indicating on job postings or the school website that it is an LGBTQ+-friendly school (Taiwan Tongzhi Hotline Association, 2019), acknowledging gender pronouns, and promoting a discourse of difference (Trinh, 2022, in press). A more direct approach toward establishing LGBTQ+ presence would include organizing LGBTQ+ social groups that welcome both LGBTQ+ individuals and allies, potentially acting as a site for building the community and solidarity needed for queer allyship.

Author

Eric K. Ku is a specially appointed associate professor at Hokkaido University, in Japan, and author of the book *Teachers of Multiple Languages: Identities, Beliefs, and Emotions*. His current research interests include language teacher identities, multilingualism, linguistic landscapes, and arts-based qualitative research.

References

Achyldurdyyeva, J., Wu, L. F., & Datova, N. (2021). Understanding LGBT individuals' employment environment in Taiwan: A relational framework perspective. *Equality, Diversity and Inclusion, 42*(5), 656–684. https://doi.org/10.1108/EDI-02-2020-0042

Adamczyk, A., & Cheng, Y. H. A. (2015). Explaining attitudes about homosexuality in Confucian and non-Confucian nations: Is there a "cultural" influence? *Social Science Research, 51*, 276–289. https://doi.org/10.1016/j.ssresearch.2014.10.002

Braun, V., & Clarke, V. (2006). Using thematic analysis in psychology. *Qualitative Research in Psychology, 3*(2), 77–101.

Brockenbrough, E. (2012). Agency and abjection in the closet: The voices (and silences) of Black queer male teachers. *International Journal of Qualitative Studies in Education, 25*(6), 741–765. https://doi.org/10.1080/09518398.2011.590157

Chang, Y. J. (2022). (Re)imagining Taiwan through "2030 Bilingual Nation": Languages, identities, and ideologies. *Taiwan Journal of TESOL, 19*(1), 121–146. https://doi.org/10.30397/TJTESOL.202204_19(1).0005

Chao, S., Kuo, L., & Liu, A. (2008). 認識同志教育資源手冊 [*Understanding tongzhi: A manual of educational materials*]. Ministry of Education.

Chen-Dedman, A. (2022). Seeing China differently: National contestation in Taiwan's LGBTQ (tongzhi) movement. *Nations and Nationalism, 28*(4), 1212–1229. https://doi.org/10.1111/nana.12833

Cheung, E. (2023, May 16). Taiwan grants right of adoption to same-sex couples in latest move toward full equality. *CNN*. https://edition.cnn.com/2023/05/16/asia/taiwan-same-sex-adoption-marriage-equality-lgbtq-intl-hnk/index.html

Chiang, W. S., & You, M. H. (2022). 朝向容納多元性別教育：中學教師推動同志教育之經驗探析 [Toward "LGBT+ inclusive education": Insights from secondary school educators]. *Journal of Curriculum Studies, 17*(2), 39–57. https://doi.org/10.53106/181653382022091702003

Coda, J. E. (2021). "I'm not sweet, bro": LGBQ Spanish teachers' experiences in the Southeastern U.S. In J. M. Paiz & J. E. Coda (Eds.), *Intersectional perspectives on LGBTQ+ issues in modern language teaching and learning* (pp. 87–113). Palgrave Macmillan. https://doi.org/10.1007/978-3-030-76779-2_4

Cui, L. (2022). "I had to get married to protect myself": Gay academics' experiences of managing sexual identity in China. *Asian Journal of Social Science, 50*(4), 260–267. https://doi.org/10.1016/j.ajss.2022.05.007

Cui, L. (2023). "Teach as an outsider": Closeted gay academics' strategies for addressing queer issues in China. *Sex Education, 23*(5), 570–584. https://doi.org/10.1080/14681811.2022.2103109

Ferfolja, T. (2009). State of the field review: Stories so far: An overview of the research on lesbian teachers. *Sexualities, 12*(3), 378–396. https://doi.org/10.1177/1363460708099116

Ferrer, A., & Lin, T. B. (2021). Official bilingualism in a multilingual nation: A study of the 2030 bilingual nation policy in Taiwan. *Journal of Multilingual and Multicultural Development*, 1–13. https://doi.org/10.1080/01434632.2021.1909054

Forbes, T. D., & Ueno, K. (2020). Post-gay, political, and pieced together: Queer expectations of straight allies. *Sociological Perspectives, 63*(1), 159–176. https://doi.org/10.1177/0731121419885353

Graham, K. M., & Yeh, Y. F. (2023). Teachers' implementation of bilingual education in Taiwan: challenges and arrangements. *Asia Pacific Education Review, 24*, 461–472. https://doi.org/10.1007/s12564-022-09791-4

Gray, E. M. (2013). Coming out as a lesbian, gay or bisexual teacher: Negotiating private and professional worlds. *Sex Education, 13*(6), 702–714. https://doi.org/10.1080/14681811.2013.807789

Griffin, P. (1992). From hiding out to coming out: Empowering lesbian and gay educators. *Journal of Homosexuality, 22*(3–4), 167–196. https://doi.org/10.1300/j082v22n03_07

Jhang, J. (2018). Scaffolding in family relationships: A grounded theory of coming out to family. *Family Relations, 67*(1), 161–175. https://doi.org/10.1111/fare.12302

Khayatt, D. (1997). Sex and the teacher: Should we come out in class? *Harvard Educational Review, 67*(1), 126–143. https://doi.org/10.17763/haer.67.1.27643568766g767m

Khayatt, D., & Iskander, L. (2020). Reflecting on "coming out" in the classroom. *Teaching Education, 31*(1), 6–16. https://doi.org/10.1080/10476210.2019.1689943

Ku, E. K. (2020). "Waiting for my red envelope": Discourses of sameness in the linguistic landscape of a marriage equality demonstration in Taiwan. *Critical Discourse Studies, 17*(2), 156–174. https://doi.org/10.1080/17405904.2019.1656655

Lander, R. (2018). Queer English language teacher identity: A narrative exploration in Colombia. *Profile: Issues in Teachers Professional Development, 20*(1), 89–101. https://doi.org/10.15446/profile.v20n1.63658

Lau, S. M. C. (2016). Language, identity, and emotionality: Exploring the potential of language portraits in preparing teachers for diverse learners. *The New Educator, 12*(2), 147–170. https://doi.org/10.1080/1547688X.2015.1062583

Li, H. (2012). Wǒ zài guózhōng jiàoxué xiànchǎng shíshī tóngzhì jiàoyù de jiàoxué cèlüè yùnyòng jí fǎnsī [Teaching LGBT education in the secondary classroom: Strategies and reflections.] *Xìngbié Píngděng Jiàoyù Jìkān* [*Gender Equity Education Quarterly*], *59*, 76–82. https://doi.org/10.6486/GEEQ.201208.0076

Llewellyn, A., & Reynolds, K. (2021). Within and between heteronormativity and diversity: Narratives of LGB teachers and coming and being out in schools. *Sex Education, 21*(1), 13–26. https://doi.org/10.1080/14681811.2020.1749040

Martin, B. (2012). Coloured language: Identity perception of children in bilingual programmes. *Language Awareness, 21*(1-2), 33–56. https://doi.org/10.1080/09658416.2011.639888

Mayo, J. B. (2020). Queer teacher to queer teacher: Reflections, questions, and hopes from current and aspiring educators. *Teaching Education, 31*(1), 32–44. https://doi.org/10.1080/10476210.2019.1709813

McKenna-Buchanan, T., Munz, S., & Rudnick, J. (2015). To be or not to be out in the classroom: Exploring communication privacy management strategies of lesbian, gay, and queer college teachers. *Communication Education, 64*(3), 280–300. https://doi.org/10.1080/03634523.2015.1014385

Minei, E. M., Hastings, S. O., & Warren, S. (2020). LGBTQ+ sensemaking: The mental load of identifying workplace allies. *International Journal of Business Communication, 60*(3), 823–843. https://doi.org/10.1177/2329488420965667

Ministry of Education. (2022, January 19). Gender Equity Education Act. http://law.moj.gov.tw/Eng/LawClass/LawAll.aspx?PCode=H0080067

Ministry of Labor. (2018, November 28). Employment Service Act.

Ministry of Labor. (2022, January 12). Act of Gender Equality in Employment. https://law.moj.gov.tw/ENG/LawClass/LawAll.aspx?pcode=N0030014

Mizzi, R. C. (2016). Heteroprofessionalism. In N. M. Rodriguez, W. J. Martino, J. C. Ingrey, & E. Brockenbrough (Eds.), *Critical concepts in queer studies and education* (pp. 137–147). Palgrave Macmillan. http://dx.doi.org/10.1057/978-1-137-55425-3_15

Mizzi, R., Schmidt, C., & Moura, G. (2021). Complexity amidst diversity: Exploring the lives of LGBTQ international teachers. *Comparative and International Education, 50*(1), 1–17.

Moore, A. R. (2019). Interpersonal factors affecting queer second or foreign language learners' identity management in class. *Modern Language Journal, 103*(2), 428–442. https://doi.org/10.1111/modl.12558

Msibi, T. (2019). Passing through professionalism: South African Black male teachers and same-sex desire. *Sex Education 19*(4), 389–405. https://doi.org/10.1080/14681811.2019.1612346

National Changhua University of Education Student Psychological Counseling & Guidance Center. (2010, April 30). 向陽花木–導師通訊 [*Xiangyang huamu—Advisor newsletter*]. https://ncuecounseling.ncue.edu.tw/ezfiles/9/1009/attach/83/pta_6776_7020993_27069.pdf

National Cheng Kung University Gender Equity Education Committee. (2022, July 10). 多元性別LGBTQ報你知 [*Diverse gender and LGBTQ report*]. https://genderequity.web2.ncku.edu.tw/p/412-1061-2136.php?Lang=zh-tw

National Kaohsiung University of Hospitality and Tourism Division of Student Counseling Office of Student Affairs. (2011, October 25). 認識多元性別 [*Getting to know sexual and gender diversity*]. https://gender.nkuht.edu.tw/var/file/41/1041/img/57_4c80d2fb.pdf

National Pingtung University Student Counseling Center. (2005). 同志圈的專業術語 [*LGBTQ+* terminology]. https://counsel-s.nptu.edu.tw/p/412-1078-138-1.php

National Taichung University of Education Office of the Secretary. (2007, July 17). LGBT~擁抱多元性別建構性別友善中教大 [*LGBT—Embracing sexual and gender diversity and building a gender-friendly NTCU*]. https://sec2020.ntcu.edu.tw/front/Gender_Equality/Educational_Resources/news.php?ID=bnRjdV9zZWNyJkVkdWNhdGlvbmFsX1Jlc291cmNlcw==&Sn=226

Neary, A. (2013). Lesbian and gay teachers' experiences of "coming out" in Irish schools. *British Journal of Sociology of Education, 34*(4), 583–602. https://doi.org/10.1080/01425692.2012.722281

Nelson, C. D. (2004). A queer chaos of meanings: Coming out conundrums in globalized classrooms. *Journal of Gay & Lesbian Issues in Education, 2*(1), 27–46. https://doi.org/10.1300/J367v02n01_05

Paiz, J. M. (2019). Queering practice: LGBTQ+ diversity and inclusion in English language teaching. *Journal of Language, Identity & Education, 18*(4), 266–275. https://doi.org/10.1080/15348458.2019.1629933

Rudoe, N. (2010). Lesbian teachers' identity, power and the public/private boundary. *Sex Education: Sexuality, Society and Learning, 10*(1), 23–36. https://doi.org/10.1080/14681810903491347

Smith, L. C., & Shin, R. Q. (2014). Queer blindfolding: A case study on difference "blindness" toward persons who identify as lesbian, gay, bisexual, and transgender. *Journal of Homosexuality, 61*(7), 940–961. https://doi.org/10.1080/00918369.2014.870846

Taipei City Government Gender Equality Education Committee. (2019, October 4). 多元性別平等及同志議題資源 [*Resources for sexual and gender diversity and equality and LGBTQ+ issues*]. https://www.gender.tp.edu.tw/cht/index.php?code=list&flag=detail&ids=88&article_id=384

Taipei City Office of Commerce. (2023, July 14). 台北友善店家認識性別友善 [*Taipei friendly stores: Getting to know LGBTQ+ friendliness*]. https://friendlystore.taipei/files/Gender_Friendly.pdf?06

Taiwan Tongzhi Hotline Association. (2019, October 1). 同志友善職場指南 [*Workplace equality guidebook*]. https://hotline.org.tw/news/2869

Taiwan Tongzhi Hotline Association. (2020, May 5). 2020年台灣同志（LGBTQ+）職場現況調查 [*2020 Taiwan LGBTQ+ workplace survey*]. https://hotline.org.tw/news/2946

Trinh, E. (2022). Supporting queer SLIFE youth: Initial queer considerations. In L. J. Pentón Herrera (Ed.), *English and students with limited or interrupted formal education: Global perspectives on teacher preparation and classroom practices* (pp. 209–225). Springer. https://doi.org/10.1007/978-3-030-86963-2_12

Trinh, E. (in press). Queer allyship in TESOL: We need to ACTS now! *TESOL Journal.*

Weick, K. E. (1995). *Sensemaking in organizations* (Vol. 3). Sage.

Wong, A. D. (2015). Tongzhi. In A. Bolin & P. Whelehan (Eds.), *The international encyclopedia of human sexuality*. Wiley. https://doi.org/10.1002/9781118896877.wbiehs513

Yang, C. L. (2020). Challenges to LGBTI inclusive education and queer activism in Taiwan. In D. A. Francis, J. I. Kajaran, & J. Lehtonen (Eds.), *Queer social movements and outreach work in schools: A global perspective* (pp. 65–92). Palgrave Macmillan. https://doi.org/10.1007/978-3-030-41610-2_4

Appendix: LGBTQ+ Language Teacher Portrait Prompt

This is a picture of you as a teacher. How does being LGBTQ+ affect who you are as a teacher? Maybe it affects you a lot, or maybe it doesn't affect you at all.

Color the person below to best represent how being LGBTQ+ affects who you are as a teacher. Use any colors/patterns/illustrations/words to show who you are as an LGBTQ+ teacher. Also, you can draw outside of the outlined person.

PART 2

THE MEDITERRANEAN

Creating Queer Allyship in the English Language Teaching Classroom Through Critical Pedagogies With Young Migrants and Refugees in Greece

Christina Fakalou

In charting possible avenues of further global queer thinking, pedagogies, and research in English language teaching (ELT), Ethan Trinh (2022) urged "to first become thinkers of how to 'mess' and play with fixed knowledge, turn them upside down, and ask, *What else can I do differently to benefit the students?*" (p. 220). Voicing Trinh, Coda (2018) and Paiz (2019) advocated for queering ELT and contributed to inclusion, equity, and diversity in the classroom. This chapter engages with these considerations by turning the attention to the Greek context. Acknowledging education's central role in disrupting and transforming the backlash regarding LGBTQ+ issues, critical scholars and pedagogues who are informed by a queer theory agenda have provided insights for practices inclusive of and supportive to gender and sexuality in ELT contexts around the world (Sauntson, 2016). Despite the important work on critical pedagogical practices affirming queer visibility and creating allyship in the classroom, contexts affected by migration are rarely explored (but see Nelson, 2009, 2012, for notable exceptions).

To redress this academic oversight, this chapter draws on elements of critical pedagogies, multimodality, and queer linguistics and unites them into a queer pedagogy aimed at advancing queer allyship at the intersection of human mobility, forced displacement, and ELT. By offering a concrete example of practice of queer allyship, this pedagogical endeavour responds to recent calls (see Coda, 2018; Paiz, 2019; Trinh, 2022) strongly urging for queering ELT education and building a community of allies and advocates to collaboratively debunk normative societal assumptions in the classroom.

I begin by providing a definition of a few terms that are used in this chapter, which I need to clarify so as to position myself in relation to them. Then I offer a brief overview of the theoretical framework that informs this study, describing the context and the method, before I turn to data presentation and a discussion of the findings and their implications.

Queer Visibility and Queer Allyship: Notes on Definitions

Queer here is understood as at odds with heteronormativity, "the normative cultural enmeshment of biological sex (male/female) and gender (masculinity/femininity) that has been used to justify the 'natural' status of heterosexuality and the gender binary while legitimising the concomitant gender oppression and homophobia" (Milani, 2014a, p. 76). In line with the antinormative queer spirit of language, gender, and sexuality scholarship (Hall et al., 2019), this chapter espouses a definition of visibility and its place in queer pedagogy that encapsulates the different ways that non-normative genders and sexualities are made visible through and in discourse (Butler, 2015; Milani & Lazar, 2017). This resonates in making "queer subjects socially, culturally, and politically seen, heard, and supported" in terms of queer visibility (Trinh, 2021, p. 756). In particular, queer visibility as taken up in this chapter is associated with discursively displaying LGBTQ+-related allyship using different semiotic resources such as posters with antihomophobia slogans, images of rainbow flags, and nonheteronormative use of grammatical gender (Milani, 2013; Motschenbacher, 2014).

Queer allyship as used in this chapter refers to allies with different backgrounds (linguistic, ethnic, gender, sexuality, age, religion, social status) who work together in classroom settings to question common heteronormative and cisgender assumptions about themselves so as to queer their own thinking and actions and build systems of support (Trinh, in press). This includes dominant gender discourses around female-male binariness and heterosexuality as normal and, therefore, preferable (Motschenbacher, 2013).

Critical Pedagogy and Queer Linguistics: An Effective Pedagogical Synergy

One premise underpinning critical pedagogy is its inherently political nature, aimed at interrogating and changing all social oppressions and inequalities (Giroux, 2020; hooks, 2014). Therefore, the tenets of critical pedagogy create an educational landscape of promise for teachers and students in which to challenge and transform power structures and dominant discourses in relation to gender and sexuality given heteronormativity (Darder et al., 2017; McLaren, 2015; Meyer, 2014). Importantly, at the root of critical pedagogy is the focus on praxis, a process of "reflection and action upon the world in order to transform it" (Freire, 1973, p. 52). Rooted in the promotion of egalitarian relationships and democratic processes between educators and students, such a pedagogy prioritizes communal voices and collective actions in setting out praxis (McLaren, 2017).

One of the major pillars of critical pedagogy is critical literacy. Literacy, however, is not reduced to language skills mastery or neutral teaching. Viewed as a political and emancipatory process, it entails not only to read the *word* but also to read the *world* (Freire & Macedo, 1968). In the context of students' critical readings of the world, special emphasis is placed on the use of different forms of visual media in the classroom as a way of developing transformative change (Kellner & Share, 2019).

Critical Media Literacy

Acknowledging the rapid technological changes and the new ways of communication in the contemporary era, critical media literacy (CML) valourizes meaning making in media texts in a multimodal way (Kress, 2010). Multimodality pays equal attention to all the semiotic resources used, writing, colour, fonts, speech, images, and layout included (Adami, 2015). Moreover, all semiotic resources are socially shaped, revealing how individuals position themselves towards established value systems such as the gendered assumptions of what counts as feminine or masculine (Adami, 2016). Crucially, CML capitalizes on students' engagement by producing multimodal media texts that advocate social change (Morrell, 2017). As Morrell (2012) reminded us, this perspective "enlightens students to the potential that they have, as media producers, to shape the world they live in, to help to turn it into the world they imagine" (p. 302). Thus, CML can help students position themselves differently and create queer allyship through their media text productions that challenge heteronormativity. Essentially, CML, as critical literacy, is the vehicle through which critical pedagogy is implemented and enacted.

Queer Pedagogy

Queer pedagogy (QP), in line with the critical pedagogy originated in the Freirean term praxis (Freire, 1973), is defined "as an educative practice enabling students to deconstruct normalcy as social and cultural construction" (Bryson & de Castell, 1993, p. 285). In conjunction with critical pedagogy, QP extends the process promoted by queer theory to destabilize social, cultural, and structural power norms (Kincheloe, 2012). Therefore, it allows students and teachers to unsettle dialogically fixed and uninterrogated knowledge and explore norms that regulate gender and sexuality given heteronormativity (Meyer, 2014; Miller, 2014).

Queer Linguistics

Underpinned by queer theory, queer linguistics is heavily concerned with interrogating and deconstructing the normative consolidation between sex, gender, and sexuality through language use (Leap, 2011; Milani, 2013; Motschenbacher, 2011; Motschenbacher & Stegu, 2013). As Hellinger (2011) posited,

> Language is not simply a neutral tool for the transmission of referential meaning: as an instrument of social practice it contributes to the communication, maintenance, and change of ideologies, attitudes and stereotypes. Language is used to perform acts of inclusion and exclusion, and is therefore invested with the potential to protect or disrupt social relations. (p. 565)

Most directly influenced by the work of Judith Butler (1990, 1993, 1997, 2004), queer linguistics is focused on the examination of contextualized linguistic practices related to normative and non-normative discursive formations of gender and sexuality, including binary notions of sex (male/female), gender (man/woman, masculine/feminine), and sexual desire (homosexuality/heterosexuality; Motschenbacher, 2010). Hence, queer linguistics offers a helpful theoretical framework for engaging LGBTQ+ issues in language classes (Sauntson, 2016). In this approach, the linguistic representation of individuals and social groups who do not neatly fit into binarily gendered language use is central (Milani, 2014a). In principle, one of the strategies that can be put into action in classrooms is subversive practices of linguistic gender crossing (Motschenbacher, 2014). Following Butler's (1990) analysis of drag, linguistic gender crossing refers to ways in which language use undermines grammatical gendered systems—for example, the use of female/feminine forms in reference to men and masculine/male forms in reference to women (Motschenbacher, 2014).

Research Context and Methodology

After a friend invited me to do so, I placed myself, as a volunteer, within a nonprofit organization offering nonformal English language courses to migrants and refugees in urban Greece. In this context, a critical action research (Hinchey, 2016) was conceived (as a master's study project) aimed at challenging heteronormative assumptions and building queer allyship (Trinh, in press). Echoing, however, Blommaert's (2005) words "that some things can only be said at certain moments, under certain conditions ... some things can only be researched at certain moments under certain conditions" (p. 65), I had one month of informal discussions with the gatekeepers before I tentatively introduced my critical research to them. After consultations, I was formally given their permission to conduct my study. In light of the study's critical context, the students' vulnerability being migrants and refugees, and the culturally bounded sensitive topics of gender and sexuality, I asked for and obtained the participants' consent to publish the research data anonymously.

The data are drawn from the critical action research discussed previously, deployed in three cycles. Being an educator-researcher (working twice a week) in the English language classroom, I gathered the data through participant observations, focus group discussions, and students' artefacts. The classroom comprised 14 students, ten males and four females, between 16 and 24 years old. The data collection spanned from May 2019 to March 2020. The data were transcribed into field notes supported by photographs. To analyse the data, I drew upon queer multimodal discourse analysis, which is concerned with the study of the relationship between texts (spoken, written, multimodal, digital), discourse (communicative events), and queer practices (Milani, 2013; Motschenbacher, 2023). Such an eclectic combination of analytical apparatus allows the capture of all the semiotic resources indexing queer allyship-related meaning-making practices in an ELT classroom. Specifically, the multimodal queer linguistic analysis of the data was focused on identifying particular lexical items, metaphors, evaluative language, intertextual meanings, and visuals in the students' discursive constructions of allyship.

Multimodal Students' Productions of Queer Allyship

The following two examples are taken from the context of the critical pedagogies (see the earlier section Critical Pedagogies and Queer Linguistics) exploring gender and sexual diversity implemented in the classroom. Compatible with the goal of heteronormativity critique, the queer readings and activities included the incorporation of Beyoncé's "Formation" video and advertising posters into the teaching and learning resources. In particular, the students were asked to critically engage with gender nonconforming representations (a person's appearance or behaviour that does not conform to the gender norms expected of them) in the video "Formation." They were also asked to critically reflect on "sexed" signs and messages pushing strictly defined binary boundaries displayed on the posters (e.g., advertising safe places for queer refugees and same-sex relationships) decorating the organization's walls.

As a result of favouring the activity of creating multimodal texts at the end of intervention evaluations, the students espoused support for gender- and sexuality-inclusive discourse. Drawing upon Morrell (2012), I argue that the students' creation of media texts that speak back to heteronormative discourses is a tool that can effect positive social change, be it small or large, as the following two examples show. Consider Figure 1, which presents a handmade poster produced collaboratively by the whole class:

Figure 1. Students' inclusion poster.

To begin with, what is most striking here is that the whole space at the bottom part of this multimodal text is occupied by the phrase "Welcome" written in large letters and accompanied by an eye-catching multicoloured rainbow. First, we observe the employment of the positive grammatical structure through the use of the word "Welcome." This lexical choice is indicative of a verbal gesture welcoming the audience into the community. The absence of an overtly queer sexual identity lexicon with reference to who or what is welcomed is also remarkable. Instead, the students invoked a visual element, the rainbow, to clarify the semantic ambiguity surrounding the word "Welcome." Although Kress and van Leeuwen (2021) cautioned against simplistic assumptions in multimodal texts, whenever verbal text is juxtaposed with an image, the former always explains the latter; I concur that this resonates well in this specific case. Indeed, it is the LGBTQ+ people who are welcomed. More specifically, from a queer multimodal point of view, the use of rainbow colours evokes one of the most historically poignant icons of the LGBTQ+ movement, the rainbow flag (Milani, 2013).

Furthermore, the students added handwritten heart shapes in red that are repeated, over the "welcome" statement and the rainbow, not once or twice, but 10 times. Interestingly, this repetition of the red hearts is gradually built up to a climax. As we see, by the end of the word "welcome" the hearts are starting to get bigger. In addition, above the rainbow, there is the most salient red heart, in terms of size. In this regard, the mobilization of a large icon and its placement right above the rainbow image serves as a semiotic device through which the students gave greater prominence to the "welcome" statement in their poster. This is additionally enhanced by the use of a red colour that connotes warmness and marking something as important (Machin, 2016). Moreover, the articulation of the heart symbol stands as an iconic declaration of love (Milani, 2014b).

Read together, through this multimodal combination of written language and iconic visual references, allyship for an all-encompassing community in terms of gender and sexuality is discursively achieved. Importantly, this statement is not solely constative but also performative (Austin, 1975), as it is a wall poster on display in the organization, thereby making visually prominent a welcome to the space for all genders and sexualities. Either way, this artefact exemplifies a queer allyship atmosphere, as similarly expressed in commercial signs in public (Iqani, 2012; Milani, 2014b).

By the same token, consider Figure 2, which presents an artefact produced by the students, as a whole class activity, using a word cloud application.

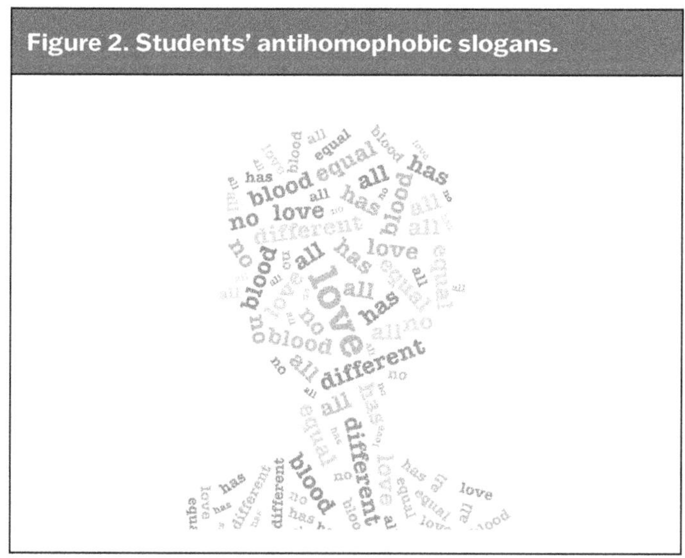

Figure 2. Students' antihomophobic slogans.

Here we see the students' own antihomophobic slogans: "all equal, all different" and "love has no blood." A silent element in this small semiotic artefact is the employment of a human form stretching from the head to shoulders in its design. Looking more closely, we also note the employment of provocative slogans that counter the dominant societal ideas circulating heteronormativity. Of interest is the mobilization of dual discourses through the use of the nouns "equal" and "different" and the comparison of semantically opposed lexical concepts serves as a basis for advocating for both equality and diversity. Despite an explicit reference to gender and sexuality, the "all equal, all different" slogan in particular carries connotations of the broader LGBTQ+ quest of speaking about equal recognition and celebration of difference (Milani, 2013). As such, queer allyship is foregrounded by generic references.

By contrast, the slogan "love has no blood" holds no semantic ambiguity in terms of its content. Through using this metaphor, the sentence makes clear that love is not connected to the traditional formation of heteronormative family relationships defined by considering biology ("blood") as the norm. Against standard narratives of romance embedded in conventional logic, such as marriage and the nuclear family lying at the heart of normal life, here a queer love is discursively constructed that functions as a subversive way of loving that is unknown to the heteronormative culture (Halperin, 2019).

Finally, these slogans are incorporated into a colourful palate. Visually, the stylized sentences and the words constituting them are multicoloured. Again, the students use here a particular colour combination that evokes LGBTQ+ connotations in a similar way as the rainbow flag. The repetitive typographic character of the word cloud application further produces a visual *synaesthesia* (see van Leeuwen, 2016), whereby combinations of sensory stimulations are deliberately produced to contribute to making queer allyship discourses "visually seen."

Gendered Language Alternatives

Linguistically speaking, personal pronouns and nouns provide a means of gendering human beings (boy/girl, she/he; Butler, 2004). In English, despite being heteronormative and anachronic, the third person singular pronouns (i.e., she, her, he, him, his) are inflected for gender, denoting male or female individuals grammatically or lexically (Motschenbacher, 2014). In addition, such heteronormative grammar causes confusion about linguistic choices regarding gender nonconforming individuals. Furthermore, seemingly heteronormative terminology like this is often strategically appropriated for non-normative purposes into discourse by gender nonconforming individuals to describe themselves as either females or males (see Milani, 2014a).

The following examples are drawn from a series of interactions that took place in the context of the teaching and learning activity "Adopting Alternatives to Gendered Language." Based on participant observations, I noticed that Julien's gender nonconforming self-expression, as someone assigned male at birth but female aligned, troubled the students in relation to third person singular pronouns as well as to gendered terms such as woman and man. Confusion aside, I also noticed that the students privileged the use of male forms (e.g., he is late, man, bro) and even homophobic labelling (he wears "unmanly" colourful clothes; the sunglasses he wears are womanish) when talking about Julien. By contrast, in informal conversations between Julien and me, she had self-identified as female. Acknowledging these linguistic gendering mismatches, I initiated classroom discussions in order for the students' misgendering practices to be challenged towards gender nonconforming allyship. After the students had been introduced to the concept of misgendering, they were encouraged to critically reflect on the practice and deconstruct it. More specifically, in the following extracts, the focus was on examples detailing how gendered language alternatives are discursively adopted in the classroom. Extract 1 shows an excellent example of implementing such practice.

Extract 1

1. Teacher-researcher: So, can you name any good practices in terms of pronouns and names usage when in doubt?

2. Tiara: We don't use them.

3. Everyone: (laughs)

4. Marcos: First...we must stop making wrong thoughts.

5. Teacher-researcher: Thoughts?

6. Marcos: To guess something because it might be the opposite.

7. Teacher-researcher: And when we use the opposite, what we should do?

8. Ben: We should change it.

9. Tiara: Say sorry and use the right pronouns and names?

10. Teacher-researcher: How we can change it? How can we tell which pronouns and names are right?

11. Mike: Asking the person about it; this will save us from wrongs.

12. Maria: Yes, I think it's always better ... to ask if we are not sure which pronoun to use.

13. George: We should give them this opportunity ... I agree.

Taking advantage of Maria and George's contributions to the discussion, I initiated an educational activity using an example from our immediate environment. The aim of the "Being a Language Ambassador" activity was to engage students in a real-world scenario of demonstrating queer allyship when referring to individuals. I divided students into two mixed-gender groups, and each group had a language ambassador, who acted as representatives of the groups. The first group was assigned to ask Julien about the preferred pronouns and names to best represent her. This then had to be communicated to the second group. The second group was assigned to make a short oral presentation on Julien's appearance in which her preferred pronouns and names would be acknowledged. As Extract 2 shows, the first group's language ambassador steps up as an ally to gender nonconforming persons.

Extract 2

1. Language ambassador: Hi, Julien. My name is Rita, and I am a language ambassador in this class. I would like to ask you this: What gender names and pronouns you want to use when we talk about you? We are not sure what to use and we want to remember so as to not make mistakes next time.

2. Julien: Hello, Rita. Thank you for asking me. Don't use male names and pronouns, please. I feel like a woman; I am a woman.

3. Language ambassador: OK, Julien. Thank you. We will use only female words.

In Extract 3, we see the ambassador of the second group present on Julien's appearance.

Extract 3

Julien is our classmate. She is very thin and not so tall. Today, she wears a nice pink sweater. On her ears, she wears silver earrings. Julien also has a silver ring on her fingers. We think that she likes to wear colorful and tight clothes. We are happy that she is in our class.

On another occasion, the following informal after-class discussion took place.

Extract 4

Maria: Miss, do you want to have a coffee with two beautiful women?

Teacher-researcher: Oh, thank you, but actually I am very hungry. I want to go home and eat something.

Maria: She can cook some traditional curry food if you want. Come to her flat to have lunch together. She cooks well. You are invited.

To begin with Extract 1, the teacher's role in this interaction is particularly interesting, as she is setting the scene, in Turn 1, to promote queer allyship in the classroom. Largely, her supportive attitude is discursively constructed thought the use of the phrase "good practices" with reference to pronouns and names. In addition, the accompanying phrase "when in doubt" has an evaluative function, acknowledging the discursive formation "haunting" (Leap, 2020). Indeed, assumptions resulting from male–female linguistic contrasts continue to cause doubts. Even if there is a pragmatic ambiguity arising from the absence of deictic expressions to indicate who is in doubt, the teacher still evaluates this practice as problematic. She continues working towards shared actions, asking the students to recommend "good practices" for countering gender-biased language. In this way the classroom is portrayed as a place that assumes an oppositional stance to practices of misgendering. Whilst Tiara's contribution in Turn 2 ("we don't use them") caused everyone to laugh, presumably in an ironic manner, from a queer linguistic point of view her statement clearly resists heteronormative gendering linguistic practices by making a radical suggestion of not using pronouns at all. In response, assuming a rather aggressive tone, manifested in the imperative mood ("we must stop making") and coupled with the semantic context of the words "wrong thoughts," Marcos is engaged in the gender conversation as a vocal supporter by proposing an "end" to assuming someone's pronouns as it might be "the opposite" or "wrong."

Along similar lines, albeit in a milder tone as the modal verb "should" indicates, Ben takes up an allyship position suggestive of action/transformation, as stressed by the verb "change." Tiara's comment, in Turn 9, is also of interest. By using the word "sorry," she evaluates language gendering as a failure to respond to human diversity. Next, Mike (in Turn 11), Maria (in Turn 12), and George (in Turn 13) powerfully attempt to offset widespread grammatical norms in terms of pronouns usage by naming a number of ways to be allies, as the verbs "ask" and "give" indicate. The extensive use of deictic pronouns in the plural form ("we," "us") in contrast to single forms usage ("I") is also noticeable. In this way, allies are collectively constructed and framed in this classroom as an entity unit. Although ambiguous, as it is not clear whether it addresses only this classroom or society more broadly, this language use nevertheless constructs a network of allies in which the hegemony of gendering by pronouns "must stop" and even "change."

Turning now to Extract 2, we observe allyship in action, which is discursively achieved by countering linguistic gendering practices. As the short dialogue depicts, the evaluative "we are not sure" and "making mistakes" are strongly opposed by the employment of good practices. Here, we see Rita, on behalf of the classroom, employing queer language when requesting Julien's preferred names and pronouns ("what gender names and pronouns you want to use when we talk about you?") so that "mistakes" can be avoided "next time." What is most interesting in this example is the mobilization of the strategy of self-labelling. Clearly, this linguistic act is in contrast with the binary-established grammar norms, which assert we should refer to a man only by male forms and to a woman only by female ones. Importantly, there is explicit recognition of Julien's misgendering ("we are not sure what to use," "make mistakes"). However, this practice is not left unchallenged but is contested, as the phrase "we want to remember so as not to make mistakes next time" clearly denotes. Butler (1997), using Austinian terminology, cogently reminded us that "acts of self-labeling are typically less problematic than when the labelling is done to other people, being more a matter of perlocutionary effect it has on the hearer than of its illocutionary force or intention of the speaker" (p. 17).

Turning now to Extracts 3 and 4, what is most striking is that the gendered personal reference forms are grammatically and lexically gendered with semantic female features. Here, Julien, a gender nonconforming peer, is discursively constructed by the class according to her desired female gender, which reflects what Cameron (1995) has called practices of "verbal hygiene" and is broadly understood as nonheteronormative and queer-friendly language use. This is done by appropriating female singular third personal pronouns ("she," "her") and lexically personal nouns ("women"). Notably, these very gendered linguistic devices are resignified through the process of resemiotization, in which "meaning making shifts from context to context, from practice to practice, or from one stage of a practice" (Iedema, 2003, p. 41). Essentially, the use of female forms to refer to an individual assigned male gender at birth is indeed a gender-crossing and subversive practice (Butler, 1990). Whether it is at odds with the idea of queer theory (Milani, 2014b) as building on the discursive gender binary formation, what should not be downplayed here is that this linguistic subversion serves as an important semiotic resource offering allyship to gender nonconforming individuals. Thus, seemingly gendered forms are queerly rephrased into an alliance of shared repertoires.

Discussion and Conclusion

This chapter has brought queer allyship in ELT into closer focus in the underexplored migrant and refugee educational contexts in Western societies (but see Nelson, 2009, 2012, for notable exceptions). Bringing queer allyship found in those spaces into the research spotlight redresses this academic oversight. If queer pedagogical inquiry is true to its radical roots of promoting gender and sexuality diversity through language education (Britzman, 1995), I argue that migrant and refugee sites cannot be left out of this endeavour. The examples discussed in this chapter make a case for doing so.

Moreover, I believe that an eclectic theoretical apparatus combining critical pedagogy, CML, QP, and queer linguistics in ELT can be a powerful tool for enacting praxis (Freire, 1973) as related to queer allyship (Trinh, in press). My findings also resonate well with the critical and queer pedagogical potential for advocating for sexual and gender difference in classroom settings through community-based and discussion-oriented practices (Darder et al., 2017; McLaren, 2015; Trinh, 2022).

In order to teach our students how to read the word and the world (Freire & Macedo, 1987) from a queer perspective, educators can build on CML as a way to cultivate transformative change that promotes social equity (Kellner & Share, 2019). Drawing on Morrell (2012, 2017), I argue that investing in students' multimodal media production can enable a productive arena for the manifestation of queer allyship in ELT classrooms. Although sometimes overlooked, I consider all semiotic resources as equally important to meaning-making practices, and thus I assign a more multimodally central role to the study of queer discourse analysis, in line with Milani (2013) and Motschenbacher (2023). Against this logocentric bias in research, the analysis highlighted that allyship in the students' discourse was accomplished in the company of a range of semiotic resources: written, spoken, material, spatial, and visual. I concur that queer allyship is shaped along the lines of multimodality (Adami, 2015, 2016; Kress, 2010) and, in turn, pushes queer linguistics beyond its epistemological limit, language (Milani, 2014a). In messing up and playing with fixed knowledge, turning it upside down, and asking, "What else can I do differently"? (Trinh, 2022, p. 220), I prompt ELT teachers to advance queer allyship in their classrooms by engaging students with multimodality.

Responding to queer linguistic calls for expanding the methodological and analytical frameworks in education (Sauntson, 2012, 2016, 2020), I have applied this dimension to capture nonheteronormative language use in terms of allyship formation in the English language classroom. Although limited to personal nouns and names, it is evident in this study that gender binary structures are employed as a strategy supportive of queer allyship. However, it was used in a radical manner, one through which gender crossing was realized (Butler, 1990). Though this tactic seems to polarize gender difference and capitalize on essentialist social categories discourses, and thus to clash with queer theory and its sidekick queer linguistics, I agree with Motschenbacher (2014), who argued that alternative linguistic choices should also include traditional ones, such as gendered language. Serving as a point of reflection, educators should recognize that sometimes something as simple as the personal pronouns we use in everyday speech can provoke systems of support such as queer allyship (Trinh, in press).

In conclusion, though we should be cautious to avoid oversimplifications due to the specific context of this study, the theoretical and analytical framework presented earlier has shown to be of use in gaining queer understandings of allyship in ELT at the intersection with migration and displacement. Hopefully, this chapter serves as a reflective piece—theoretically, methodologically, and analytically—so that educators might further develop queer allyship in other contexts. Failure to do so perpetuates social injustice and inequality. However, the queer pedagogy presented in this chapter cannot be read as a manual that could be simply applied to the ELT classroom, irrespective of context. Rather, it functions as an example to be attempted and modified in other educational settings.

Author

Christina Fakalou holds an MA in language education for refugees and migrants. She has been working in Greek educational contexts with various social groups who have experienced migration for the past 6 years. Her research interests include queer studies, multimodality, and critical discourse analysis.

References

Adami, E. (2015). A social semiotic perspective on digital mobility. *Media Education, 6*(2), 184–207.

Adami, E. (2016). Multimodality. In O. Garcia, N. Flores, & M. Spotti (Eds.), *The Oxford handbook of language and society* (pp. 451–472). Oxford University Press.

Austin, J. L. (1975). *How to do things with words.* Harvard University Press.

Blommaert, J. (2005). *Discourse: A critical introduction.* Cambridge University Press.

Britzman, D. P. (1995). Is there a queer pedagogy? Or, stop reading straight. *Educational Theory, 45*(2), 151–165. https://doi.org/10.1111/j.1741-5446.1995.00151.x

Bryson, M., & de Castell, S. (1993). Queer pedagogy: Praxis makes im/perfect. *Canadian Journal of Education, 18*(3), 285–305.

Butler, J. (1990). *Gender trouble: Feminism and the subversion of identity.* Routledge.

Butler, J. (1993). *Bodies that matter: On the discursive limits of "sex."* Routledge.

Butler, J. (1997). *Excitable speech: A politics of the performative.* Routledge.

Butler, J. (2004). *Undoing gender.* Routledge.

Butler, J. (2015). *Notes toward a performative theory of assembly.* Harvard University Press.

Cameron, D. (1995). *Verbal hygiene.* Routledge.

Coda, J. (2018). Disrupting standard practice: Queering the world language classroom. *Dimension*, pp. 74–89.

Darder, A., Baltodano, M., & Torres, R. D. (2017). *The critical pedagogy reader* (3rd ed.). Routledge.

Freire, P. (1973). *Pedagogy of the oppressed.* Penguin.

Freire, P., & Macedo, D. (1987). *Literacy: Reading the word and the world.* Routledge.

Giroux, H. A. (2020). *On critical pedagogy* (2nd ed.). Bloomsbury Academic.

Hall, K., Levon, E., & Milani, T. (2019). Navigating normativities: Gender and sexuality in text and talk. *Language in Society, 1*, 481–489. https://doi.org/10.1017/S0047404519000447

Halperin, D. (2019). Queer love. *Critical Inquiry, 45*(2), 396–419. https://doi.org/10.1086/700993

Hellinger, M. (2011). Guidelines for non-discriminatory language use. In R. Wodak, B. Johnstone, & P. Kerswill (Eds.), *The Sage handbook of sociolinguistics* (pp. 565–582). Sage.

Hinchey, P. (Ed.). (2016). *A critical action research reader*. Peter Lang.

hooks, b. (2014). *Teaching to transgress: Education as the practice of freedom*. Routledge.

Iedema, R. (2003). Multimodality, resemiotization: Extending the analysis of discourse as multi-semiotic practice. *Visual Communication*, *2*(1), 29–57.

Iqani, M. (2012). *Consumer culture and media studies*. Palgrave Macmillan.

Kellner, D., & Share, J. (2019). *The critical media literacy guide: Engaging media and transforming education*. Brill Sense.

Kincheloe, J. L. (2012). Critical pedagogy in the twenty-first century: Evolution for survival. *Counterpoints*, *422*, 147–183.

Kress, G. (2010). *Multimodality: A social semiotic approach to communication*. Routledge.

Kress, G., & van Leeuwen, T. (2021). *Reading images: The grammar of visual design* (3rd ed.). Routledge.

Leap, W. L. (2011). Queer linguistics, sexuality, and discourse analysis. In J. P. Gee & M. Handford (Eds.), *The Routledge handbook of discourse analysis* (pp. 558–571). Routledge.

Leap, W. L. (2020). *Language and sexuality before Stonewall*. Palgrave.

Machin, D. (2016). The need for a social and affordance-driven multimodal critical discourse studies. *Discourse & Society*, *27*(3), 322–334.

McLaren, P. (2015). *Life in schools. An introduction to critical pedagogy in the foundations of education* (6th ed.). Routledge.

McLaren, P. (2017). Critical pedagogy: A look at the major concepts. In A. Darder, M. P. Baltodano, & R. D. Torres (Eds.), *The critical pedagogy reader* (3rd ed., pp. 56–79). Routledge.

Meyer, E. J. (2014). She's the man: Deconstructing the gender and sexuality curriculum at "Hollywood high." In A. Ibrahim & S. R. Steinberg (Eds.), *Critical youth studies reader* (pp. 252–259). Peter Lang.

Milani, T. (2013). Expanding the queer linguistic scene: Multimodality, space and sexuality at a South African university. *Journal of Language and Sexuality*, *2*(2), 206–234. https://doi.org/10.1075/jls.2.2.02mil

Milani, T. (2014a). Querying the queer from Africa: Precarious bodies—precarious gender. *Agenda*, *28*(4), 75–85. https://doi.org/10.1080/10130950.2014.963940

Milani, T. (2014b). Sexed signs—Queering the scenery. *International Journal of the Sociology of Language*, *228*(228), 201–225. https://doi.org/10.1515/ijsl-2014-0011

Milani, T., & Lazar, M. (2017). Seeing from the South: Discourse, gender and sexuality from southern perspectives. *Journal of Sociolinguistics*, *21*, 307–319. https://doi.org/10.1111/josl.12241

Miller, sj. (2014). Moving an anti-bullying stance into schools: Supporting the identities of transgender and gender variant youth. In A. Ibrahim & S. R. Steinberg (Eds.), *Critical youth studies reader* (pp. 161–171). Peter Lang.

Morrell, E. (2012). 21st-century literacies, critical media pedagogies, and language arts. *The Reading Teacher*, *66*(4), 300–302.

Morrell, E. (2017). Toward equity and diversity in literacy research, policy, and practice: A critical, global approach. *Journal of Literacy Research, 49*(3), 454–463. https://doi.org/10.1177/1086296X17720963

Motschenbacher, H. (2010). *Language, gender and sexual identity: Poststructuralist perspectives.* John Benjamins.

Motschenbacher, H. (2011). Taking queer linguistics further: Sociolinguistics and critical heteronormativity research. *International Journal of the Sociology of Language, 212,* 149–179. https://doi.org/10.1515/ijsl.2011.050

Motschenbacher, H. (2013). Gentlemen before ladies? A corpus-based study of conjunct order in personal binomials. *Journal of English Linguistics, 41*(3), 212–242. https://doi.org/10.1177/0075424213489993

Motschenbacher, H. (2014). Grammatical gender as a challenge for language policy: The (im)possibility of non-heteronormative language use in German versus English. *Language Policy, 13,* 243–261. https://doi.org/10.1007/s10993-013-9300-0

Motschenbacher, H. (2023). Affective regimes on Wilton Drive: A multimodal analysis. *Social Semiotics, 33*(1), 168–187. https://doi.org/10.1080/10350330.2020.1788823

Motschenbacher, H., & Stegu, M. (2013). Queer linguistic approaches to discourse. *Discourse & Society, 24*(5), 519–535. https://doi.org/10.1177/0957926513486069

Nelson, C. (2009). *Sexual identities in English language education: Classroom conversations.* Routledge.

Nelson, C. (2012). Emerging queer epistemologies in studies of "gay"-student discourses. *Journal of Language and Sexuality, 1*(1), 79–105. https://doi.org/10.1075/jls.1.1.05nel

Paiz, J. M. (2019). Queering practice: LGBTQ+ diversity and inclusion in English language teaching. *Journal of Language, Identity & Education, 18*(4), 266–275. https://doi.org/10.1080/15348458.2019.1629933

Sauntson, H. (2012). *Approaches to gender and spoken classroom discourse.* Palgrave.

Sauntson, H. (2016). Language, sexuality and education. In S. Wortham, D. Kim, & S. May (Eds.), *Discourse and education, encyclopedia of language and education* (3rd ed., pp. 1–13). Springer.

Sauntson, H. (2020). Applying queer theory to language and sexuality research in schools. In J. Angouri & J. Baxter (Eds.), *The Routledge handbook of language, gender and sexuality* (pp. 339–353). Routledge.

Trinh, E. (2021). Visibility. In K. K. Strunk & S. A. Shelton (Eds.), *Encyclopedia of queer studies in education* (pp. 756–757). Brill.

Trinh, E. (2022). Supporting queer SLIFE youth: Initial queer considerations. In L. J. Pentón Herrera (Ed.), *English and students with limited or interrupted formal education: Global perspectives on teacher preparation and classroom practices* (pp. 209–225). Springer.

Trinh, E. (in press). Queer allyship in TESOL: We need to ACTS now! *TESOL Journal.*

van Leeuwen, T. (2016). A social semiotic theory of synesthesia? A discussion paper. *Hermes Journal of Language and Communication in Business, 53,* 105–119. https://doi.org/10.7146/hjlcb.v0i55.24292

Queer Inclusion and Allyship in the Turkish English Language Teaching Sphere

Elizabeth S. Coleman

This chapter explores how I have drawn on concepts of intersectionality to de-other LGBTQ+[1] persons in the English language teaching (ELT) environment. Working with English learners at the A1–B2 levels on the Common European Framework of Reference for Languages[2] who are studying primarily in medical faculties and university personnel, I have attempted to foster an understanding of the normalcy of queerness and de-other LGBTQ+ persons by speaking publicly about the harm of heteronormativity in order to generate allies in my communities of practice. This chapter explains the Turkish social context and how heteronormativity dominates there, my personal position as an educator in this context, and diversity, equity, and inclusion–related training given in tertiary institutions in Türkiye with the aim of enhancing allyship. Forbes and Ueno (2020) found that "allyship is not fixed but can vary within a marginalized population, having different meanings for different people" (p. 173). Reason and Broido (2005) noted that to be an ally, one must be aware of one's dominant position and the impact it has on the minoritized group (p. 82). Further, Reason and Broido established three key "ally actions": educating and inspiring members of the dominant group, bringing about cultural and institutional change, and supporting members of the minority group (pp. 83–85). Therefore, in this chapter, I work from the following concept of allyship: supporting minority rights while not being a member of that particular minority group. In this context, allyship pertains to the efforts of heterosexual cisgender (non-trans) learners

1. Though this is the acronym I use to refer to lesbian, gay, bisexual, transgender, queer, and other (+) members of the community, several variations on this term appear throughout this chapter. In instances where other forms are present, they are the forms used by the original author or source being referenced. This has been done to preserve the voice of the original authors as much as possible. All variations of this acronym refer to the same community.

2. The Common European Framework of Reference for Languages spans six levels, from A1 to C2, with A1 and A2 being basic users, B1 and B2 independent users, and C1 and C2 proficient users. A1–B2 levels can be expressed as covering basic to upper intermediate levels. C levels are considered to be native-level proficiency.

and educational professionals to support the needs and inclusion of queer, transgender, and gender-queer learners and colleagues. Allyship here is considered an active process in which the ally takes action to effect change or offer support, rather than merely stating that they support a minority. For further definitions of terms used in this chapter, please see the terminology section at the end of the chapter.

Social Context

To give some context, it should be noted that Türkiye is a country founded on neoliberal Islam, and while still technically secular, the country is experiencing an increasing rightward swing toward tendencies of an Islamic state. Homosexuality is not illegal in Türkiye, and, in fact, the country often finds itself a route of passage for those seeking asylum from gender- and sexuality-related persecution. While the past 10 to 15 years have seen queerness becoming more visible, the same period has also seen the state cracking down on expressions of queer freedom. Homogeneity, which is to say the condition of everyone being the same, is important in Turkish culture, and as outliers members of the LGBTQ+ community find themselves to be the nail that gets hammered down. Homogeneity shows up in various forms in Turkish society, such as in the requirement to complete military service and the shunning of those who do not complete their service, especially if they are excluded on grounds of homosexuality. When it comes to masculinity, the ritual of *sünnet,* or circumcision, when a boy is 7 or 8 years old is a significant event. All boys are expected to undergo this procedure, and it is considered their entry into manhood. Masculinity is highly coded in Türkiye, and those who fall outside of the prescribed norms are often described as soft or faggots[3] (Atencio & Koca, 2011; Bakacak & Öktem, 2014; Cengiz et al., 2004). Atencio and Koca (2011) note that although members of a community adopt gendered identities through the communities to which they are exposed, "they also come to influence social practices and take up diverse positions of power" (p. 60).

In present-day Türkiye the LGBTQ+ community is under attack. The current state of affairs is somewhat different from that of 10 years ago, when Istanbul was able to hold its largest ever Pride march of 100,000 people. This followed the Turkish equivalent of the Occupy movement, the Gezi Park protests. These protests were a radical push for social change and an uprising against the government. The Turkish regime ultimately quashed these demonstrations and 2 years later the 2015 Pride march was banned at the last moment by the city governorate, leading to demonstrations and civil unrest. No Pride protests have been able to successfully take place since then, mirroring the state's repression of the queer community across Türkiye. President Recep Tayyip Erdoğan has stated both that there are no LGBT+ people in Türkiye and that queer individuals exist and must be quashed as we are a threat to family order (Baume, 2021). In March 2010, then minister for Women and Family Affairs Selma Aliye Kavaf stated, "Homosexuality is an illness.... I think it is something that should be

3. Though readers may find this term offensive, I include it here purposefully as a direct translation of the Turkish term *ibne*, which is often used to subjugate men who do not fit within the highly coded hegemonic masculinity endemic in Turkish society. The term has been directly translated precisely to show the level of violence enacted upon members of the LGBTQ+ community in Türkiye.

cured" (Savcı, 2020, p. 29). Under the shadow of this pervasive government view, the Council of Higher Education, which oversees all Turkish universities, issued a decree in 2019 that amended the way gender was to be taught ("YÖK'ten "Cinsiyet Eşitliğinde" Geri Adım!", 2019). The president of the Council, Yekta Saraç, stated, "It is necessary to take care to determine the curriculum of the courses for women's studies within the understanding of *Justice-Based Women's Studies* rather than *Gender Equality* and to highlight the superior values of the Turkish society, especially the concept of family" ("YÖK'ten "Cinsiyet Eşitliğinde" Geri Adım!", 2019, para. 5). The message from the government was very clear: Progressive gender is not something that aligns with the Islamic values of Türkiye and therefore must not be taught. Outside of circles working on gender and sexuality issues, this largely went unchallenged, yet for those of us working on gender and sexuality issues, this meant the need to step very carefully to get our work done.

In spring 2019, the gender studies club at Middle East Technical University (METU, or in Turkish Orta Doğu Teknik Üniversitesi [ODTÜ]) was prohibited from organizing an event in which LGBTI+ families would talk about their experiences. The reason for the ban by the rectorate was "the relation of LGBTI+ and rainbow" [to the event] ("Ban at METU," 2019). The rectorate also reminded the students of the Ankara governate's prohibition on LGBT-related activities. Such bans have become pervasive across Türkiye, often under the guise of public safety. METU LGBTIQAA+ Solidarity, the university's LGBTQ+ group, stated that the canceling of the event was not only discrimination but a bar to academic freedom—particularly considering the institution's membership in the Effective Gender Equality in Research and the Academia group, which comprises eight institutions across the European Union and Türkiye with a commitment to research on gender equality. METU has seen other bans against queer events. In June 2022 the rectorate again banned LGBT-related activities on campus, prohibiting what should have been the 10th Pride march on campus. An announcement from the rectorate read, "A certain group is trying to present the campus of our university as a place where they can make their illegal march." Pride marches, however, are not illegal in Türkiye, merely made to be by last-minute pronouncements from offices of authority; there is a constitutional right to demonstrate in the nation. METU LGBTIQAA+ Solidarity announced that they would push ahead with the march and would not allow themselves to be criminalized after 25 years of working on such issues on campus and organizing nine previous marches. Both of these events saw participants arrested and tried, with a court in 2021 ruling that no offense had been committed by the holding of the march ("Turkish Court Acquits Students," 2021). Marches across the country are often met with arrests and violence. Since 2015, it has been impossible to hold a peaceful march in any city in Türkiye, despite historically large crowds at Istanbul's 2013 and 2014 Pride marches causing no civil or security issues, a reason often cited for last-minute bans by regional authorities.

This is the context in which activists and educators in Türkiye are trying to cultivate allyship. Though students try to run solidarity groups, which require, by law, faculty support, they are often rejected by university management. Rulings such as that by the Higher Education Council mean many academics are wary of getting involved in struggles, and in the field of ELT the lack of diversity education in preservice training combined with the pervasive homogeneity of Türkiye leave educators wondering what any of it has to do with them.

Positionality

As a queer woman, the need for solidarity has always been clear to me and it has been a commitment in my work, often to the point that my work will out me before I can out myself. It is this belief in the need for solidarity that has meant that, for the past 6 years, I have been bringing the message of equality and harm reduction to Turkish ELT events. Delivering various conferences and trainings aimed at highlighting the harm done by heteronormativity and queer erasure in the ELT industry, it has been possible to highlight to colleagues the need to include diversity, equity, inclusion, and access-related topics in their classroom presentations. It is also through these sessions that I have found allies across institutions and among preservice ELT teachers. Due to the stigma around queer issues and the difficult position of working at a conservative institution, it is not always possible to come out and directly declare oneself to be discussing queer issues.

Queer-Related Training and Workshops

At the start of the 2019–2020 academic year, it was made very clear to me that I could not lead a training on LGBTQ+ issues as part of our annual staff orientation. In order to circumvent this, I expanded the session to cover several other topics, although my primary focus remained on issues of gender and sexuality discrimination. This provided an excellent opportunity for instructors to analyze their own privilege and consider what course of action they would take in given situations. The discussions that developed during these sessions brought to light issues that some colleagues had not previously considered, including a healthy dose of analysis on the use of they/them pronouns. Following modeling, attendees were asked to summarize their own identities and consider how the different factors interrelate. They were then asked to complete a buying privilege activity (see Appendix) in which it would not be possible to have all the comforts they usually have. In short, groups are allocated a budget and given a list of privileges that are rights and freedoms cisgender heterosexual nondisabled individuals take for granted. Each group must buy privileges from the list with their budget. The exercise is designed so that it will not be possible for everyone to select all the rights they want. Colleagues in this session began to break down the notion of identity and understand the intersectional nature of being, and that while they may be unfamiliar with one aspect of a person's identity—their sexuality—they can understand the person through other facets of identity. Thus, understanding that sexuality is a small but challenging component of a person's being allows for the cultivation of deeper understanding and allyship.

Though many colleagues responded well to this session, one even feeling comfortable enough to disclose their own sexuality to me afterward, some colleagues failed to see the relevance of inclusion to their own teaching. While it saddens me that members of my own department may not see the need to be inclusive, despite rising numbers of LGBTQ+ students in our classrooms, this particular session did lead to colleagues knowing that they could approach me on related issues that arose in their classrooms. Presently, my department holds a small group of instructors committed to actively working on LGBTQ+ issues and bringing queer philosophy into their classroom practice.

One of the most successful allyship programs that arose from my work was the establishment of a cross-institutional working group aimed at developing a handbook for university ELT teachers on how to tackle issues around gender and LGBT topics in their classrooms. In 2018, I presented at a conference at another Istanbul university discussing academic drag. *Academic drag* is a term coined by Samek and Donofrio (2013) to describe the hiding of things such as our queerness from the academy: "part and parcel of our academic socialization into the professortariat, our notions of intention and expression are shaped to comply with the standards of the profession" (p. 30). Attendees at the presentation welcomed the opportunity to discuss identity and ask questions about terminology, ultimately enabling them to discuss these topics better in their own departments and classrooms. A faculty member of the host institution saw the hosting of my speech as a sign that their department was amenable to queer-related projects. Thus, they began to work on LGBTQ+ issues at that institution along with several other colleagues. Simultaneously, the same faculty member and I developed a separate working partnership looking at queer classroom issues.

The following year the same colleague proposed a working group to develop a handbook on queer inclusion in the ELT classroom, complete with a glossary of terminology for the uninitiated. The Queer ELT Initiative was born. Reaching out to colleagues from various institutions, we established a small group of academics and ELT practitioners from both inside and outside the queer community who were committed to improving the state of affairs. The group met on a monthly basis and began by examining prominent texts on LGBT+ issues in ELT, such as the work of Britzman (1995), Liddicoat (2009), and Nelson (1999, 2010). Once all members of the group had a good grounding in the area, a chart was drawn up to highlight key concepts that would be relevant to practitioners in the field. Alongside this, each meeting saw a member discussing problematic material that they had worked with and how they had amended it. Materials included authentic texts from news articles that were adapted as reading and discussion materials in one institution. The original teacher shared how she reframed some of the questions to provoke critical thinking in her class. Upon discussing the material together, the group proposed that the text be replaced with one that relied less on stereotypes or, if it could not be replaced, that questions set to provoke criticism of the presented ideas be constructed.

By reaching out to different universities, we were able to bring multiple cisgender heterosexual colleagues into the working group and expand their knowledge of queer issues. Although the working group folded during Türkiye's extended COVID-19 lockdown, these group members remain better able to support queer learners and tackle issues of discrimination in the classroom following their work on the project. Members of this team have taken ideas they were not previously exposed to back to their classrooms and, in some cases, other countries and exposed their learners to more diversified identities. Cisgender heterosexual colleagues gained an understanding of how not seeing oneself represented in materials can make learners excluded. Those instructors now include diverse identities in their materials and have an expanded recognition of who is and is not present in materials and classrooms. In this way, they themselves are expanding the network of allies among our Gen Z student body. Those of us who identify as queer also found an enhanced support network and a sense of invigoration in knowing that we were not alone in facing the challenges of a heteronormative classroom environment.

One very clear thread runs throughout all of these events: my coming out and sharing first person experience alongside theory. In every conference session and workshop I have delivered in the past 6 years, I have come out in no uncertain terms. Though it may be argued that announcing one's sexuality in an environment such as staunchly conservative Türkiye is not the best idea, it feels vital to lend that first person perspective to the theory that I share. Though there is no doubt some preaching to the choir, given that we know queer folks tend to attend queer presentations, each session is greeted with voices from the heterosexual community who describe how they have not previously considered particular aspects or the impact of materials used in their classrooms. This authenticity is what facilitates the finding of allies. Vulnerability allows people to feel comfortable enough to mirror their own vulnerability in not knowing and wanting to do more and better. In a wonderful hybrid article/letter to his mother, Ono (1997) talked of wanting to cultivate courageous voices. In order to do this, we must first have courage ourselves; declaring one's identity is an act of this courage. The conversations that arise when we speak authentically of identity and the needs of our community not only allow us to cultivate courage in others in the same position but also allow us to find allies and supportive educational families as they become aware of our existence.

I am a firm believer in queer pedagogy, and a key part of that in my practice is putting myself on the front line and risking the backlash. Queer pedagogy brings queer theory into the classroom alongside critical theory and traditional teaching methodologies. Nemi Neto (2018) offers a simple definition: "Queer pedagogy offers a critical view of the practices of exclusion that are naturalized in the classroom by a banal heteronormativity that makes all those who don't fit into a certain standard invisible" (p. 591). It is not common for educators in Türkiye to out themselves, which, considering the attitudes outlined previously, is not surprising. Yet I am a firm believer in the notion that you cannot be what you cannot see. Both students and colleagues need to see representation that shows being "progressive" is possible in the restrictive confines of the Turkish establishment.

Classroom Allyship

Inside the classroom, allies can be found and cultivated in much the same way. Allowing students to discuss topics that naturally arise and share their thoughts without policing benefits them greatly. Though one should be mindful that anti-queer students should not be allowed to espouse hate, allowing them to be present in a discussion where they can be exposed to the idea that homosexuality and transness are usual may begin to create a shift in their ideology. A subtle sneaking in of queer concepts while offering the chance to take a perspective that is not that of their identity can create space for students to find their support for others. This can be the inclusion of same-gender couples in an example sentence or the sharing of additional details regarding straight-washed celebrities represented in materials; see Oxford University Press's representation of Keith Haring in its *Lecture Ready* series (Frazier & Leeming, 2013) and Pearson's inclusion of Jack Monroe in *Speak Out Pre-intermediate* (Clare & Wilson, 2015).

A personal favorite way of introducing diverse identities is building on lessons on first impressions to elicit ideas about famous and less well-known real-life personalities. I present paired students with a photograph of a person and ask them to write down any ideas they have about them based on how the person looks and their surroundings. This often draws out some very normative and heterosexual ideas—he is wearing a ring, so he has a wife; she looks old, she could be a mother; and so on. Students are often surprised to find that the people they have been introduced to are not straight, not necessarily married despite their jewelry choices, and in fact may not even fit the category of man or woman.

A photo of the late great Leslie Fienberg is a wonderful inclusion here as it allows for discussion of neo pronouns and nontypical gender presentation. (I strongly recommend using Leslie's self-portrait from 2011, available on hir website.) Neo pronouns are third person pronouns that are not the standard pronouns of he/she/they. Such pronouns tend to be used by genderqueer or nonbinary individuals as there is no traditional attachment of gender to these words and they are therefore gender neutral. Following the she/her/hers pattern, examples include *hir/hir/hirs*, *zie/zir/zirs*, *ey/em/eirs*, and *xe/xem/xyrs*.

Expansive language such as zie and hir can be a revelation to higher level students, providing them with a linguistic challenge while reminding them that what we believe is not always true. In the Turkish context, the inclusion of photos of James Baldwin's time in Istanbul centers the idea of difference in the local context. To see a person they believe to be other sipping tea at a *kıraathane*, a traditional coffee house often used for reading and generally favored by middle-aged men, which is a cornerstone of Turkish culture, brings home the message that like-minded souls can be found everywhere. Ultimately, removing the foreignness of queer identities and the taboo around discussing them allows students to express their support. Though it would be misleading to say all students embrace the LGBTQ+ community, members of my classrooms have become vocal in their support and will challenge bigoted ideas espoused by others. Once students know they are able to share these views safely, I often see queer ideas cropping up in their work, such as one student who, during a character design project, crafted a story of a character who had to flee to another planet to escape persecution for his sexuality, which she reminded her class was a very natural thing.

When it comes to demonstrating how natural such things are, it is important not to make a fuss when students make reference to minority sexual identity, whether their own or someone else's. Should the reference be discriminatory, a quick shutting down of the discussion with a reminder that we do not use language such as that will do the trick. When it comes to showing support, being open, but not over-referring to queer students when it comes to queer topics or making a show of being accepting, will signal one's own allyship without making anyone uncomfortable or feel the need to out themselves. The easiest way to show openness is to ask your students what they want to be called; you may be amazed at how many of them will not have been asked before.

Allyship in Preservice Teaching Programs

One of the biggest challenges is to reach preservice ELT teachers. Many educators share that topics of equality and inclusion were not taught during their training. As instructors and teacher trainers, we must push the concept of inclusion when working with future colleagues. Some attempts are happening here in Türkiye, with an LGBTQ project happening through Sinop University's ELT department. ELT students were able to engage in a social justice project that allowed them to consult with members of the local LGBTQ community and develop

LGBTQ+-inclusive pedagogies. The students reported that they had found this refreshing and learned a great deal from the experience. Students heard directly from community members and were asked by the facilitator what they would do if they were in that position; their reflections showed how deeply impacted and even distressed they were upon learning about the experiences of members of the queer community. Students were familiarized with terms relating to LGBTQ+ life and issues, guided in creating "anti-slur" policies, and engaged in critical thinking to reduce prejudice. By critical thinking, I mean that they examined the ideas presented to them and questioned the validity of the ideas put forward. Thinking through the reasons that these ideas are presented, and the author's purpose in articulating them, the learners were able to form their own conclusions and respond to the original input. Having met these students through my work at Sinop University, it is clear that engagement in these types of projects positively impacts and expands allyship. The students involved have requested guidance on how to be better allies and asked for opportunities to work further in the area of queer-aligned ELT. It is again through my self-outing that these students have been able to find me and know that they have a safe person to approach to discuss their ideas with and to ask for assistance.

What's Next?

Following the reelection of Recep Tayyip Erdoğan in May 2023, it seems the wider LGBTQ+ community in Türkiye will continue to suffer. Immediately following his acceptance speech, President Erdoğan again marked out the queer community as being away from Turkish and family values ("LGBTİ+ dernekleri," 2023, para. 4; Michaelson & Narlı, 2023, paras. 1, 4). The 2023 election process saw LGBT+ individuals be called terrorists, threatened with strangulation ("LGBTİ+ dernekleri," 2023, para. 11), and the whole concept of LGBT existence described as a "religion" imported from the United States ("Erdoğan'ın cumhurbaşkanlığı zaferi sonrası," 2023, para. 7). At present, the LGBTQ+ community in Türkiye is both fearful and exhausted. The attitude of the state has become suffocating, and many community members are unsure of how they will continue to exist inside Türkiye's borders.

With the ruling party set to preside over the country for 5 more years, it will be difficult for LGBTQ+ individuals to find freedom. This will in turn make it harder for queer educators to be out and offer inclusive education. However, such activities are more vital than ever if educators are to support their learners. The community of queer teachers and allies in Türkiye must redouble their efforts to create safe spaces for sexual- and gender-minority students while being mindful of their own safety. At this juncture, the subtle inclusion of queer identities may be the best route for instructors to signal themselves and their classrooms as safe spaces.

Conclusion

Time and time again in my practice, I have found that people are more than willing to listen to discussions of queer topics and share their ideas, often in agreement regarding the problems we face in supporting LGBTQ+ learners. Those unfamiliar with the issues welcome the chance to ask questions in a supportive environment. What is universally true is that people in Türkiye are amazed to finally have a space in which to speak about such topics. Millennial and Gen Z educators are much more relaxed around ideas of sexuality than those before them, and Gen Z in particular has access to more knowledge about such topics than prior generations. These young educators and students, who have massive global input thanks to the ever-expanding internet, are primed to become allies. What is necessary in the Turkish context is to model a way in which they can do so—despite fears of recrimination from the state. Demonstrating that there are simple practices, such as simply recognizing complex identities, allows members of the Turkish educational community to take those first steps toward allyship. Considering the increasingly hostile attitudes toward the LGBTQ+ community in Türkiye, it is more important than ever to offer a supportive environment to queer learners and colleagues. Therefore, it falls to LGBTQ+ members of the educational community and our allies to be courageous and create safe spaces; now more than ever, those in the Turkish ELT sphere need support from allies at home and abroad.

Dedication

This chapter is dedicated to my late friend and colleague, Selin Nur Hürmüz. Selin was always authentically herself, believed strongly in the strength of queer community and hoped for better days for Türkiye. Beloved by friends, family and students, her passing is a great loss to those who knew her, and to our educational community. May we one day achieve the world she wished to see.

Author

Elizabeth S. Coleman has been in ELT for over 15 years and is currently an English lecturer and CPD (continuous professional development) specialist. A firm believer in education as a transformative and developmental tool, Elizabeth is engaged in research around social constructions, gender, and the representation of minorities in education.

References

Atencio, M., & Koca, C. (2011). Gendered communities of practice and the construction of masculinities in Turkish physical education. *Gender and Education, 23*(1), 59–72. https://doi.org/10.1080/09540250903519444

Bakacak, A. G., & Öktem, P. (2014). Homosexuality in Turkey: Strategies for managing heterosexism. *Journal of Homosexuality, 61*(6), 817–846. https://doi.org/10.1080/00918369.2014.870453

Ban at METU due to "the relation of rainbow-LGBT." (2019, March 27). *Kaos GL*. https://kaosgl.org/en/single-news/ban-at-metu-due-to-the-relation-of-rainbow-lgbt

Baume, M. (2021, February 5). Turkish president says LGBTQ+ people don't exist amid national protests. *Them*. https://www.them.us/story/turkish-president-lgbtq-erasure-amid-national-protests

Cengiz, K., Tol, U. U., & Küçükural, Ö. (2004). Hegemonik erkekliğin peşinden [Pursuing hegemonic masculinity]. *Toplum ve Bilim, 101*, 50–70.

City University of New York. (2009). *The other*. http://academic.brooklyn.cuny.edu/english/melani/cs6/other.html

Erdoğan'ın cumhurbaşkanlığı zaferi sonrası "LGBTQ+ toplumunda korku katlanarak arttı" [After Erdoğan's presidential victory, "fear has increased exponentially in LGBTQ+ society"]. (2023, May 29). *Euronews*. https://tr.euronews.com/2023/05/29/erdoganin-cumhurbaskanligi-zaferi-sonrasi-lgbtq-toplumunda-korku-katlanarak-artti

Forbes, T. D., & Ueno, K. (2020). Post-gay, political, and pieced together: Queer expectations of straight allies. *Sociological Perspectives, 63*(1), 159–176. https://doi.org/10.1177/0731121419885353

LGBTİ+ dernekleri: Bir kere açıldık, bir daha kapanmayız [LGBTI+ associations: Once out, we won't be hidden again]. (2023, May 29). *Bianet*. https://m.bianet.org/1/126/279509-lgbti-dernekleri-irademiz-degerlidir-kudretlidir

Michaelson, R., & Narlı, D. B. (2023, May 12). "We're against LGBT": Erdoğan targets gay and trans people ahead of critical Turkish election. *The Guardian*. https://www.theguardian.com/global-development/2023/may/12/lgbt-recep-tayyip-erdogan-targets-gay-trans-rights-critical-turkish-election

Nemi Neto, J. (2018). Queer pedagogy: Approaches to inclusive teaching. *Policy Futures in Education, 16*(5), 589–604. https://doi.org/10.1177/1478210317751273

Ono, K. A. (1997). A letter/essay I've been longing to write in my personal/academic voice. *Western Journal of Communication, 61*(1), 114–125. https://doi.org/10.1080/10570319709374566

Reason, R. D., & Broido, E. M. (2005). Issues and strategies for social justice allies (and the student affairs professionals who hope to encourage them). *New Directions for Student Services, 2005*(110), 81–89. https://doi.org/10.1002/ss.167

Samek, A. A., & Donofrio, T. A. (2013). "Academic drag" and the performance of the critical personae: An exchange on sexuality, politics, and identity in the academy. *Women's Studies in Communication, 36*(1), 28–55. https://doi.org/10.1080/07491409.2012.754388

Savcı, E. (2020). *Queer in translation: Sexual politics under neoliberal Islam*. Duke University Press.

Turkish court acquits students of organising 2019 gay pride march. (2021, October 8). *Euronews*. https://www.euronews.com/2021/10/08/turkish-court-acquits-students-of-organising-2019-gay-pride-march

YÖK'ten "cinsiyet eşitliğinde" geri adım! [A step back in "gender equality" from YÖK!]. (2019, February 19). *Gazzette Duvar*. https://www.gazeteduvar.com.tr/gundem/2019/02/19/yokten-cinsiyet-esitliginde-geri-adim

Additional Resources

Britzman, D. P. (1995). Is there a queer pedagogy? Or, stop reading straight. *Educational Theory, 45*(2), 151–165. https://doi.org/10.1111/j.1741-5446.1995.00151.x

Clare, A., & Wilson, J. J. (2015) *Speak out pre-intermediate* (2nd ed.). Pearson.

Frazier, L., & Leeming, S. (2013). *Lecture ready 3* (2nd ed.). Oxford University Press.

Liddicoat, A. J. (2009). Sexual identity as linguistic failure: Trajectories of interaction in the heteronormative language classroom. *Journal of Language, Identity, and Education*, *8*(2–3), 191–202. https://doi.org/10.1080/15348450902848825

Nelson, C. (1999). Sexual identities in ESL: Queer theory and classroom inquiry. *TESOL Quarterly*, *33*(3), 371–391. https://doi.org/10.2307/3587670

Nelson, C. (2010). A gay immigrant's perspective: Unspeakable acts in the language class. *TESOL Quarterly*, *44*(3), 441–464. https://doi.org/10.5054/tq.2010.226853

Appendix: Privileges for Sale

Aims: For participants to discuss what privileges are most important for them. To provoke an understanding of how certain minority groups are less privileged and to increase empathy for such groups.

Materials: List of privileges (see below), play money/money values written on paper

Suggested time: 20 minutes

Method:

1. Group participants into small groups, ideally around four people in each.
2. Give each group the list of privileges and make sure the price for each privilege is clear.
3. Allocate an amount of money to each group.
4. Instruct groups that they can buy as many privileges as they want with their money, but they cannot go over the amount given and they may not borrow money from another group. The group members all have to agree on each privilege they buy.
5. Set the timer and allow the groups to discuss their choices and make their purchases.
6. At the end of the allocated time, bring the groups back together and ask each group what they bought, why, and how they found the experience. Draw out any difficulties they had and elicit from them what they gained from the activity.

Privilege List

Instructions: Please look at the following list of privileges. Each privilege costs 100 Turkish lira to purchase. As a group, please decide which privileges you would buy with the money you are given.

1. Being safe in your own home
2. Having your partner(s) accepted by your family
3. Celebrating your marriage with your family, friends, and coworkers
4. Being able to speak about your life without fear of attack

5. Living openly with your partner(s)
6. Sharing health insurance with your partner(s)
7. Being able to marry without suffering financial consequences or loss of benefits
8. Sponsoring your partner(s) for citizenship
9. Being able to complete forms and paperwork honestly so it accurately reflects who you are
10. Receiving paid compassionate leave after the death of a partner/lover/companion
11. Inheriting from a partner/lover/companion automatically after their death
12. Being able to see your partner(s) immediately in an emergency
13. Having others comfort and support you when a relationship ends
14. Having your identity be seen as normal
15. Being accepted by those around you
16. Seeing yourself represented in the media
17. Having people recognize your illnesses and health conditions as real
18. Being able to feel safe in your interactions with the police
19. Having and being able to show identification documents without fear you'll be mocked or questioned on your identity
20. Using public restrooms without fear of threat or punishment
21. Being able to be promoted in your job without your identity playing a factor
22. Having access to multiple family planning options
23. Being able to discuss your sexual health openly with medical professionals
24. Being able to go to a doctor and receive treatment that doesn't conflict with your identity
25. Being able to obtain child custody
26. Being able to adopt or foster a child
27. Raising children without worrying about people rejecting them because of your sexuality
28. Being employed as a teacher without people assuming you will corrupt/recruit/groom the children
29. Having your ancestry celebrated

30. Having people accept your country as an independent state
31. Being free from living paycheck to paycheck
32. Having equal access to education as and when you choose
33. Receiving support from your religious community
34. Being able to access social services without fear of discrimination or denial based on your identity

Privileges adapted from The Safe Zone Project: https://thesafezoneproject.com/activities/privilege-for-sale/

Lived Experiences of English as a Foreign Language Teachers and Their (LGBTQ+) Students in Türkiye: Building Queer Allyship Even When You Do Not Have the Means

Özge Güney

Türkiye is a secular and democratic republic bound by a constitution with 99% of the population specified as Muslim (U.S. Department of State, 2022). Since its foundation in 1923, the country has undergone several modernization and secularization reforms. However, the lesbian, gay, bisexual, transgender, queer/questioning (LGBTQ+) community is still disadvantaged in terms of health, education, income, employment, and participation in social life (Yılmaz & Göçmen, 2016). Though there has been a rise in LGBTQ+ awareness, activism, visibility, and respectability of both queer public figures and individuals (Ozbay, 2015), the LGBTQ+ community continues to be exposed to hate crimes and honor killings, and the laws in place are not adequate or not applied properly to protect individuals (Yılmaz, 2008). Due to the dominant heteropatriarchy[1] and religious concerns, reinforced by state policies of the Islamist-rooted ruling party, the LGBTQ+ community has faced considerable violence that has extended into every walk of life including

> murders of both gays and transgenders; the homophobic approach that popular press and even politicians do not hesitate to use out of blue; ... the scarce academic and scholarly research about queer lives and sexualities; and the intense marginalization and exclusion experienced by those intellectuals who think or write about sexualities. (Ozbay, 2015, p. 873)

Discussing sexuality is a taboo in the Turkish social and educational context (Gelbal & Duyan, 2006); therefore, LGBTQ+ students may face oppression from not having their identities recognized in the heteronormative school environment (Saraç & McCullick, 2017).

---

1. Heteropatriarchy refers to the social, political, and economic systems that promote cisgender heterosexual men as the ideal through their social and state institutions. In educational settings, educational policies, curricula, and social norms privilege cisgender heterosexual men as the source of knowledge and science (Kelley & Arce-Trigatti, 2022).

Regardless, teachers should be able to employ agency to build queer allyship (i.e., nonqueer individuals acting in solidarity with the LGBTQ+ community) so that LGBTQ+ students can achieve internal safety being their authentic selves in the classroom (Leonardi & Meyer, 2016; Leonardi & Saenz, 2014; Miller, 2015). However, research conducted with EFL preservice teachers in Türkiye showed that teacher education programs mostly avoid queer pedagogies, and preservice teachers are not prepared to handle sexuality issues in the classroom (Güney, 2018, 2022; Ordem & Ulum, 2020). The practices of in-service teachers regarding sexuality issues and the experiences of LGBTQ+ learners in the English classroom remain to be explored in the Turkish context. Thus, this study aimed to give voice to EFL teachers and their (LGBTQ+) students at a Turkish university with the following research questions:

1. What are the lived experiences of EFL teachers and their (LGBTQ+) students regarding sexuality issues?
2. In what ways do Turkish EFL teachers help build and maintain queer allyship in a restrictive school environment?

The study, more specifically, explored how EFL teachers and their learners work to build queer allyship against heteropatriarchy when they do not have the means (i.e., without any educational policies and curricula, school services and staff, and pre-/in-service teacher education that deals with sexual diversity issues).

Literature Review

Queer Theory, Queer Pedagogy, and Queer Allyship

Queer theory rejects any labeling of sexual identities, including the terms *gay* and *lesbian* themselves, as such categorization prioritizes heteronormativity[2] in all walks of life (Jagose, 1996). Thus, *queer* is used as an umbrella term to cover any nonheteronormative sexual orientation (Chase & Ressler, 2009).

According to queer theory, sexual identity, or heteronormativity, is constructed discursively (Foucault, 1978) and performatively (Butler, 1990). Any laws, state and educational policies, and related practices in schools that erase queer identities reinforce heteronormativity. This erasure could be realized in different ways such as school curriculum that does not recognize queer individuals (Leonardi & Meyer, 2016; Miller, 2015); instructional materials that promote heterosexual families, relationships, and fixed gender roles (Paiz, 2015; Selvi & Kocaman, 2021; Thornbury, 1999; Trinh & Tinker Sachs, 2023); English language teacher education programs that skip queer pedagogies (Andrews & Govender, 2022; Barozzi & Ojeda, 2016; Güney, 2018, 2022; Ordem & Ulum, 2020; Tran-Thanh, 2020); and English language teachers who ignore sexual diversity and remain silent toward homophobia (Dumas, 2010; Güney, 2021; Kaiser, 2017; Kappra & Vandrick, 2006; Nelson, 1993).

---

2. Heteronormativity is the construct that assumes only heterosexual identities, relationships, and social arrangements are natural and normal and enforces fixed, binary gender roles such as male gender behaving in masculine ways versus female gender behaving in feminine ways (Staley, 2022).

Informed by queer theory, queer pedagogy is an educational approach that seeks to challenge *hidden curricula of heteronormativity* by promoting inclusive educational praxis for LGBTQ+ learners to engage in the learning process meaningfully and safely (Meyer, 2007; Thomas-Reid, 2018). Queer pedagogy, with its focus on praxis, empowers teachers to initiate discourses of sexuality against discrimination and helps educators question how they reinforce or challenge heteronormativity in their classrooms (Meyer, 2019). It is the responsibility of nonqueer teachers, as they enjoy the privilege of being heterosexual, to practice queer pedagogies to create a welcoming classroom environment for learners of diverse sociosexual backgrounds as allies of the queer community (Meyer, 2007; Nelson, 1993; Vandrick, 2001). Here, the term *ally* refers to any individual who works toward social change in solidarity with stigmatized communities of which they are not a member (Crawley, 2022). Heterosexual teachers may enact *queer allyship* in diverse ways to be determined by their social and educational context. Queer allies may adopt a passive role by simply being a listener, being open-minded, and engaging in pro-LGBTQ+ social media content (Crawley, 2022; Jones et al., 2022). They could also play a more active role by protecting the LGBTQ+ community against bullying, participating in pro-LGBTQ+ events, being vocal against discrimination (Crawley, 2022), and making culturally relevant discussions of sexuality a part of the classroom instruction (Trinh, in press). My understanding of allyship resonates with Boler's (1999) "pedagogy of discomfort," which calls for action because "passive empathy" does not guarantee transformation (p. 179). This action is possible collectively with both teachers and students "learning to live with ambiguity, discomfort, and uncertainty" and taking "ethical responsibilities" (Boler, 1999, p. 198). Thus, queer allyship is more meaningful if it involves action, especially in restrictive communities of practice. The transformative teachers and their students in this study took action in different ways and showed that building queer allyship is possible even in challenging school settings as they engaged in pedagogy of discomfort.

In conservative settings, classrooms might be the only safe spaces for LGBTQ+ community. Therefore, performing queer allyship is particularly important where discussions of sexuality are rare, as in Japan (Ó'Móchain, 2006) and China (Paiz & Zhu, 2018) as well as with conservative Middle Eastern populations such as Kuwaiti and Saudi Arabian learners of English (Güney, 2021). If teachers fail to indicate their queer allyship, LGBTQ+ learners may tend to hide their sexual identity and are sometimes silenced when they are expected to discuss private issues such as family, relationships, hobbies, and individual likes and dislikes in the English classroom (Kappra & Vandrick, 2006; Knisely & Paiz, 2021; Nelson 1993; Vandrick, 1997). To this end, teachers, as agents of change, need to be able to create spaces that promote queer learners' identity as autonomous, self-determined individuals with a sense of self-love and acceptance, which Leonardi and Saenz (2014) call *internal safety*. To guarantee and improve queer learners' internal safety, teachers need to realize their potential as they have the power to decide about what identities are represented and whose experiences are shared in the classroom (Andrews & Govender, 2022). Teachers should be able to recognize and critique how the norms in their society and educational context as well as their discourse reinforce heteronormativity and guide their students to do the same, irrespective of their gender and sexual identity (Leonardi & Meyer, 2016; Leonardi & Saenz, 2014; Miller, 2015).

LGBTQ+ in the Turkish (Educational) Context

In Türkiye, although homosexuality is not a crime, same-sex marriage is not recognized legally (Ozbay, 2015). The president of the country explicitly announced that his Islamist-rooted ruling party has worked toward raising a pious generation for the past two decades (Lüküslü, 2016). The president proposed a constitutional amendment to legally define a family as a union between a male and a female gender to protect families against "perverse trends" as he called it (Bektas, 2022). He also built his 2023 election campaign on anti-LGBTQ+ rhetoric and accused all the opposition parties of being pro-LGBTQ+ at every election rally, although none of them had an agenda to protect LGBTQ+ rights (Stockholm Center for Freedom, 2023). Türkiye ranked 48th among 49 countries regarding human rights for the LGBTQ+ community, with the interior minister defending the crackdown against LGBTQ+ people as he stated that

> the Turkish nation was conservative and religious and did not embrace LGBT values ... Pride events were funded and organized by the United States and Europe ... LGBT+ threatens the traditional Turkish family structure, [and] ... Turkey should never allow space for the LGBT+ community. (Stockholm Center for Freedom, 2022, paras. 2–3)

In line with restrictive government policies, four college students who joined protests against violence faced by the LGBTQ+ community on their campus were arrested (VOA News, 2021). Such government crackdowns have also influenced educational policies in the country. First, the Ministry of National Education and then Türkiye's Higher Education Council canceled their gender equality programs as the authorities announced these projects were against the country's social values and norms ("Turkey's Educational Authorities," 2019). Overall, sexual orientation is not addressed in the national education system as discussions of sexuality are considered a taboo both in daily life and at schools, where no formal sex education is offered (Saraç & McCullick, 2017).

Research conducted with preservice teachers indicated that teacher education programs in Türkiye mostly avoid discussions on how to address sexuality issues in the classroom (Dedeoğlu et al., 2012; Güney, 2018, 2022; Ordem & Ulum, 2020). Preservice teachers of English at a rural university stated that sexuality issues are a taboo and should not be a part of daily or academic conversations (Ordem & Ulum, 2020). On the other hand, research conducted at three state universities in Ankara showed that preservice teachers of English were positive toward discussions of sexuality issues in teacher education programs and in their future classrooms (Güney, 2018, 2022). The practices of Turkish teachers once they enter the English classroom upon graduation remains to be explored, hence the motivation for the current study.

As for the attitudes of learners, two transformative EFL teachers successfully incorporated sexual identity issues in their high school (Michell, 2009) and college-level classes (Tekin, 2011), and they reported positive attitudes from their students toward discussions of "homosexuality." Similarly, a case study conducted with a self-identified gay male student at a Turkish state university showed that the student got the support of his peers after disclosing his sexual orientation (Saraç & McCullick, 2017). Despite such allyship with peers, the student did not reveal his sexual identity publicly due to the social pressure and religious sensibility of people because Islam "explicitly rejects and condemns homosexuality and accepts same-sex acts as a sin" (Saraç & McCullick, 2017, p. 351). Religiosity is known to influence the attitudes of students; Turkish students with high religiosity were found to have more negative attitudes toward "homosexuality" than those with liberal views (Gelbal & Duyan, 2006). Despite such bleak conditions, it might be possible to create a safe classroom space for LGBTQ+ students through allyship with peers and transformative teachers as this study sought to explore.

Methods

The Study

This study explored the lived experiences of Turkish EFL teachers and their (LGBTQ+) students at an intensive academic English language program (ELP) of a state university in Türkiye through case study analysis. The data mainly draw from semistructured individual interviews conducted with the teachers ($n = 3$) and their students ($n = 2$) in Turkish, with my observations and sample classroom artifacts incorporated as relevant. The students preferred to participate in the interviews at a downtown café as they stated they felt more comfortable outside the campus.

For data analysis, I translated the interviews into English and used reflexive thematic analysis (Braun & Clarke, 2021). Throughout the interpretation and editing stages, I was in touch with the participants to check for clarification. To make sure that my interpretations reflected the experiences and ideas of the participants, I also did a member check by sharing an initial draft of the manuscript with them (Dörnyei, 2007).

The teachers, Sena, Sara, and Mine, were self-identified as Muslim, female (cisgender), and heterosexual. They all held bachelor's degrees in English language teaching (ELT) and master's degrees from different Turkish universities (see Table 1). None of the teachers had taken any undergraduate or graduate courses informed by queer pedagogies.

Table 1. Background Information on Teachers

Pseudonym	Bachelor's degree	Master's degree	Gender, sexual identity	Their student (pseudonym)
Sara	ELT	ELT	Female, cishet	Volkan
Mine	ELT	Communication	Female, cishet	Kaan
Sena	ELT	European studies	Female, cishet	Braveheart

The students, Volkan and Kaan, both self-identified as Muslim and LGBTQ+. They had been taking English classes for two semesters before they could proceed to their academic programs. In the ELP, students take English classes for 5 hours, Monday through Friday, and spend each semester in the same classroom with two partner teachers. As this study took place toward the end of the second semester, Volkan and Kaan had built close relationships with their peers and teachers.

The university where the current study took place is one of the leading, well-established urban universities with more than 20 faculties and 50,000 national and international students. The ELP alone hosts more than 1,000 students. There are no LGBTQ+ associations, policies, staff, or support services to protect LGBTQ+ students or faculty. The school leadership is known for openly supporting a right-wing, conservative, nationalist political movement in the country. There is a student association politically affiliated with this movement and supported by the school leadership. The members of this association are known to police and attack other students who do not conform to the "local values"; for example, male students with an earring or long hair have been attacked for threatening masculinity.

Researcher Reflexivity

I am a cisgender, heterosexual teacher researcher of TESOL with around 15 years of teaching experience in Türkiye. My motivation for queer scholarship derives from my observations of the struggles of LGBTQ+ students in Türkiye. When I invited participants to tell their lived experiences, I informed them about my advocacy for social justice issues.

Findings and Discussion

In the ELP where this study took place, all the teachers use the same instructional materials, follow the same syllabus, and use the same tests provided by the school administration. When you enter the school building, you can see the cafeteria across the main entrance, where the aforementioned student association has a desk with representatives present at all times.

In what follows, I discuss the findings related to each EFL teacher and their students in three subsections, with each one of them telling a different story. Sara and Volkan's story focuses on why LGBTQ+ students may prefer to remain hidden from their peers and how they find an ally in their EFL teacher. Mine and Kaan's story recounts the struggles of an openly gay student and their teacher to create queer allyship. Sena and Braveheart's story is about how Sena and her students unite in the face of institutional homophobia.

Considering the situated nature of queerness and queer research, the findings and discussions need to be conceived in their own context. When the participants talk about their classroom environment, the benchmark is the bigger, conservative Turkish educational and social context. As a result, what might look like an unfriendly environment for a reader more familiar with a liberal context could be perceived as a relatively comfortable environment for readers from more repressive societies.

Sara and Volkan: The English as a Foreign Language Teacher as a Mentor for Hidden Sexualities

Based on her experience of teaching English at her current school for 9 years, Sara's overall approach toward sexuality issues was to assume that there are hidden LGBTQ+ students in her classroom:

> At the beginning of each semester, I underline that all is welcome and as the semester proceeds if I recognize any issues like hate speech or homophobia, then I am extra careful and will interrupt whenever needed.... My coverage of sexuality issues is somehow embedded in cultural diversity because I don't have any pedagogical or psychological training [on sexuality].... I mean, I am concerned about misleading them when trying to help them.... Like there was a quote that resonated well with how I feel about this: "Do not open the boxes you cannot close."

Sara stated that she was not able to incorporate instructional materials with LGBTQ+ content in her classes because of the preplanned syllabus the school provided and her lack of teacher training on queer-inclusive instruction. Thus, she stated that her discussions of sexuality issues were more about promoting a peaceful classroom environment and cultural diversity for her learners' future encounters than a deliberate effort to incorporate LGBTQ+ issues in the instructional materials. However, her recount of several "queer" encounters in her classes showed that queer discussions are an inherent part of the language classroom even if the teacher or the textbook does not systematically address them:

> You know about ELT textbooks. The discussion somehow relates to family and relationships, like we talk about who they like to buy gifts for ... and how they spend Valentine's Day.... These kids [LGBTQ+ students] tend to be shy or lie.... Sometimes, since we are not native speakers [of English], sometimes we make mistakes and just say *she* instead of *he* when we refer to their partners [because their first language, Turkish, is not a gendered language]. I also remember once I said *boyfriend* when I should have said *girlfriend*. Then all the students laughed like "Hahahaha, *Hoca* [teacher] said boyfriend." Then, I revised my statement like, ... "your girlfriend or boyfriend, which is also acceptable." If you have an LGBTQ+ student in such cases, you realize that student is shy and sometimes just fakes laughing because everybody else is laughing.

This excerpt shows that Sara was aware how the classroom discourse triggered discussions of sexuality and recreated her discourse to use every single chance to promote diversity. This mindful discourse encourages LGBTQ+ students to express their authentic self, as Sara's experiences revealed:

> Our approach [to social justice] as teachers is intuitive. You recognize the kids [LGBTQ+ learners] and just do your best to promote equity and respect. This is somehow about who you are, like, if you are a humanist personality.... Then, my LGBTQ+ students observe my stance and positive attitude towards diversity and come out about their sexual orientation in a private conversation with me, although they hide their sexual identity in the classroom.... In certain cases, I feel like some

> students do not agree with me but remain silent either out of respect or not to attract my criticism.

When I inquired about the reasons why her LGBTQ+ students would prefer to hide their identity in the classroom, the main reason, according to Sara, was that LGBTQ+ students are emotionally and physically threatened at this school:

> The university is very strict, and the LGBTQ+ community here isn't acknowledged because it is just not acceptable or tolerable for the conservative ideology the school has supported for many years. That is the main reason why LGBTQ+ students hide their identity.... They are scared. When I say they are scared, it is not only because they might be emotionally disturbed. It is also because they might be physically attacked. I have never had an LGBTQ+ student coming out about their sexual identity in the classroom.

In her current classroom, Sara had similar experiences with Volkan, who had been extremely careful not to reveal their sexuality among peers. Sara talked about Volkan's struggles during in-class activities: "So Volkan talks like he has a girlfriend, but I have always felt the truth. He tries to act as if he was heterosexual.... He just replaces *he* with a *she* when talking about his partner, and sometimes he is blocked trying to make up a story."

The first time Sara witnessed a homophobic remark from one of Volkan's peers, she reminded her students, "There is no space for hate speech in my classroom." Sara expressed that this conversation encouraged Volkan to go talk to her in person, disclosing their sexual identity and revealing their struggles. Volkan's own experiences completed Sara's story. Volkan talked about how they were depressed starting the ELP program, indicating the main reason was because "the school is populated by conservative people, and they think God will curse you if you are gay." Volkan referred to the sociopolitical context of their school as the main issue:

> I am not a person who likes to lie, but I cannot tell the truth in class because this is an extremely nationalist, conservative university. Your friends may share the same ideologies [as school] and get away from you. So I lie to almost all my friends in and outside the classroom.

Despite the constrictive school environment, Volkan talked about how they felt comfortable starting a private conversation about their sexual identity with Sara:

> I trust in my instincts, and when I first saw teacher Sara, I thought she would be such a nice mentor for me because she was such understanding, humanist, and open-minded. So I just wanted to talk to her considering her mindset.... There were such bad things I had gone through until then, and now [looking back] I am like "I did a great thing having shared my feelings and experiences with her."... She is the only teacher that I have had this conversation with.

Unfortunately, Volkan wanted to end the interview when his friends walked into the café where we were having the interview. I could easily observe how nervous and worried Volkan looked at the time. Thus, we shifted the topic of the conversation to some daily issues, had some lunch together chatting, and departed on good terms. Eventually, Volkan was happy to have contributed to this study and thanked me for the opportunity.

Looking at their story, it looks like Volkan found a reliable ally in their EFL teacher as Sara was the only teacher Volkan disclosed their identity to. This was a step toward self-acceptance, acknowledging their sexual identity for the first time explicitly in a conversation with a teacher. As Miller (2015) stated, "Students must be allowed to self-identify however they choose and to be provided opportunities to see themselves reflected back in a positive manner" (p. 40). It is such recognition and legitimization that fosters LGBTQ+ learners' self-expression and internal safety. Sara contributed to Volkan's internal safety by promoting an inclusive classroom space as she somehow disrupted the dominant ideology at school. She relied on her experiences and intuition and started every semester assuming a diversity of sexual identities in her classroom. Sara made diversity part of the classroom discourse and maintained it throughout the semester, which has actually become a part of her teaching philosophy. This is what Trinh (2022) calls *discourse of difference* as the teacher utilizes in-class conversations spontaneously to remind her students that gender and sexual identity is not fixed, and diverse possibilities need to be acknowledged.

Mine and Kaan: Protecting an Openly Gay Student

Both Mine and Kaan were happy with their overall classroom climate despite prevailing issues at their school. Mina reported that she had to deal with many classroom management issues to protect Kaan because they had disclosed their sexual identity in the classroom. For instance, she reported how her students' comments about Kaan sometimes caught her off guard:

> So one day, this student asked me, "*Hocam* [teacher], aren't you upset you have a student like Kaan?" I said, "Just the opposite. I am very happy to have him in my classroom." To be honest, I wasn't prepared for this kind of question.... If I happen to criticize him [Kaan] in any way, not only about his sexuality, they will behave more unfavorably.

Mine observed her students becoming more negative when Kaan revealed his sexuality more openly, for example, when Kaan acted more effeminately:

> For example, one day, Kaan was late and walked into the classroom in an effeminate way. Then, some students rolled their eyes and said, "There he comes again." Another day, Kaan took out a nail file from his pencil case, a pink one, very cute.... I immediately realized how other students looked at him, right? Some of them were so surprised with their eyes wide open. Then, I just stepped in and said, "Oh my god, I love this file! Where did you get it? I definitely want one of these." So Kaan's peers definitely found some of his attitudes weird.

Mine reported that she generally talked to her students when Kaan was not around and asked them to be mindful about their manners. Mina talked about a student's reaction in one of these conversations and associated his attitude with the school's culture:

> There is this student … he doesn't want to sit next to Kaan in the classroom. When there was this night out, … when I mentioned in class Kaan would be attending, he was like, "I'm happy I won't be there." From his attitudes and the way he talked, I could see he adopted [school name]'s culture.

At the end of our interview, Mine shared one of Kaan's writing assignments where they talk about the differences between South and North Korea: "In North, you can't listen to pop music or you can't cut your hair with queer style" (see Figure 1). This assignment proves that Mine was able to establish trust in her relationship with Kaan as they can talk about their ideas without having to censor them, in a way reworking classroom norms.

Figure 1. Kaan's queer statement in a writing assignment.

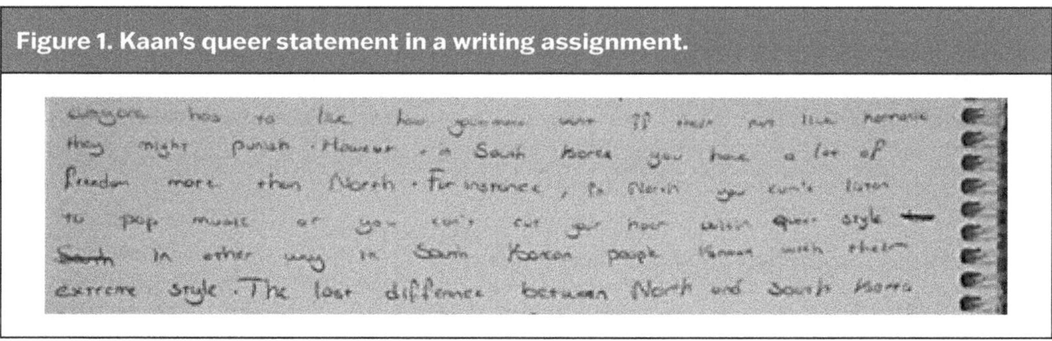

[illegible] has to like how [illegible] [illegible] if [illegible] [illegible] like [illegible]
they might punish. However, in South Korea you have a lot of
freedom more than North. For instance, in North you can't listen
to pop music or you can't cut your hair with queer style ←
~~South~~ In other way in South Korean people [illegible] with their
extreme style. The last difference between North and South Korea

Looking at Kaan's part of the story, they had foreseen the challenges even before they started to study in the ELP and had planned to remain hidden:

> At the beginning of the first semester, because I had too many reservations about the school, I was determined not to disclose my sexual identity in the classroom. I used to take care of my clothing, trying to wear less colorful, plain clothes. Now I'm wearing an earring, but then I did not have one. I had planned not to stick out and remain hidden as much as I could.

Kaan mentioned diverse factors that made their school environment particularly challenging, including "the political stance of the school supporting nationalist conservative ideologies," "sexuality being a taboo in Turkey," "religious norms that consider homosexuality as perversion," and "patriarchy" combined with "nationalist ideologies that require Turkish men to pass on their 'supreme' breed to the following generations." To make things worse, as Kaan reported, their parents were not supportive of their sexual identity. Kaan showed me a text message from their father where he said, "I would rather you died than have a child like you," due to his nationalist and patriarchic tendencies. As for Kaan's mother, she believed that Kaan would "get better" if they prayed enough and Kaan would sometimes wake up to find their mother citing Qur'an by their bedside. It was in this context and mood that Kaan preferred not to express their true self at this school, which did not offer an environment different from Kaan's home and general surroundings.

Kaan told me that it was not easy to keep silent about his sexual identity because they were exposed to private questions and had to lie or make up stories:

> In speaking activities or exams, I have acted as if I was heterosexual and talked about my sister as if she was my girlfriend. I haven't had any issues with any one of my teachers [in the ELP] because I know, from their conversations, that they are open-minded. However, they somehow initiate conversations about your private life.

When I asked Kaan if teachers initiated such conversations based on the textbook, Kaan was affirmative and reflected on their experience of learning English in the ELP versus German at Goethe-Institut (a German cultural institution offering German courses in Türkiye):

> English textbooks are really sexist. For example, there was a reading text about Neil Patrick Harris that talked about when he got married and had kids but never mentioned who he was married to or how they adopted the kids.... You know, German books are not like that. For example, we have this book *Menschen (A2)*. It is more life-like. There is a unit on marriage ... also a discussion on changing gender roles.... In English textbooks, it's all about the ideal family. Everything has to look nice and sweet like a cotton candy. English textbooks are more about, like, read the text, check vocabulary, and then do some grammar and listening; then, you are all set. It feels like you are just preparing for an exam.

Considering the differences, I asked if Kaan felt more comfortable in the English or the German classroom, and they promptly said,

> German without a single doubt! Because I feel more comfortable after I've been exposed to German culture. Also, teachers of German encourage more incorporation of European culture. They were born and raised in Germany, and even if not, have frequently visited European countries.

As a result, with sexuality issues treated more liberally in the textbook and by the teachers given their cultural background, Kaan observed more authenticity in the German classroom, which increased the possibility for Kaan's identity to be socially accepted and legitimized. Regardless of all the challenges in Türkiye, Kaan expressed his main expectation from EFL teachers was to be brave in the face of all the challenges:

> I understand this is a taboo in Turkey, and people are not fine with homosexuality.... Despite the pressure from society, teachers need to be informed about how LGBTQ+ students are different in their emotional and biological development, and how you need to handle the challenges they encounter in the classroom. I also understand that these issues will not be addressed in the textbooks in our country in the near future, but teachers need to know how to cover these issues and be brave enough to talk about homosexuality explicitly in their classes.

Pseudonyms are used to refer to participants to maintain their privacy and confidentiality. The teacher, Roberto, collected data as part of a collaborative action research project with me, the researcher. Due to heavy workloads, two jobs, and a family with three children, Roberto—perhaps for political reasons—declined the opportunity to coauthor this chapter as he would not be able to commit to contributing to the writing process. He has been a very critical friend, to whom much gratitude is extended. Students were given informed consent and had the action research project explained to them. Eight students (four pairs) agreed to being audio-recorded for research purposes. Data from three of the four pairs are reported here.

Data Collection and Analysis

Data were obtained from audio-recorded conversations of six students (three pairs). Content analysis was utilized to examine teachers' reflective notes. Coding categories emerged directly from the data (Creswell & Creswell, 2018; Dawson, 2007, 2009), which allowed for the generation of emerging themes, or conversational episodes deemed relevant to address the research question. A similar approach to the analysis of classroom interactions was employed. Though this data may have been analyzed through the lens of conversation analysis by looking at "the architecture of conversations" (Jones, 2008), the search for specific meaning-focused cues along with underlying ideologies in the participants' discourse that would help address the research question in the study is more closely aligned with CDA. Approximately 20–25 minutes of pair interaction were recorded and transcribed. Due to the extensive length of the transcribed data, the teacher and the students were sent the transcriptions of the first and last 5 minutes of interactions to ensure accuracy and fidelity to what they discussed during their interactions. Though this was a retrospective exercise, participants appreciated having the opportunity to see and analyze extracts of their conversations.

The Teaching Activity

The class activity, conducted by Roberto, was based on two news articles from public media sources. One was news coverage of the marriage equality law passed in the Chilean Parliament. The second showcased stories of the first same-sex marriages held in Chile after the law came into effect. The lesson comprised three stages. The first part of the lesson focused on gender diversity vocabulary building through explicit teaching and group discussion. This was followed by peer interactions and discussions about the news articles. The peer discussions, which constitute the focus of attention in this chapter, centered around two open-ended prompts: (1) What are your views of this new law? (2) Do you think this law was needed in Chilean society? Why? The third part of the lesson comprised a reflective writing task in which students were asked to write about the perceived benefits of a same-sex marriage law for the wider community.

Findings and Discussion

The discussion of extracts of conversations is undertaken in response to the following research question: How do Chilean EFL students navigate and negotiate their allied positionalities toward gender diversity through peer discussions in a classroom-based task?

It is noteworthy that Kaan understood the challenges that go beyond their teachers, but they also saw that teachers have different responsibilities than a layperson. Given their experiences in the German classroom, Kaan was also aware that it is possible to create a different classroom environment that goes beyond the traditional norms and gives more comfort to marginalized students.

It was with this idea of comfort that Kaan disclosed his sexual identity in the English classroom. It was sometime around midsemester that Kaan's school friends saw them at a Halloween party with their partner. Having enjoyed the comfort of sharing their sexual identity with others, Kaan wanted to enjoy the same comfort when they went back to school and started to give real answers to private questions: "When you go back to school, you have this urge, some kind of an inadvertent relaxation. When you move from a very comfortable environment to some restrictive space, that urge somehow finds a way out."

After coming out, Kaan experienced a few cases where their peers did not want to be seen together, saying that people would misunderstand their relationship. Nevertheless, Kaan underlined, "Ours is not a typical classroom compared with the others at this school," remaining positive about the overall climate:

> Today, we were taking pictures all together and he [a classmate] said, "Bro, can you not stand next to me?" I don't even consider this negative. My class is not bad compared with this school, and people have changed for the positive. I even introduced my partner to them when we organized this night out. I can be myself around my peers, and I can take care of my clothing the way I like.

Mine and Kaan's story shows that their union improved their classroom environment, with peers adopting a more positive attitude toward the end of the semester. Mine constantly interrupted heteronormativity by "positively discriminating in favor of Kaan," as she put it. Thus, Mine promoted Kaan's social acceptance whereby Kaan was able to express their true self and became more autonomous in the classroom. This, in turn, contributed to their internal safety (Leonardi & Saenz, 2014). Kaan's emphasis on comfort during the interview is further proof of their search for having authentic conversations with peers.

Having said that, Kaan was looking for further improvement in the English classroom considering their experience of learning German. Because his German textbook was more culturally diverse and teachers of German tended to incorporate European culture more in their classes due to their background, Kaan developed a better sense of internal safety in the German classroom. It is known that English resources overall lack references to sexuality issues, but teachers can always teach students to think queer even with the traditional textbook (see Trinh & Tinker Sachs, 2023). Another factor is the school context, as Goethe-Institut displays a completely different culture than the state school described in this study. Regardless, according to Kaan, teachers "need to be different [than laypeople] given their educational background," which could be considered a call for queer-informed teacher education.

Sena and Braveheart: United Against Institutional Homophobia

In this final subsection, Sena provides us with a solid example of how to build queer allyship with the help of her students. Sena aspired for inclusivity in her classroom: "I want my students to feel free.... I want a classroom where my students can be their authentic self." To this end, she talked about how she put an *All are welcome!* poster on their classroom door that welcomes all genders, nationalities, religions, and races.

Sena and Braveheart's story begins with an in-class speaking activity that Sena called "What's In Your Mind?" In this activity, learners are randomly given a worksheet of empty male and female portraits of their choosing and fill them in with "ideas, dreams, or worries through self-reflection." Sena underlined that she would tell her students to choose any gender they like. When they were done, learners then discussed their portraits with their partners. As Sena reported, the students had a lot of fun and came up with such creative portraits that she wanted to put them up on the back of the classroom door so that her students could "develop a sense of belonging to the classroom." One of the students, Braveheart, was an LGBTQ+ ally and put the statement *Love is love* in her portrait. The problems started when they had a break as the classroom door opened toward the hallway. Hence the portraits ended up being explicitly displayed to others. When the break was over, Sena went to her classroom to find approximately 10 homophobic students from other classrooms having an argument with her students with the LGBTQ+ poster torn down. Sena reported:

> You know, we have a student association against such stuff.... I will say, a conservative, nationalist group of students raised with this school's culture. As my students told me, one of them sees the poster with the LGBTQ+ content and storms into our classroom during the break, asking who made the poster. My student says, "I made it, so what?" She is such a brave heart [laughs]. As the homophobic student tries to grab and tear the poster on the door, he says, "You don't have the right to write this. Your teacher doesn't have the right to put that poster up on the door." My students then get worried thinking that I might be in trouble.

In the end, Sena said that she spent 10 minutes of her class time negotiating with the intruders and their "leader" (as she called them) outside her classroom, trying to explain how they were committing a crime occupying her classroom and tearing materials and that she was well aware of her rights as a teacher of 10 years' experience in that school. Afterward, as Sena recounted, she talked to the administration and demanded that the leader of the association apologize both to her and to Braveheart, which they did, and the issue was thus "resolved." When Sena reflected on this incident and her overall experience at this school, she remained positive:

> Homophobic students think it is a threat to social values and masculinity. However, ... the new generation is beautiful, not that narrow-minded. In my other classroom, I have a kid, who I believe to be LGBTQ+, and one day when we were playing one of those online games, something like Kahoot or Jeopardy, he said, "Let's name the group *Nonoş*" [the Turkish slang for fruit/fruitcake]. When his peers asked why, he simply said, "Because I'm Nonoş." When I looked at his friends' faces, I was so relieved to see no one was condemning or saying anything offensive, as it should be the case. That makes me think that such conversations are welcome in my classroom.

Sena and Braveheart's story clearly indicates the influence of the school culture as they stood against homophobia reinforced by the institution. As stated by Giroux (1994), "The culture of the school is often representative of those features of the dominant culture that it affirms, sustains, selects, and legitimates.... [S]ymbolic rewards to different groups indicates how politics work" (p. 36). It is not possible to isolate the school culture from the bigger restrictive social context of Türkiye. Nevertheless, Sena and Braveheart showed that building queer allyship and protecting your territory is possible despite the overwhelming social and educational context.

Unfortunately, having a positive attitude toward diversity does not always translate into teachers' practices. Sena achieved this diversity in many ways. First, she incorporated her support of the LGBTQ+ community into her classroom discourse and practice by putting an *All are welcome!* poster on the door. Second, during in-class activities, she gave her students an opportunity to express their authentic selves. For instance, she offered options by letting students choose any gender portrait they liked instead of giving male portraits to male students and female portraits to female students. Third, she disrupted the institutional, heteronormative ideology by putting the *Love is love* portrait on the door and standing against the homophobic school association.

What Sena and Braveheart achieved is precious, especially when their restrictive environment is considered. Even teachers in so-called liberal, Western countries like the United States and Canada may avoid sexuality issues and ignore homophobia in classrooms populated by students from conservative backgrounds (e.g., Muslim, Chinese) because ESL teachers think sexuality issues might be too overwhelming for these students (Güney, 2021; Kaiser, 2017; Kappra & Vandrick, 2006; Nelson, 1993). Despite the risks in their depressive environment, Sena and Braveheart troubled the normativity, becoming agents of change.

Conclusion

The teachers and their (LGBTQ+) students in this study showed that queer allyship is possible even in a restrictive environment by taking on ethical responsibilities (Boler, 1999). Hopefully, the participants here were able to answer the question raised by Trinh (in press): "What have you done to disrupt heteronormative activities and thinking with your students and colleagues?" To answer that question, the EFL teachers in this study created an *All are welcome!* discourse in their classroom and in some cases reconstructed their discourse if it sounded heteronormative (e.g., Sara's confusion about *he* versus *she* and *boyfriend* versus *girlfriend*). Also, the teachers assumed they had LGBTQ+ learners in every classroom as it is not typical for queer learners to come out in conservative Turkish schools. This assumption and queer-friendly discourse encouraged LGBTQ+ learners seeking support to disclose their identity to their EFL teachers. Thus, LGBTQ+ learners and their allies experienced internal safety as their identity was socially accepted and legitimized in their classroom (Leonardi & Meyer, 2016; Leonardi & Saenz, 2014). Finally, EFL teachers and their students maintained and reinforced queer allyship by uniting and acting against institutional heteronormativity. In Sena and Braveheart's case, their classroom was occupied, and their *Love is love* portrait was torn down by members of the homophobic student association. As Miller (2015) stated, "Schools are not just unsafe, they are restrictive, constrictive, and reinforcers of multiple forms of systematic oppression" (p. 39). By taking risks, queer allies showed that it is possible to stand against such systematic, institutionalized oppression. This incident will hopefully be an inspiration for those interested in a pedagogy of discomfort in the sense of Boler (1999).

Participants discussed several reasons why and how the Turkish social and educational context is oppressive for the LGBTQ+ community. First, due to the patriarchic family structure and the higher status assigned to masculinity, the LGBTQ+ community is perceived to be against traditional values and family structure. This is a discourse legitimized by the current government (Stockholm Center for Freedom, 2022). Second, people with high religiosity tend to cast out LGBTQ+ community members because they perceive Islam to forbid any sexual orientation other than heterosexuality. Although Türkiye is a secular country, with the current ruling party aspiring for a pious generation (Lüküslü, 2016), LGBTQ+ learners in this study were concerned about negative reactions from their religious peers (see also Saraç & McCullick, 2017). Despite sexuality being a taboo in schools, this study revealed that queer discussions are not only inevitable but also needed in language classrooms to achieve equity and diversity. EFL teachers were able to contribute to a positive classroom environment in this study; as one of the LGBTQ+ learners said, "I can be myself" in the English classroom and considered this an opportunity that may not be afforded in other classrooms of the same school.

The EFL teachers acknowledged that their practices were bound by the preplanned syllabus and the materials determined by the school administration. Also, they did not receive any formal training on how to incorporate sexuality issues in their instruction or how to deal with homophobia as part of classroom management. With English textbooks heavily relying on fixed genders and heterosexual relationships, they were not able to incorporate queer issues in their classes in a systematic or planned fashion. Nevertheless, the EFL teachers acted intuitively and adopted a discourse of difference by using spontaneous classroom conversations as an opportunity to disrupt heteronormativity. The teachers also performed queer allyship by being good listeners and open-minded intellectuals, offering emotional support to their LGBTQ+ students and their ally peers. To support teachers in constrictive settings, English textbooks need to offer more cultural diversity, at least by reflecting the true nature of relationships and family structure in the real world (Paiz, 2015; Selvi & Kocaman, 2021; Thornbury, 1999; Trinh & Tinker Sachs, 2023). Also, considering the lack of attention devoted to queer-informed teacher education (Andrews & Govender, 2022; Barozzi & Ojeda, 2016; Güney, 2018, 2022; Ordem & Ulum, 2020; Tran-Thanh, 2020), teacher training programs need to inform pre- and in-service teachers about how to handle diversity issues and homophobia in the language classrooms.

This study had certain methodological limitations, partly due to the situated nature of queer research. As this was a case study, the findings are most relevant for the context the study took place in. Future research conducted at a different institution (maybe a private university) or in a different city may yield different results. Also, future research conducted with a greater number of LGBTQ+ participants may yield different experiences and would increase their representation in the literature. Despite the limitations, EFL teachers in the study offered great insights into how to promote allyship against all odds, which will hopefully be an inspiration to teachers of English and teacher educators working in challenging settings.

Author

Özge Güney's research interests include queer pedagogy, preservice teacher education, and Global Englishes.

References

Andrews, G., & Govender, N. (2022). Queer critical literacies and initial teacher education: Transnational moments. In D. Banegas & N. Govender (Eds.), *Gender diversity and sexuality in English language education: New transnational voices* (pp. 11–28). Bloomsbury. https://doi.org/10.5040/9781350217591.ch-001

Barozzi, S., & Ojeda, J. R. G. (2016). Sexual identities in EFL at primary school level: A pre-service teachers' perspective from Spain. *Porta Linguarum, 25*, 9–20. https://doi.org/10.30827/Digibug.53885

Bektas, U. (2022, October 31). Erdogan says constitutional change will protect families against "perverse trends." *Reuters.* https://www.reuters.com/world/middle-east/erdogan-says-constitutional-change-will-protect-families-against-perverse-trends-2022-10-31/

Boler, M. (1999). A pedagogy of discomfort: Witnessing and the politics of anger and fear. In M. Boler (Ed.), *Feeling power: Emotions and education* (pp. 175–202). Routledge.

Braun, V., & Clarke, V. (2021). One size fits all? What counts as quality practice in (reflexive) thematic analysis? *Qualitative Research in Psychology, 18*(3), 328–352. https://doi.org/10.1080/14780887.2020.1769238

Butler, J. (1990). *Gender trouble.* Routledge.

Chase, B., & Ressler, P. (2009). An LGBT/queer glossary. *English Journal, 98*(4), 23–24.

Crawley, S. A. (2022). Allies and allyship. In K. K. Strunk & S. A. Shelton (Eds.), *Encyclopedia of queer studies in education* (pp. 19–25). Brill. https://doi.org/10.1163/9789004506725_005.

Dedeoğlu, H., Ulusoy, M., & Lamme, L. L. (2012). Turkish preservice teachers' perceptions of children's picture books reflecting LGBT-related issues. *Journal of Educational Research, 105*(4), 256–263.

Dörnyei, Z. (2007). *Research methods in applied linguistics.* Oxford University Press.

Dumas, J. (2010). Sexual identity and the LINC classroom. *Canadian Modern Language Review, 66*, 607–627. https://doi.org/10.3138/cmlr.66.4.607

Foucault, M. (1978). *The history of sexuality. Volume 1: An introduction* (R. Hurley, Trans.). Pantheon Books.

Gelbal, S., & Duyan, V. (2006). Attitudes of university students toward lesbians and gay men in Turkey. *Sex Roles, 55*(7–8), 573–579. https://doi.org/10.1007/s11199-006-9112-1

Giroux, H. A. (1994). Teachers, public life, and curriculum reform. *Peabody Journal of Education, 69*(3), 35–47. https://doi.org/10.1080/01619569409538776.

Güney, Ö. (2018). *Queering teacher education programs: Perceptions of pre-service EFL teachers towards queer issues* [Unpublished master's thesis]. Bilkent University.

Güney, Ö. (2021). Discussing LGBTQ+ issues with Muslim students in the ESL classroom: The interface of culture, religion, and sexuality. In J. M. Paiz & J. E. Coda (Eds.), *Intersectional perspectives on LGBTQ+ issues in language teaching and learning* (pp. 55–85). Palgrave Macmillan. https://doi.org/10.1007/978-3-030-76779-2_3

Güney, Ö. (2022). Pre-service teachers discussing queer-inclusive pedagogies in Turkish EFL classrooms. In C. E. Poteau & C. A. Winkle (Eds.), *Advocacy for social and linguistic justice in TESOL: Nurturing inclusivity, equity, and social responsibility in English language teaching* (pp. 166–182). Routledge. https://doi.org/10.4324/9781003202356

Jagose, A. (1996). *Queer theory: An introduction.* New York University Press.

Jones, K. N., Hoover, S., Glaeser, E., Woods, C. J., Clark, M., & Brewster, M. (2022). Thematic qualitative content analysis of cishet allies' activism: Perceptions of igniting events and barriers to activism. *Journal of Homosexuality, 69*(9), 1501–1523. https://doi.org/10.1080/00918369.2021.1917220

Kaiser, E. (2017). LGBTQ+ voices from the classroom: Insights for ESOL teachers. *CATESOL Journal, 29*(1), 1–21.

Kappra, R., & Vandrick, S. (2006). Silenced voices speak: Queer students recount their experiences. *CATESOL Journal, 18*(1), 138–150.

Kelley, J., & Arce-Trigatti, A. (2022). Heteropatriarchy. In K. K. Strunk & S. A. Shelton (Eds.), *Encyclopedia of queer studies in education* (pp. 256–259). Brill. https://doi.org/10.1163/9789004506725_051

Knisely, K. A., & Paiz, J. M. (2021). Bringing trans, non-binary, and queer understandings to bear in language education. *Critical Multilingualism Studies, 9*(1), 23–45.

Leonardi, B., & Meyer, E. J. (2016). Internal safety. In N. M. Rodriguez, W. J. Martino, J. C. Ingrey, & E. Brockenbrough (Eds.), *Critical concepts in queer studies and education: An international guide for the twenty-first century* (pp. 173–183). Palgrave Macmillan. https://doi.org/10.1057/978-1-137-55425-3

Leonardi, B., & Saenz, L. (2014). Conceptualizing safety from the inside out: Heteronormative spaces and their effects on students' sense of self. In D. Carlson & E. Meyer (Eds.), *Gender and sexualities in education: A reader* (pp. 202–229). Peter Lang.

Lüküslü, D. (2016). Creating a pious generation: Youth and education policies of the AKP in Turkey. *Southeast European and Black Sea Studies, 16*(4), 637–649. https://doi.org/10.1080/14683857.2016.1243332

Meyer, E. J. (2007). "But I'm not gay": What straight teachers need to know about queer theory. In W. F. Pinar & N. M. Rodriguez (Eds.), *Queering straight teachers: Discourse and identity in education* (pp. 15–29). Peter Lang. https://digitalcommons.calpoly.edu/coe_dean/13

Meyer, E. J. (2019). Ending bullying and harassment: The case for a queer pedagogy. In C. Mayo & N. M. Rodriguez (Eds.), *Queer pedagogies: Theory, praxis, politics* (pp. 41–59). Springer. https://doi.org/10.1007/978-3-030-27066-7

Michell, M. (2009). When consciousness dawns: Confronting homophobia with Turkish high school students. *English Journal, 98*(4), 67–72. https://www.jstor.org/stable/40503267

Miller, S. (2015). A queer literacy framework promoting (a)gender and (a)sexuality self-determination and justice. *English Journal, 104*(5), 37–44. http://www.jstor.org/stable/24484578

Nelson, C. D. (1993). Heterosexism in ESL: Examining our attitudes. *TESOL Quarterly, 27*(1), 143–150. https://doi.org/10.2307/3586966

Ó'Móchain, R. (2006). Discussing gender and sexuality in a context appropriate way: Queer narratives in an EFL college classroom in Japan. *Journal of Language, Identity, and Education, 5*(1), 51–66. https://doi.org/10.1207/s15327701jlie0501_4

Ordem, E., & Ulum, Ö. G. (2020). Gender issues in English language teaching: Views from Turkey. *Acta Educationis Generalis, 10*(1), 25–39. https://doi.org/10.2478/atd-2020-0002

Ozbay, C. (2015). Same-sex sexualities in Turkey. In *International encyclopedia of the social and behavioral sciences* (2nd ed., Vol. 20, pp. 870–874). Elsevier. https://doi.org/10.1016/B978-0-08-097086-8.10219-3

Paiz, J. M. (2015). Heteronormativity in ESL reading texts and textbooks. *Journal of Language and Sexuality, 4*(1), 77–101.

Paiz, J. M., & Zhu, J. (2018). Queering the classroom: A teacher's action and a student's response. *TESOL Journal, 9*, 565–568. https://doi.org/10.1002/tesj.371

Saraç, L., & McCullick, B. (2017). The life of a gay student in a university physical education and sports department: A case study in Turkey. *Sport, Education and Society, 22*(3), 338–354. https://doi.org/10.1080/13573322.2015.1036232

Selvi, A. F., & Kocaman, C. (2021). (Mis-/under-)representations of gender and sexuality in locally produced ELT materials. *Journal of Language, Identity and Education, 20*(2), 118–133. https://doi.org/10.1080/15348458.2020.1726757

Staley, S. (2022). Heteronormativity. In K. K. Strunk & S. A. Shelton (Eds.), *Encyclopedia of queer studies in education* (pp. 250–255). Brill. https://doi.org/10.1163/9789004506725_050

Stockholm Center for Freedom. (2022, August 30). *Turkish interior minister targets LGBT+ community in Victory Day speech.* https://stockholmcf.org/turkish-interior-minister-targets-lgbt-community-in-victory-day-speech/

Stockholm Center for Freedom. (2023, May 5). *Anti-LGBT rhetoric becomes pillar of Erdogan's election campaign.* https://stockholmcf.org/anti-lgbt-rhetoric-becomes-pillar-of-erdogans-election-campaign/

Tekin, M. (2011). Breaking the shell: A study on Turkish students' reactions towards sexual identity issues in the language classroom. *GLIP Review, 7*, 216–230.

Thomas-Reid, M. (2018). Queer pedagogy. *Oxford research encyclopedia of education*. Oxford University Press. https://doi.org/10.1093/acrefore/9780190264093.013.405

Thornbury, S. (1999). Window-dressing or cross-dressing in the EFL subculture. *Folio, 5*(2), 15–17.

Tran-Thanh, V. (2020). Queer identity inclusion in the EFL classroom: Vietnamese teachers' perspectives. *TESOL Journal, 11*(3), Article e00512. https://doi.org/10.1002/tesj.512

Trinh, E. (2022). Supporting queer SLIFE youth: Initial queer considerations. In L. J. Pentón Herrera (Ed.), *English and students with limited or interrupted formal education: Global perspectives on teacher preparation and classroom practices* (pp. 209–225). Springer.

Trinh, E. (in press). Queer allyship in TESOL: We need to ACTS now! *TESOL Journal.*

Trinh, E., & Tinker Sachs, G. (2023). Thinking queer with Vietnamese EFL textbooks. *Critical Inquiry in Language Studies*. https://doi.org/10.1080/15427587.2023.2190524

Turkey's educational authorities cancel gender equality programmes. (2019, February 23). *Ahval News*. https://ahvalnews.com/gender-equality/turkeys-educational-authorities-cancel-gender-equality-programmes

U.S. Department of State. (2022, June 2). *2021 report on international religious freedom: Turkey*. https://www.state.gov/reports/2021-report-on-international-religious-freedom/turkey/

Vandrick, S. (1997). The role of hidden identities in the postsecondary ESL classroom. *TESOL Quarterly*, *31*(1), 153–157. https://doi.org/10.2307/3587980

Vandrick, S. (2001, February 28). *Teaching sexual identity issues in ESL classes*. Paper presented at the Annual Meeting of TESOL, St. Louis, MO. https://files.eric.ed.gov/fulltext/ED474464.pdf

VOA News. (2021, February 4). Turkey's Erdogan calls student protesters terrorists, intensifying anti-LGBT rhetoric. *VOA News*. https://www.voanews.com/a/extremism-watch_turkeys-erdogan-calls-student-protesters-terrorists-intensifying-anti-lgbt-rhetoric/6201631.html

Yılmaz, H. (2008). Conservatism in Turkey. *Turkish Policy Quarterly*, *7*(1), 57–63.

Yılmaz, V., & Göçmen, İ. (2016). Denied citizens of Turkey: Experiences of discrimination among LGBT individuals in employment, housing and health care. *Gender, Work & Organization*, *23*(5), 470–488. https://doi.org/10.1111/gwao.12122

PART 3

THE AMERICAS

It Is Not Weird Pedagogy, It Is Queer! Unpacking Assumptions, Beliefs, and Attitudes Toward LGBTQ+ in an English Language Classroom in Chile

Leonardo Veliz

Historically, the field of English language teaching (ELT) around the world has been mainly preoccupied with the forms and functions of formal properties of language and how these are taught to and learned by English language learners. Despite the emergence and adoption of a variety of teaching approaches, and the strong impetus for an enlightened approach/method (Brown, 2007), most English language classrooms, especially in periphery contexts, or countries in the Global South (Block & Cameron, 2002), continue to focus so heavily on the development of language skills that they often relegate the needs, individualities, and positionalities of language learners to a secondary role.

Much of the effort to create learning environments that are inclusive of learners' needs has focused mainly on the social, cultural, and linguistic needs of students. An example of this is the well-established place of culturally responsive pedagogy (CRP) as "a student-centered approach to teaching in which the students' unique cultural strengths are identified and nurtured" (Lynch, 2016, para. 2). Though this approach, or "instructional stance" (Thomas & Carvajal-Regidor, 2021, p. 91), is broadly grounded in the premise of embracing inclusively the lived experiences of disadvantaged and marginalized groups, it has not made its way into recognizing the complex gender and sexual identities of English language learners, especially of those who battle against heteronormative views of gender diversity.

In contexts of English language learning, whether it be second, foreign, or additional language learning environments, there is a strong impetus for attending to the fluidity of diverse views, understandings, and experiences of language learners (Cahnmann-Taylor et al., 2022). Though an inclusive lens is needed when it comes to embracing language learners' positionings, identities, and subjectivities, this must adopt a critically liberatory stance on issues of race, ethnicity, class, and sexuality (Pennycook, 2001). This means that when issues of, for instance, gender diversity are addressed in the ELT classroom, they should not be dealt with tangentially, peripherally, or tokenistically, but rather in ways that visibility and representation of sexual identities of "minority groups" are given full consideration. This, according to Paiz (2019), can be achieved by queering all aspects of ELT practice. Paiz described *queering* as acts in which students are engaged in critical pedagogies that allow for the questioning of dominant discourses of identity. Zacho-Smith and Smith (2010) pointed out that sexual identity is seen through the lens of queer theory as multiple and shifting rather than fixed and static. This means that any attempt to create inclusive learning environments in ELT classrooms must problematize normative assumptions and practices that perpetuate those binaries that have endured in the ELT field. Furthermore, though we recognize that queer pedagogies must serve the purpose of destabilizing norms and what is certain (Reynolds, 2010) through awareness-raising processes of social injustices and of "privileged" and "disadvantaged" peoples in the community, it is essential that meaningful opportunities be created in ELT environments for students to learn language and about the language, but most importantly about the powerful ways in which language perpetuates inequality and oppression against marginalized and minoritized peoples.

This chapter lies at the heart of these issues of queer pedagogy and allyship in ELT classrooms. Situated in the context of Chile, where English is not a dominant language nor a medium of instruction but a foreign language, this chapter reports on a study that examined students' classroom interactions and conversations that took place in an English lesson on gender diversity. The study aimed to unpack students' perceptions, opinions, and positionalities toward gender diversity through the analysis of news media articles on the (then) recently passed same-sex marriage law in Chile. The research question that arises from this context is: How do Chilean EFL students navigate and negotiate their allied positionalities toward gender diversity through peer discussions in a classroom-based task?

Queer Pedagogy and Allyship in ELT

The increasing diversity in our ELT classrooms, motivated by transnational mobility and global migration, has partly shifted the focus of teaching and learning English from linguistic forms to the sociocultural needs of learners. This has materialized in attempts to humanize the ELT curriculum (e.g., Burke et al., 2008) in ways that it becomes more learner centered so as to "recognize the wealth of experiences, resources and cultural capital that learners bring to the learning session" (Nunan, 1988, p. 23). However, despite these efforts for inclusion, issues relating to gender diversity and gender equality have not been accounted for in learner-centered curricula. Ordem and Ulum (2020) asserted that "queer and LGBT identities have been intentionally ignored in ELT disciplines and departments" (p. 25).

The absence of much-needed discourses and practices of difference, acceptance, and tolerance in ELT requires that urgent and prompt action be taken to embed issues of race, ethnicity, class, religion, and sexuality in classroom practice. These issues, often used as weapons to silence anyone who does not fall within binary boundaries, can be integrated into almost any aspect of ELT pedagogy—design, planning, implementation, resources/materials, assessment, and so on. Merse (2014) advocated for the promotion of sexual literacy through the intentional use of queer texts. In this way, through the lens of queer pedagogy, all sexual identities, not just those of sexual minorities, are normalized through our discursive practices.

Though the intentional integration of queer materials and resources in the ELT classroom may be seen as inappropriate or even harmful by those who uphold strong heteronormative views, research has shown that students, even at a young age, are able and willing to engage with LGBTQ+ issues. A study with Brazilian middle school students found that learners showed a desire and motivation to partake in work and discussions about LGBTQ+ issues (Moita-Lopes, 2006). However, an interesting aspect of the study was that, perhaps driven by pedagogical unpreparedness, heteronormative ideologies, and fear of parents' or administration's reprimands, teachers would suppress these conversations. Irrespective of the reasons for restricting, avoiding, or eliminating opportunities for these discussions, given the central role of teachers in the classroom, it is pivotal that teachers exercise their agency to challenge not only their own normative worldviews, but those of students (Allen, 2015). As a democratizing endeavor, and in an attempt to queer their pedagogies, McBeth and Pauliny (2018) challenged the boundaries and normative practices of academia by integrating queerness into their writing classes with first-year college students. Students in composition classes were asked to compose a writing piece in response to the prompt "How are you queer?" Though the prompt was unsettling, challenging, and, perhaps, uncomfortable, the intent was mainly to encourage students to think about their educational otherness, which was reflected in papers (compositions) that foregrounded students' non-normative subject positionings about several personal, social, and cultural matters. These instances, whether it be in the form of pedagogical interventions or intentional teaching adjustments aimed to embed queerness in the ELT classroom, help develop a critical awareness of how our daily social and cultural practices contribute to the (de)construction of what is perceived to be normal in society.

Greater efforts for social justice, inclusion, and safety can be achieved in classrooms by having allied teachers. As alluded to earlier, the central role of teachers in the classroom is pivotal to the creation of safe spaces for all students, where an awareness of everyone's sexual identities can be developed along with a greater sense of empowerment to disrupt thinking and practices that privilege heteronormativity (Selvi & Kocaman, 2021). Nelson (2009), for instance, explored the intersection of teachers' own sexual identities and their teaching practices. She found that teachers' reflective narratives about their sexualities served as valuable resources for classroom discussion about how heteronormativity in ESL and EFL classrooms marginalizes and disadvantages sexual minorities. These instances constitute critical sites for raising awareness of inequalities and social injustices that involve LGBTQ+ students. Most importantly, they act as a catalyst for value-based conversations that stimulate opinion-based activism, allyship, and potential collective action. According to Sharma (2019), an ally is best described as a person from a privileged, dominant group who intentionally advocates for the rights of those who are racialized, minoritized, or disadvantaged. In the ELT classroom, allied teachers can acknowledge students' fluid and dynamic identities (Trinh, in press), demonstrate respect and self-reflection (Potvin, 2016), and foster what Love (2018) called "a liberatory consciousness" aimed "to create change and increase social justice" (Reynolds, 2010, p. 13).

The Chilean Context

To understand the educational and sociopolitical context that drove the present study, there must be some reference to the various significant effects of the military government (1973–1990) on education as well as the neoliberal and neoconservative ideologies that shaped the current Chilean educational system. The military takeover in 1973 brought about a series of radical social, political, economic, and educational changes in Chilean society. Based on the premise "absolute control of the nation" (Beltrán & Preller, 2003, p. 11), Chile witnessed military intervention in almost every human activity, which legitimized power imbalances as well as social injustice and inequalities, and, at the same time, neutralized any possible form of sociopolitical activism, reformation, or social transformation. In education, for example, several drastic measures were taken to extirpate the "Marxist cancer," that is, any views and ideologies perceived as posing a threat to the prevailing military order. One of these measures was the development of a policy of control with the intent to eradicate all existing teachers' unions (Nuñez, 1984). The suppression of teacher associations was vital for the government as these were seen as sites of social and political campaigns. In Mora's (2013) view, one of the aims of Augusto Pinochet's government was to minimize, and ideally neutralize, all possible educational instances and opportunities that could ignite commitment, social responsibility, and bravery in young people to realize that they had the power to critique and challenge the status quo.

The unprecedented impact of a military order, coupled with historical patriarchal beliefs and practices controlled by an orthodox Catholic church, have largely influenced the narrow views of diversity and tolerance upheld by a large portion of Chilean society (Movilh, 2022). This has led to increasing numbers of reported homophobic attacks in public places, many of which have sadly ended in the loss of many innocent lives.

Recently, some political unrest has unfolded due to the strong impetus for implementing the "Orientaciones para la Inclusión de las Personas Lesbianas, Gays, Bisexuales, Trans e Intersex en el Sistema Educativo [Guidelines for the Inclusion of Lesbians, Gays, Bisexuals, Trans and Intersex in the Educational System]" by the minister of education, Marco Antonio Ávila, who is a supporter and member of the LGBTQ+ community (Kogan, 2023). This has led to not only parliamentary resistance and great opposition but also seven accusations against an alleged gender agenda in favor of gender diversity (Laborde, 2023).

Methodology

This study was methodologically framed by some of the overarching principles of critical discourse analysis (CDA). CDA, sometimes understood as an extension of critical linguistics, deals mainly with the intersection of language and ideology (Waring, 2016). The interplay of language and ideology has been examined by different areas of education (e.g., critical literacy, critical pedagogy) and branches of linguistics (e.g., critical applied linguistics). Though some (e.g., van Dijk, 1993) have alluded to any form of criticality being politically driven, which is partly true, it must be noted that any "critical" strand of education or linguistics seeks to not only unveil hidden dominant ideologies that perpetuate dominant practices, but also bring about change and transformation that advances equity, social justice, and inclusion (Hall, 2016).

According to van Dijk (2001), there are different types of CDA and contexts in which it can be used. This makes CDA theoretically and analytically diverse, yet common underlying questions across the various types of CDA research are asked. The overarching question that CDA addresses is to do with "the way specific discourse structures are deployed in the reproduction of social dominance" (van Dijk, 2001, p. 353). A vast area of research that has been examined through the lens of CDA is gender inequality (Fairclough & Wodak, 1997; van Dijk, 2001). In this study, the methodological examination of the language and discourse of gender (in)equality in students' interactions was undertaken through the lens of what van Dijk called "personal and social cognition." This refers to the fact that language users as social actors possess personal memories, knowledge, and opinions along with those shared with members of their social or cultural group as a whole.

Participants

The participants in the study were a group of 18 adult EFL students studying conversational English in a private college in Santiago, Chile. The students were deemed to possess a B2 English proficiency level per the Common European Framework of Reference for Languages (Council of Europe, 2023), which enabled them to express ideas clearly, comprehend a wide range of complex texts and express ideas and opinions in a sophisticated manner. The students were taking an "advanced" English course that focused mainly on conversational English at a local English language institute in Santiago, Chile. Some demographic information on participants is provided in Table 1.

Table 1. Students' Profiles

Name	Age	Identified themselves as	Qualifications	Languages
Felipe	28	Male	Bachelor's in business (equivalent)	Spanish and English
Marina	32	Female	Master's in accounting	Spanish, English, and some Japanese
Juan	30	Male	Bachelor's in physical education	Spanish and English
Josefina	26	Supporter[1] (ally)	Bachelor's in history	Spanish and English
Daniel	33	Supporter (ally)	Master's in political science	Spanish, English, and German
Barbara	26	Female	Bachelor's in business and marketing	Spanish and English

1. Students indicated that they were "strong supporters" of the LGBTQ+ community.

To explore students' positionalities toward gender diversity through the lens of personal and social cognition, attention is paid to the interaction between Barbara and Daniel, who negotiated their understandings and views of the new law. Barbara, who did not explicitly identify herself as an ally, demonstrated a level of self-reflection that supports social justice against oppressed communities by, first and foremost, asserting that Chile has shown a degree of maturity toward inclusion and integration of "everyone in our society." This positive attitude was reinforced by Daniel, who stressed fairness and equality brought forth by this new law while also demarcating the gap between an idealized outcome that may be achieved through the law and a pressing reality that constantly perpetuates discriminatory practices.

> **Barbara:** I think it's a sign of a "mature" country, making progress about integrating everyone in our society.
>
> **Daniel:** It's a great law, more fairness, equality, and justice to everyone. We needed this for a long time. Although discrimination will continue in many areas every day, it's a big step, but a sad reality.
>
> **Barbara:** Totally agree. Discrimination is not in a law but in people's minds, and that is hard to remove from everyone against different sexualities, but even this class and discussion is a good starting point.

Though Barbara reaffirmed Daniel's views on fairness, equality, and social justice, she alluded to discrimination as a "socially situated cognitive representation and practice" (van Dijk, 2001, 2003) that resides in the social cognitions of individuals (i.e., people's minds) and enacted by members of society. This interaction typifies the collective thinking about the complexities around eradicating discrimination and oppression against gender-diverse people. Furthermore, it demonstrates the feasibility of an ELT classroom as a safe space (Trinh, 2022) for queer students to voice their support, allyship, and advocacy for marginalized communities.

As a self-identified ally, it is interesting to observe Josefina's use of inclusive language in her discourse. Though she emphasized not being a lesbian, the use of "we," first person plural pronoun, evokes a great sense of support, allyship, to a large extent group membership, and respect toward LGBTQ+ communities.

> **Josefina:** Absolutely amazing! From a legal point of view, we can now get married, and get official recognition of our bonds. I'm not lesbian, but a fond supporter. Go gay people! This is my favorite class so far!
>
> **Juan:** Yes, it's needed for equality in our country and gay people can now legally marry, but if you think about it, what's then for them and us? What do we get as a society?
>
> **Josefina:** More fairness. It's a change in how we think about diversity, and this also shows how much we need to change.
>
> **Juan:** ...understand, what's a priority for some is not for others, but that's life.

Josefina's inclusive discourse situated her in a vulnerable position as she was challenged by Juan's othering, which foregrounds a rhetoric of difference and separation between "them" and "us." Though Juan did not appear to foresee any societal benefits of the same-sex marriage law, he showed a level of understanding and respect for diverse opinions and positions after Josefina stressed the necessity to transform individual and collective cognitions about diversity. Despite the different views and positions toward the implications of the adoption of the law, it is apparent that this interactional encounter in the context of the broader activity created an ally-filled environment that "contribute[s] to the making of a space in which the person who is oppressed gets to have their voice heard and listened to" (Reynolds, 2010, p. 14).

A similar discourse of difference and otherness is perceived in Felipe's response, whereby he positioned himself as one not needing or benefiting from this law. The significance of a same-sex marriage law was downplayed by an underlying ideology that prioritizes colonial and capitalist endeavors such as economic wealth and education over recognizing the oppression, discrimination, and racialization of minority groups.

> **Felipe:** ...not a medical breakthrough but needed by some. Yeah, it's fine for me but at the same time there are some many other important issues that should happen in Chile that we should be celebrating.
>
> **Mariana:** Like what...?
>
> **Felipe:** Come on, Mariana! The divide between the rich and the poor, poor-quality education, crime rates, people feeling vulnerable, discrimination of Indigenous peoples, and so many other things.
>
> **Mariana:** Couldn't agree more but one step at a time, but social activism for people who suffer discrimination is more important.
>
> **Felipe:** Yeah, it's needed for some, but it could have been a different step, but it's OK.
>
> **Mariana:** Mmm...but it's needed because Chile is a very unjust country, and I don't want a country like this.

Though Mariana agreed that other social issues should also be tackled, she located herself in a position of advocacy and strong social responsibility for those who are victims of the oppressive discourse of heteronormativity. Mariana's position can be seen as "allyship as intrapersonal growth, interpersonal connections, and collectivist actions" (Catalano & Chrisiaens, 2022, p. 97). Love (2018) argued that allyship from a liberatory consciousness perspective must be viewed as everyone's responsibility rather than of only those who enjoy a certain privilege in society.

In these short extracts, it can be observed that though students' different positionalities toward gender diversity may be seen as contentious, they reflect healthy and respectful dialogic interactions whereby "ELT practitioners [can] trouble dominant disciplinary and societal discourses through a pedagogy of inquiry and disruption" (Paiz, 2019, p. 271).

Thinking Back

By the end of the lesson, students were asked to share their thoughts and opinions about the activity. Through the discussions, it becomes clear that students positioned themselves in favor of the ways the lesson had disrupted the well-established rigid structures of the architecture of a "normal" class.

> **Daniel:** This lesson has been totally unusual to what we normally do in English, but I loved it, I loved it. We need more of this. Everyone in the community needs to develop a better understanding of gender diversity to be more tolerant.
>
> **Barbara:** It was a great lesson. These discussions should be happening in schools, like in...in history classes, in Spanish classes, because there's so much homophobia in Chile.
>
> **Daniel:** Yeah, but teachers need to be prepared to do things a bit different because it takes courage.
>
> **Barbara:** Not easy...!

Besides the usefulness and value added to the lesson, the class activity was viewed by the students as a disruption to normative lesson structures. Seen as "totally unusual" to what is normally done in an English class, clear traces of queer pedagogy are observed in how the lesson activity was lived and experienced by students. Though Alexander (2005) posited that queer pedagogy is about deconstructing normalcy, a greater focus should be on introducing queerness to all students to empower them to think deeply about the complex ways in which their lives operate in a heteronormative society. The interaction between Barbara and Daniel also hints at the necessity for queer activism and anti-oppressive education as they recognized the impetus for broader and more pervasive discussions about sexualities and gender diversity, not only across school subjects but in the wider community. In addition to the need for a change in people's social cognitions and social representations of gender, Daniel alluded to teachers' pedagogical preparedness to deal with content and instruction that resides outside the boundaries of monolithic social and cultural institutions. Paiz (2019) asserted that "queering ESL/EFL teaching must begin with teacher preparation" (p. 270). The fact that queerness in teaching "takes courage" implies that teachers must be equipped with the pedagogical and epistemological knowledge and skill sets to reposition and renegotiate their own (sexual) identities along with those of all students.

An element of teacher (un)preparedness was also perceived by Felipe, who noted that the teacher did not appear to know how to proceed when he was challenging Mariana in an earlier conversation. Whether it was fear, discomfort, or actual unpreparedness to deal with what appeared to be conflicting or opposing opinions, what is clear in the following interaction is that teachers have the responsibility to create a safe space for all students—those who position themselves as allies and those who are willing to show respect and tolerance toward diversity while sustaining a heteronormative view of the world.

Felipe: It's been a good conversation, but you could see that the people in other tables didn't really like my honest opinion about this issue. We can't like everything or everyone, so that is tolerance, too, and the teacher didn't seem to know what to do then.

Mariana: Yeah, it's like tolerance has to be in one way only, but not both ways, and maybe the teacher didn't make this clear.

Felipe: Exactly! This happens all the time. I respect gay people and lesbians, but I don't think the world works this way. I have a gay friend, and we respect each other, but this "gender diverse" idea is not in my head.

Mariana: It doesn't have to be as long as we show respect, support, and help these people be a part of our community because they are so discriminated.

Felipe and Mariana negotiated a safe space of two-way tolerance that, despite clearly articulated differing positions and attitudes toward diversity, highlights their inclinations to inclusion, respect, and tolerance. Irrespective of how peripheral or tokenistic this might sound, this has been the political rhetoric of postmilitary governments, one that brings multiple perspectives, political parties, and ideologies together in the best interests of society.

At the onset of their article on queering English language classrooms, Trinh (2022) asserted that working with queer English language learners requires close attention to their emotions and feelings. The conversational encounter between Juan and Josefina accentuates their attempts to humanize marital relationships, irrespective of sexualities or sexual identities, by bringing the importance of happiness, compassion, and kindness to the fore.

Juan: The article about the marriage was good because it shows "human happiness" and anyone deserves to be happy, and...

Josefina: ...that's what's showing, just happiness. I know you said it would be difficult for you to accept this in your children, but you understand the emotional side of these people.

Juan: ...these people have been killed and treated like animals, and that's so sad. I understand that...

Juan: ...and also, and it doesn't really cost anything to show human kindness and compassion.

Josefina: Mmm...what's you're saying really sounds like they were lower than us and because of that we have to show compassion.

Juan: Not lower but discriminated in every sense, with our language, actions, and everything, especially from those that think they are superior.

Josefina: Yeah, but we can show human kindness to anyone, White, Black, gay, not gay.

Sadly, what becomes salient in this interaction is the disastrous consequences of underlying patriarchal, heteronormative, and hegemonic thinking that has demonized nonbinary practices, often resulting in homophobic attacks, assaults, and murders. It is in this context that Juan and Josefina called for compassion and kindness toward LGBTQ+ communities, which seems to reify their commitment to equity, social justice, and allyship.

It becomes apparent that though the intentional discussions about the selected texts in class served as a basis for critical dialogue that reflected the complex discursive constructions and representations of gender and sexual identities upheld by students, they seem to have formed a safe space for students to voice their attitudes and positionalities toward LGBTQ+ communities. In line with Moita-Lopes's (2006) study, it was evident in students' discussions that they felt a sense of motivation and desire to partake in this "unusual" class activity, which served the purpose of destabilizing classroom norms and structures (Reynolds, 2010).

Conclusion

This study sought to explore EFL students' beliefs and attitudes toward LGBTQ+ communities through the analysis of their dialogic classroom discussions about the same-sex marriage law passed in Chile in 2022. In particular, it explored the complex, dynamic, and multifaceted ways in which students navigated their positionality and allyship moves in their conversations. Though a common storyline running across all interactions featured students' deep concerns about existing and continuing manifestations of unequal power structures that perpetuate marginalization of LGBTQ+ communities in Chile, all students, irrespective of their attitudes toward the benefits of the law and its broader community benefits, placed themselves in a position to show support, tolerance, and respect for those who are silenced, marginalized, and invisibilized in society. Besides the central elements of allyship and criticality evidenced in the discussions, students showed great appreciation for the nature, depth, and orientation of the conversations generated in class. The discussions revealed that while a level of marginalization and discrimination against gender diversity may continue to be prevalent in Chilean society, greater efforts should be made in and out of school to engage in discussions that increase awareness of the dominant social cognitions of the privileged and powerful, and of the ways in which these can be destabilized and disrupted.

Author

Leonardo Veliz, PhD, is an associate professor in language and literacy in the School of Education at the University of New England, in Australia.

References

Alexander, J. (2005). "Straightboyz4Nsync": Queer theory and the composition of heterosexuality. *JAC: A Journal of Rhetoric, Culture and Politics, 25*(2), 371–395.

Allen, L. (2015). Queer pedagogy and the limits of thought: Teaching sexualities at university. *Higher Education Research and Development, 34*(4), 763–775. https://doi.org/10.1080/07294360.2015.1051004

Beltrán, A., & Preller, J. (2003). *Impacto de la dictadura militar (1973–1990) en la nueva narrativa Chilena. Análisis de casos* [The impact of military dictatorship (1973-1990) on the new Chilean narrative. Case study analysis. Universidad Austral de Chile. http://cybertesis.uach.cl/tesis/uach/2003/ffb548i/doc/ffb548i.pdf

Block, D., & Cameron, D. (Eds.). (2002). *Globalization and language teaching.* Routledge.

Brown, H. D. (2007). *Teaching by Principles: An Interactive Approach to Language Pedagogy* (3rd ed.). Pearson Longman.

Burke, C., Adler, M. A., & Linker, M. (2008). Resisting erasure: Cultivating opportunities for a humanizing curriculum. *Multicultural Perspectives, 10*(2), 65–72. https://doi.org/10.1080/15210960801997924

Cahnmann-Taylor, M., Coda, J., & Jiang, L. (2022). Queer is as queer does: Queer L2 pedagogy in teacher education. *TESOL Quarterly, 56*(1), 130–153. https://doi.org/10.1002/tesq.3044

Catalano, J. C., & Chrisiaens, R. (2022). Reimagining allyship: Commodification, resistance and liberatory potentials. *College Student Affairs Journal, 40*(2), 87–99.

Council of Europe. (2023). Common European Framework of Reference for Languages (CEFR). https://www.coe.int/en/web/common-european-framework-reference-languages/level-descriptions

Creswell, J., & Creswell, D. (2018). *Research design: qualitative, quantitative, and mixed methods approaches* (2nd ed.). Sage.

Dawson, C. (2007). *A practical guide to research methods.* How to Books.

Dawson, C. (2009). *Introduction to research methods: A practical guide for anyone undertaking a research project* (4th ed.). How to Books.

Fairclough, N. L., & Wodak, R. (1997). Critical discourse analysis. In T. A. van Dijk (Ed.), *Discourse studies: A multidisciplinary introduction* (pp. 258–284). Sage.

Hall, C. (2016). A short introduction to social justice and ELT. In C. Hastings (Ed.), *Social justice in English language teaching* (pp. 3–10). TESOL Press.

Jones, R. (2008). Turns, topics and tyranny: Conversation analysis and power in Alan Ayckbourn's absurd person singular. *Innervate: Leading Undergraduate Work in English Studies, 1,* 167–174.

Kogan, A. (2023). Polémica guía de orientación sexual en Chile [Controversial sexual orientation guide in Chile]. *La Vanguardia.* https://www.lavanguardia.com/participacion/lectores-corresponsales/20230607/9021716/guia-orientacion-sexual-polemica-chile.html

Laborde, A. (2023). La derecha Chilena fracasa en su intento de destituir al ministro de Educación de Boric en el Congreso [The Chilean right fails in its attempt to dismiss Boric's Minister of Education in Congress]. *EL País.* https://elpais.com/chile/2023-07-12/

la-derecha-chilena-fracasa-en-su-intento-de-destituir-al-ministro-de-educacion-de-boric-en-el-congreso.html

Love, B. (2018). Developing a liberatory consciousness. In M. Adams, W. J. Blumenfeld, D. C. J. Catalano, H. W. H. K. DeJong, L. E. Hopkins, B. J. Love, M. L. Peters, D. Shlasko, & X. Zúñiga (Eds.), *Readings for diversity and social justice* (pp. 599–603). Routledge.

Lynch, M. (2016). *What is culturally responsive pedagogy?* https://www.theedadvocate.org/what-is-culturally-responsive-pedagogy/

McBeth, M., & Pauliny, T. (2018). Queering the first-year composition student (and teacher): A democratizing endeavor. In E. McNeil, J. Wermers, & J. Lunn (Eds.), *Mapping queer space(s) of praxis and pedagogy* (pp. 57–69). Palgrave Macmillan.

Merse, T. (2014, October 21). *Promoting sexual literacy through queer pedagogy in EFL and ESOL classrooms: Materials and methods* [Conference session]. Queering ESOL: Towards a Cultural Politics of LGBT Issues in the ESOL Classroom, King's College, London.

Moita-Lopes, L. P. (2006). Queering literacy teaching: Analyzing gay-themed discourse in a fifth-grade class in Brazil. *Journal of Language, Identity, & Education, 5*(1), 31–50. https://doi.org/10.1207/s15327701jlie0501_3

Mora, D. (2013). *Pensamiento crítico en el currículum oficial y en los textos escolares. Propuesta didáctica: La Revolución Industrial* [Critical thinking in the official curriculum and school textbooks. Didactic proposal: Industrial Revolution; Bio Bio University]. http://repobib.ubiobio.cl/jspui/bitstream/123456789/366/1/Mora_Godoy_Danilo.pdf

MOVILH. (2022). *Informe anual de derechos humanos de la diversidad sexual y de género en Chile: Historia anual de las personas LGBTIQA+ en Chile* [Annual Human Rights report on sexual and gender diversity in Chile: Annual history of LGBTIQA+ in Chile]. http://www.movilh.cl/documentacion/2022/XX-Informe-Anual-DDHH-MOVILH.pdf

Nelson, C. D. (2009). *Sexual identities in English language education: Classroom conversations.* Routledge.

Nunan, D. (1988). *Syllabus design.* Oxford University Press.

Nuñez, I. (1984). *Las transformaciones educacionales bajo el régimen militar* [Educational transformations under the military regime] (Vol. 1). Programa Interdisciplinario de Investigaciones en Educación.

Ordem, E., & Ulum, Ö. (2020). Gender issues in English language teaching: Views from Turkey. *Acta Educationis Generalis, 10*(1), 25–39. https://doi.org/10.2478/atd-2020-0002

Paiz, J. M. (2019). Queering practice: LGBTQ+ diversity and inclusion in English language teaching. *Journal of Language, Identity and Education, 18*(4), 266–275. https://doi.org/10.1080/15348458.2019.1629933

Pennycook, A. (2001). *Critical applied linguistics.* Lawrence Erlbaum.

Potvin, L. (2016). Radical heterosexuality: Straight teacher activism in schools. *Confero, 4*(1), 9–36. https://doi.org/10.3384/confero.2001-4562.160614

Reynolds, V. (2010, October). Fluid and imperfect ally positioning: Some gifts of queer theory. *Context*, pp. 13–17. https://www.suu.edu/pridealliance/pdf/reynolds.pdf

Selvi, F. A., & Kocaman, C. (2021). (Mis-/under)representations of gender and sexuality in locally-produced ELT materials. *Journal of Language, Identity & Education, 20*(2), 118–133. https://doi.org/10.1080/15348458.2020.1726757

Sharma, A. (2019). Allyship and social justice: Men as allies in challenging men's violence and discrimination against women. In D. Baines, B. Bennett, S. Goodwin, & M. Rawsthorne (Eds.), *Working across difference: Social work, social policy and social justice* (pp. 103–119). Red Globe Press.

Thomas, M., & Carvajal-Regidor, M. (2021). Culturally responsive pedagogy in TESOL. In P. Vinogradova & J. K. Shin (Eds.), *Contemporary foundations for teaching English as an additional language: Pedagogical approaches and classroom applications* (pp. 91–99). Routledge.

Trinh, E. (2022). Supporting queer SLIFE youth: Initial queer considerations. In L. J. Pentón Herrera (Ed.), *English and students with limited or interrupted formal education: Global perspectives on teacher preparation and classroom practices* (pp. 209–225). Springer International.

Trinh, E. (in press). Queer allyship in TESOL: We need to ACTS now! *TESOL Journal.*

van Dijk, T. (1993). Principles of critical discourse analysis. *Discourse and Society, 4*(2), 249–283.

van Dijk, T. (2001). Critical discourse analysis. In D. Schiffrin, D. Tannen, & H. Hamilton (Eds.), *The handbook of discourse analysis* (pp. 352–371). Blackwell.

van Dijk, T. (2003). The discourse-knowledge interface. In G. Weiss & R. Wodak (Eds.), *Critical discourse analysis: Theory and interdisciplinarity*. Palgrave Macmillan.

Waring, H. (2016). *Theorizing pedagogical interaction: Insights from conversation analysis*. Routledge.

Zacho-Smith, J. D., & Smith, G. (2010). Recognizing and utilizing queer pedagogy. *Multicultural Education, 18*(1), 2–9.

Translation Outside Binaries: Queer Pedagogy, English Language Teaching, and First Language>Second Language Translation

Lihit Velázquez-Lora

In their introduction to *Queer in Translation*, Epstein and Gillet (2017) created a parallelism between Tiresias[1] and translators by underlining the importance of duality for both. They affirmed that translators "have unlearned essentialism" (p. 3) because they work with and in between languages. However, it would be relevant to question whether essentialism is unlearned by being a translator and, if so, how. Intercultural awareness is a very useful skill to translate and, though it can be considered an element of translation competence, it is not always so acknowledged in EFL (Rhodes & Coda, 2017) or explicitly named in translation courses (Tomozeiu & Kumpulainen, 2018). Moreover, thinking about the relationship between translators and their work languages might be revealing. For example, translating from a second language into a first language (L2>L1 translation) is a common practice, while L1>L2 translation is usually unadvised (Beeby Lonsdale, 1996b; Newmark, 1988; Stewart, 2000). Then, in general terms, the translator's abilities are considered more suited for L2>L1 translation but not the opposite. Such a view comes from a set of binary oppositions deeply embedded in translation as a discipline (Baer, 2021; Ladmiral, 2004; Spurlin, 2017).

In this chapter, I argue that including a queer pedagogy in an EFL writing course for translators[2] might help students question some assumptions they may have had previously and create a safe space in the classroom to experiment with language. I make the case that including exercises aimed at improving or practicing L1>L2 translation in such a writing course will help translators improve the needed competences for their task. Also, creating a safe space for translator trainees will give them the opportunity to question their own translation practices

1. Tiresias, considered a prophet and a mediator of disputes, is a character in Greek mythology who experienced being both a man and a woman at different stages in life.

2. Students should get at least a B1+ English level (according to the Common European Framework of Reference of Language [Council of Europe, 2023]) in their entrance exam to the translation degree.

and consider what other dichotomies they could reflect on, including, for example, gender or sexuality. All of this together will help them become allies[3] to the LGBTQ+ community.

In the first part of this chapter, I present binaries in translation and challenge them. Then, I question the hierarchy created between L2>L1 translation and L1>L2 translation. Finally, I focus on intercultural competence (IC) as a useful skill needed to face these translations. From this point of view, L1>L2 translation helps students see their own culture from another perspective. When asked for L2>L1 translation, students usually use their reading skills in their L2 and rely on their L1 to translate. Switching these elements gives students a new perspective about their process. In addition, being able to question the power systems behind the beliefs of their own profession would lead students to reflect on the ethical questions related to their practice, raise their awareness, and guide them toward other "ingredients required for effective allyship[:] analysis, accountability, and action" (Shlasko, 2017, "What Is Allyship?" para. 4).

Binary Oppositions in Translation

In translation studies (TS), there are many binary oppositions, but a fundamental one is the *author–translator dichotomy*. However, not only have the concepts changed through time, but also there are forms of translation where the author and translator are the same.[4] Another problem with the distinction is that it establishes an inherent hierarchy that privileges the author's authority as superseding that of the translator. A variation is the dichotomy of *author–reader*, which is exemplified by depicting translation either as an author-centered or a reader-centered process focused on either the foreign culture or their own culture (Schleiermacher, 1813/2000, p. 47).

Associated with this distinction is another dichotomy: *original text* or *copy*. As mentioned before, authorship is considered the original (therefore, superior) in opposition to the translator's work, a copy (Venuti, 1995). Epstein and Gillet (2017) emphasized such a view:

> It is often maintained that the ideal translation is a kind of seamless assimilation in which the status of a translation as a translation is all but invisible, in which, in other words, the translation is able to "pass." But precisely because this is not something that a non-translated text has to go through, the very existence of the idea bespeaks an operation of power and a position of subalternity. (pp. 2–3)

The binary *source text–target text* (ST-TT) also adds to the idea of an original text and a version or copy. However, it is important to remember that translations tend to be presented as originals, and the translators' voices and work are hidden while pretending to be the

---

3. Shlasko (2017) defined allyship as "supporting someone (or some group) who is impacted by oppression or inequality differently than you are," whereas Trinh (in press) characterized the concept of queer allyship as the one that "describes allies who work together to challenge common heteronormative and cisgender assumptions of oneself to think queer and provoke actions in relational systems of support (ACTS)" (p. 5).

4. For example, self-translation, which is not as uncommon as it is thought, as Santoyo (2005) has explained.

authors'. Indirect translation[5] also questions the dualism between ST and TT as translations might be considered an ST, therefore generating a "new original" (Baer, 2021, p. 35).

Another type of binary is that of the translators' mother tongue and the other languages they work with. These are usually called *foreign* or *secondary*. Regarding the first set, *mother tongue* has also been called *first language*, *A language*, *dominant language*, and *home language* (de la Cruz Trainor, 2004, p. 54; Kelly, 1997, p. 175; Pokorn, 2005, pp. 2–6), while a *foreign language* might also be called *second language* or *B language*. The different ways of naming these languages imply an ideology behind them and some problems in defining them (Pokorn, 2005, p. 1). The dichotomy presented here is based on the user's identity and culture and does not question the concept of mother tongue and the fact that there are many possibilities regarding the language(s) one might know. Furthermore, it gives a higher status to the mother tongue as it gives native speakers an authority and prestige that is not bestowed on the other languages. Pokorn (2005) showed how categorizing criteria are related to problematic aspects of immigration, prestige, and colonization (pp. 3–4) and how such terms depict a hegemonic point of view (p. 2).

The last binary opposition that I consider important to reflect on is L2>L1 translation versus L1>L2 translation. In TS, L1>L2 translation has been depicted in a negative light. An example is Stewart's (2000) title for an article on this topic: "Poor Relations and Black Sheep in Translation Studies."[6] L1>L2 translation is not one of the main topics in TS and is even seen as inferior (Stewart, 2000, p. 206). In fact, important authors have emphasized that L1>L2 translation lacks effectiveness and accuracy (Newmark, 1988, p. 3) and that even bilingual translators face limitations when translating in such a way (García Yebra, 1983, p. 348, cited in Massau, 2013, p. 283).

Moreover, some international institutions disapprove of L1>L2 translation and establish that for practicing L1>L2 translation, translators must have the same skills in their L2 as in their L1. Even assuming that the concept of mother tongue is not ambiguous, it is important to remember that "being a native speaker does not guarantee having the best linguistic competence in such language" (Yuste Frías, 2014, p. 83, my translation). It should be considered that "even being bilingual does not imply the communicative skills or the writing competence needed to translate" (Yuste Frías, 2005, p. 152, my translation). As Crystal (2019, p. 203) explained, knowing grammar and knowing about grammar are different things. Giving native speakers a higher status is problematic,[7] not only because the term can mean different things, but also because it assumes the "innate capacities of the ideal native speaker" (Pokorn, 2005, p. 117).

The restrictions on L1>L2 translation do not seem to consider that translation competence goes beyond the linguistic abilities and includes other subcompetences, such as extralinguistic, strategic, and instrumental subcompetences (Proceso de Adquisición de la

5. A translation from a minor language to a major language and then from this to other minor languages.

6. We can problematize how poverty and Blackness are stereotypically related to negative aspects and linked to L1>L2 translation. Beeby Lonsdale (1996b) presented a comparison between L1>L2 translation and Cinderella, but as such "the stepdaughter who was obliged to do the dirty work ... outshone her stepsisters at the ball" (p. 100). It would be interesting to ask translation trainees about their thoughts on the title and comparison.

7. To review some of the negative aspects of such a situation, see Holliday's (2006) article "Native-Speakerism."

Competencia Traductora y Evaluación [PACTE], 2017, p. 38–41). In fact, translators develop abilities that sometimes native speakers do not have, for example, text typology knowledge, specializing in certain topics and skills to research terminology and any contextual information necessary to translate. In this context, it would be more relevant to focus on the translator's writing abilities and their IC.

Even when L1>L2 translation is an unadvised practice, it is common for clients or agencies to ask for this type of translation (Cómitre Narváez, 2003; de la Cruz Trainor, 2004; Yuste Frías, 2014). In a survey conducted in 2017, 84% of the interviewed translators said that they translated in both directions for their most common language pair. According to Beeby Lonsdale (1996a), "The idea that translation from a second language is superior appeared in the sixteenth century when modern countries were forming, after the Reformation and the development of vernacular languages" (p. 59, my translation).

There is no clarity related to the way this type of translation is named: "indirect translation, inverse translation, marked translation, service translation, pedagogical translation, prose translation" (Stewart, 2000, p. 207) as well as "translation from the mother tongue, ... translation AL→BL" (Beeby Lonsdale, 1996b, p. 5). Yet these terms depict how L1>L2 translation is considered second class or a "deviation from the norm" (Stewart, 2000, p. 207). However, it is not only a common type of practice that clients ask for, but also it is considered "a valuable educational instrument for translator trainees, as it forces them to think about translation in a different light" (Kelly, 1997, p. 176, my translation). I would add to this that it also makes students think of themselves in a different way: both as language learners and as translators.

Nevertheless, until this point, it is possible to see that questioning concepts usually presented and conceived as a dichotomy is a first step in the process of building allyship. Such a reflective process facilitates becoming aware of the asymmetric relationships in a dual system. The fact that binaries are not the only possibility in translation mirrors what happens with nonbinary identities as they establish that there are multiple possibilities when talking about identities. The concept of passing also is relevant both for translation and LGBTQ+ identities. In translation, passing as the original is wrongly considered the goal for translators, and in the realm of sexual and gender identities, cisheteronormativity is wrongly seen as the superior identity that people should try to reach.

Even though awareness does not equal actions, noticing that there are more options than a supposedly fixed binary helps students understand their responsibility as translators and might lead them to become allies when faced with situations related to inequality. This, of course, might develop from further analysis and specific activities. As Neuhouser et al. (2022) explained, a big part of hate speech in Mexico comes from importing it via translation (pp. 9, 28, 33). Hate speech has been directed particularly toward trans people (either binary or nonbinary). Thus, becoming aware of what is at stake when translating a text related to the LGBTQ+ community is a vital aspect of becoming an ally.

Intercultural Awareness

The intercultural dimension usually tends to be less acknowledged than the other skills in language classes because activities related to it might be perceived as time-consuming or related skills are not explicitly considered on the syllabus (Rhodes & Coda, 2017). Nonetheless, such a dimension is essential for language learners as it will enable them to be "competent, adaptable communicators" (López-Rocha, 2016, p. 105). Furthermore, it is quite central for translation students as their intercultural skills are the ones that will make them "mediators who are able to engage with complexity and multiple identities" (Byram et al., 2002, p. 9). Translators work in between cultures, and without IC they cannot fully complete their labor (Tomozeiu et al., 2018). In addition, IC is the skill that could help translators reflect on essentialism.

Even when considered an important part of the syllabus, IC is not always taught in an explicit way, which is, according to Tomozeiu and Kumpulainen (2018), vital especially for translators. Currently, there is more interest in defining and researching translation competence, thus different models establish the necessary elements to achieve such competence (Tomozeiu & Kumpulainen, 2018). Yet there is still not one model on which translators agree. These models, from which PACTE's (2017) is the most quoted, tend to mention IC as a relevant aspect; however, "there seems to be a 'blank spot' in TS pedagogical literature in this regard [translator intercultural training]" (Tomozeiu & Kumpulainen, 2018, p. 21). Nevertheless, "intercultural competence is either implicit in multicomponent translation competence models, or alternatively, it is specified in a vague, and sometimes incoherent manner" (Tomozeiu & Kumpulainen, 2018, p. 21). Although there are many definitions of IC, Witte's (2005) description has explanatory value:

> the ability to become critically aware of what is "known" unconsciously and to "learn" consciously what is not "known" about one's own culture and other culture(s), as well as the ability to relate and contrast the cultures so as to be able to produce behaviours in accordance with the aim of the communication and tailored to the particular communicative situation, behaviours that account for the communicative need of at least two actors from two different cultures, so as to enable the communication between these actors. (cited in Tomozeiu & Kumpulainen, 2018, pp. 21–22)

To this, I would add Dietz's (2019) note that this competence is visible when the translator becomes aware of and questions their own point of view. Among the different contexts in which translators might encounter a different culture, Dietz includes class, ethnic group, nationality, religion, age, gender, and capacities.

IC is relevant not only when translating texts, but also when engaging "effectively and professionally with the client or translation project manager or other fellow translators that might have different cultural values and practices" (Tomozeiu & Kumpulainen, 2018, p. 23). In this sense, I argue that assuming that translators would communicate with clients, managers, or other translators only in their mother tongue is unrealistic.

By paying attention to the power system behind L1>L2 translation, students can reflect on their own place in that system and other people's expectations of them. Furthermore, they can challenge them if they disagree. According to Yajima and Toyosaki (2015), "Reflexive translators come to know how their cultural identities are implicated in the process of translating and world-making" (cited in Tomozeiu et al., 2018, p. 12). Thinking about this practice will trigger other types of questioning and might lead students to "unlearn ... essentialism" (Epstein & Gillet, 2017, p. 3).

Being able to reflect on the assumed binaries in their discipline, while considering how their cultural identity is constructed, might make students receptive to questioning other types of dichotomies and understand the power relationships involved in translation that might make them privileged in some situations and oppressed in others. For example, when translating a text that includes someone from an oppressed group, students must decide how to translate such experiences. Separating themselves from simplistic dichotomies such as good or bad translations, students might be able to consider the complexity of their discipline and how their decisions will depict specific groups.[8] Furthermore, concepts such as epistemic violence, testimonial injustice, and credibility excess or deficit (Fricker, 2007) could be analyzed and help students reflect on the complex process of translating.

Queer Pedagogy and Allyship

I consider there to be a deep connection between the space created for reflection when translating into one's additional language and allyship for the LGBTQ+ community. First of all, when talking about queering the classroom, the idea is to talk about "a queer space [not just] in terms of sexuality, but also in terms of linguistic practice" (Paiz, 2016, p. 3). This means that "dominant discourses surrounding the notion of the successful college writer and English language user" (Paiz, 2016, p. 3) can also be questioned. In these considerations, the hierarchy between the binary oppositions already mentioned is questioned and problematized, therefore demystifying the figure of native speakers. In my view, this aligns with Trinh's (2022) queer pedagogy, whose objective is to think on how to learn about the process of reading and thinking by disrupting the binarism in doing and thinking. Questioning the notion that only native speakers should translate into their mother tongues is similar to one of the attitudes Nelson (1993) questioned: "Only LGBTQ+ people can teach about LGBTQ+ issues" (cited in Paiz, 2020, p. 6).

From my point of view, showing students that they have other tools besides linguistic knowledge of their L2 empowers them to face L1>L2 translation. Furthermore, emphasizing that native speakers do not have an inherent skill in opposition to nonnative speakers is vital for students as they need to learn about their own language. At Universidad Nacional Autónoma de México (UNAM), where the course I describe in this chapter takes place, most of the students speak Spanish; nevertheless, they could also speak any of the other languages spoken in Mexico. In addition, I consider that linking the assumed binaries in translation can help students perceive how binaries in other realms are not necessarily real as there are not two exclusive positions. Furthermore, becoming aware of the systems of oppression related

8. An example concerning nonbinary identities is Velázquez-Lora (2022b).

to their field helps them reflect on how such systems work in other aspects, such as gender and sexuality.

The course that I am referring to is an academic writing course for translator trainees in their seventh semester (of nine total semesters) at a public university in Mexico City. The syllabus includes translation into English, although students get a workshop with this type of translation only in an elective course in their eighth semester. This writing course is also an elective. Up to this point, translator trainees have already been working with English and Spanish separately in courses about grammar, syntax, or writing, but also together in a contrastive grammar course.

In class, I use an adapted version of the "Get to Know You Sheet 2.0" by Shwarz (2021), which helps me open a space for students to share, if they want to, some personal information (e.g., name, pronouns, interests). I always assume that in my groups there is "at least one trans/nonbinary student" (Conrod, 2019, p. 24) or a student who belongs to one or more identities under the LGBTQ+ umbrella. This aligns with the data from the "First University Survey About the Equality Conditions of the LGBTTTIQ+ Community at UNAM" ["Primera consulta universitaria sobre condiciones de igualdad de género de la comunidad LGBTTTIQ+ en la UNAM"], conducted in 2022. Though students may not belong to the LGBTQ+ community, creating the possibility to express one's sexual orientation or gender identity establishes an environment for building a safe space in the classroom. I also share my name and my pronouns with the whole class and, even if students do not know if I identify or not with any letter under the umbrella, I must be the first ally in the classroom, because we all face different types of oppression even when we belong to similar groups. As I enact allyship by modeling it, they can envision ways they can engage as allies while translating.

Including material written by or related to the LGBTQ+ community is a powerful opportunity to raise awareness and encourage questioning certain binary preconceptions (Trinh & Tinker Sachs, 2023). Importantly, it has been shown that LGBTQ+phobia is based on lack of familiarity with people who belong to this heterogenous group and assumptions that stereotypes and prejudices against LGBTQ+ individuals are true (Rodríguez-Otero & García-Andrés, 2022, pp. 244–245). The educational system has an important role in such a situation as it can be a safe space to raise awareness, reduce stereotyping and prejudice, and build understanding and empathy—all of which are activities that allies can engage with to support the LGBTQ+ community.

Preparing Translators to Be Allies

Regarding the concept of allyship, I follow Shlasko's (2017) definition of it (presented in Footnote 3) where the author also defines allies as people whose "informed, accountable action[s]...contribute...to other people's ability to survive and thrive in a context of inequality" ("What Is Allyship?" para. 3). Here, I consider not only allyship in general but also Trinh's (in press) definition of queer allyship (see Footnote 3).

Working with texts that talk about identities different from cishetero identities might provide opportunities for students to question such prejudices and stereotypes, leading them to become allies. This allyship might spread not only to their task as translators but also to their day-to-day lives as students and their roles in society. Creating a safe space for students to talk about such identities might lead to them sharing their own, and some of them might be part of the LGBTQ+ community. Visibility can be dangerous and complicated (Trinh, 2021); thus, creating a respectful and safe space is key so that students can share who they are and learn from other identities.

When texts include content related to the LGBTQ+ community and they must be translated, it becomes a very important part of the process to research any information that we do not understand. Such a process is not different from the one followed with any other type of text; however, the result might imply very different consequences. Representation is important; when translating a text, by choosing to erase such representation or misrepresenting it, translators make a decision, and they must be accountable for it.

Démont (2018), thinking about how to translate queer literary texts, identified three possibilities: "the misrecognizing translation, the minoritizing translation and the queering translation" (p. 157). Démont underlined the importance of the third type because for him "respecting the queer meaning potential of a text should therefore be a central focus of queering translations, as this practice is instrumental to undoing the strategic erasures or assimilations of misrecognizing or minoritizing translations" (p. 166). Underlining the consequences of these types of translation helps students see how their task as translators is extremely relevant to specific minoritized groups. In addition, these reflections help students consider translation practices such as thick translation or translation critique, as Démont mentions, as a "specific 'queering' stance" (p. 157).

Even if students do not become allies, questioning binaries and including the possibility of different identities in the classroom highlight students' responsibilities for their decisions and show that, as translators, we are accountable for our choices (Baker & Maier, 2011, cited in Vigo, 2019, p. 11). If we decide to depict LGBTQ+ identities without adequate research and without reflecting on the possible strategies to do so and the probable effects of our translation, then we are engaging in an unethical practice. As a community, we can keep each other accountable for our translations, for example, through a "queer critique of existing translations" (Démont, 2018, p. 157).

Nowadays, gender and the way it is translated have gained increased importance in TS (Epstein & Gillet, 2017; López, 2019; Velázquez Lora, 2022a, 2022b, 2023). Nevertheless, the emphasis has been on how to translate gender when translating from English to Spanish. As this is an academic writing course, a possibility is to translate an article that includes direct nonbinary language (López, 2019) such as "Políticas del conocimiento: hacia una epistemología trans*" ["Knowledge Politics: Towards a Trans* Epistemology"] (Radi, 2019) or *Polarización y transfobia: Miradas críticas sobre el avance de los movimientos antitrans y antigénero en México* [*Polarization and transphobia: Critical views on the advance of the anti-trans and anti-gender movements in Mexico*] (Neuhouser et al., 2022). As Spanish and English have different characteristics and the authors use different techniques to unmark gender in some words (e.g., "lxs teóricxs trans*" [Radi, 2019, p. 38], "editore" e "investigadoræ" [Neuhouser et al., 2022, pp. 3, 11]), it would be interesting to see how the authors' intentions are translated. Another exercise could be to translate the inner communication of the university as there are students, professors, and researchers from anglophone countries at the various venues of the university in Mexico and abroad. An example could be to translate the survey mentioned earlier. This information is important for the community, and sharing it would imply a real translation project for their own university, as it includes data about the gender, pronouns, and well-being of the students and employees that belong to the LGBTQ+ community.

Working with L1>L2 translation helps students de-automatize their decisions and focus on the aspect of gender and how it is treated in English. Regardless of their final choices, students must research to learn how to transport these texts to English not only in the linguistic realm but also in the cultural aspects. Students will become accountable for their decisions. Finally, it is expected that knowing that they might share the classroom with a member of the LGBTQ+ community and learning from this group by informing themselves to translate the assigned texts might lead students to be empathetic toward this community and understand that there are power systems behind the beliefs of their own profession and behind constructs such as gender.

By creating safe spaces for students, teachers become allies to their LGBTQ+ students, but by emphasizing how translating decisions do or don't represent the LGBTQ+ community, teachers show students that they can also choose to be allies and how to do it. Going through the stages of analysis to accountability will lead students to action. Translation trainees might be more aware of nongendered vocabulary in English and might become advocates for the LGBTQ+ community. Such advocacy might not only be relevant in texts that already include the voices of the LGBTQ+ community, but also help overcome the invisibilization of such a group if translators actively suggest to their clients certain vocabulary, pronouns, or structures for all types of texts.

Moving Forward

Challenging certain fundamental concepts about translation and languages helps us see in a different light the assumptions about the discipline by showing the power systems behind it. The process of questioning these concepts can also be applied to topics related to the LGBTQ+ community. By adding this type of material to the syllabus, it is possible to think about identity and how it is formed, negotiated, and in some situations constrained by communities and definitions. Giving students the opportunity to take risks in the context of language learning helps create a safe space for them to practice their skills and develop more. This chapter comes as the result of my reflections while teaching this writing course for the first time, thinking about how to improve it, and emphasizing the relevance of L1>L2 translation.

Assuming that just because we translate we become more open to other cultures, beliefs, and ideas in general is not precise. Translators can help with peace treaties, but we can also translate texts that lead to conflicts and war (Baker, 2005). Reflecting on each aspect and what is in between is important for an ethical practice. It is vital to talk about this in an explicit way so that students do not assume that there is a neutral way of translating or that, as established at the beginning of this chapter, just because they work with more than one language and culture, translators are able to overcome essentialisms and the belief that they can see the many sides of these cultures automatically. The ability to understand two or more languages and cultures is a privilege as well as a responsibility, so we need to acknowledge it, because "whenever translators assert that there is no ideology in their translation, what they are doing, arguably, is subscribing to mainstream ideological practices" (Martínez-Carrasco, 2019, p. 49). As translators, we have a social role that "can contribute to (or refrain from) the spread of ideas, stimulate some possible changes in people's behaviours" (Vigo, 2019, p. 11).

Author

Lihit Velázquez-Lora (she/they) has a master's degree in translation from El Colegio de México, an undergraduate degree in English literature from Universidad Nacional Autónoma de México (UNAM), and an undergraduate degree in translation from Universidad Intercontinental. She currently works at UNAM giving EFL and translation courses.

References

Baer, B. J. (2021). *Queer theory and translation studies: Language, politics, desire.* Routledge.

Baker, M. (2005). Narratives in and of translation. *Skase: Journal of Translation and Interpretation, I*(1), 4–13.

Beeby Lonsdale, A. (1996a). La traducción inversa [L1>L2 translation]. In A. Hurtado Albir, (Ed.). *La enseñanza de la traducción.* (pp. 57–78). Universitat Jaume I.

Beeby Lonsdale, A. (1996b). *Teaching translation from Spanish to English: Words beyond words.* University of Ottawa Press.

Byram, M., Gribkova, B., & Starkey, H. (2002). *Developing the intercultural dimension in language teaching: A practical introduction to teachers.* Council of Europe.

Cómitre Narváez, I. (2003). La enseñanza de la traducción inversa (Español-Francés): Realidad profesional y desafío didáctico [Teaching L1>L2 translation (Spanish-French): A professional reality and a didactic challenge]. In R. Muñoz Martín (Ed.), *I AIETI: Actas del I Congreso Internacional de la Asociación Ibérica de Estudios de Traducción e Interpretación* (pp. 383–389). Asociación Ibérica de Estudios de Traducción e Interpretación.

Conrod, K. (2019). Pronouns raising and emerging [Doctoral thesis, University of Washington]. https://linguistics.washington.edu/research/graduate/pronouns-raising-and-emerging

Council of Europe. (2023). Common European Framework of Reference for Languages (CEFR). https://www.coe.int/en/web/common-european-framework-reference-languages/level-descriptions

Crystal, D. (2019). *The Cambridge encyclopedia of the English language.* Cambridge University Press.

de la Cruz Trainor, M. M. (2004). Traducción inversa: Una realidad [L1>L2 translation: A reality]. *Trans: Revista de Traductología, 8,* 53–60. https://doi.org/10.24310/TRANS.2004.v0i8.2963

Démont, M. (2018). On three modes of translating queer literary texts. In B. J. Baer & K. Kaindl (Eds.), *Queering translation, translating the queer: Theory, practice, activism* (pp. 157–171). Routledge.

Dietz, G. (2019). Competencia intercultural [Intercultural competence]. In I. Villegas, G. Dietz, & M. F. Saavedra (Eds.), *La traducción lingüística y cultural en los procesos educativos: hacia un vocabulario interdisciplinar* (pp. 43–65). Universidad Veracruzana.

Epstein, B. J., & Gillet, R. (2017). *Queer in translation.* Routledge.

Fricker, M. (2007). *Epistemic injustice: Power and the ethics of knowing.* Oxford University Press.

Holliday, A. (2006). Native speakerism. *ELT Journal, 60*(4), 385–387. https://doi.org/10.1093/elt/ccl030

Kelly, D. (1997). La enseñanza de la traducción inversa de textos «generales»: Consideraciones metodológicas [Teaching L1>L2 translation in "general" texts: Methodological considerations]. In M. A. Vega & R. Martín-Gaitero (Eds.), *VI encuentros: La palabra vertida. Investigaciones en torno a la traducción* (pp. 175–181). Universidad Complutense.

Ladmiral, J. R. (2004). Dichotomies traductologiques [Translation dichotomies]. *La Linguistique, 40*(1), 25–49.

López, Á. (2019). Tú, yo, elle y el lenguaje no binario [You, Me, Hir, and Non-Binary Language]. *La Linterna del Traductor, 19,* 142–150. http://lalinternadeltraductor.org/n19/traducir-lenguaje-no-binario.html

López-Rocha, S. (2016). Intercultural communicative competence: Creating awareness and promoting skills in the language classroom. In C. Goria, O. Speicher, & S. Stollhans (Eds.), *Innovative language teaching and learning at university: Enhancing participation and collaboration* (pp. 105–111). Research-publishing.net.

Martínez-Carrasco, R. (2019). Social action and critical consciousness in the socialization of translators-to-be: A classroom experience. In M. De Marco & P. Toto (Eds.), *Gender approaches in the translation classroom: Training the doers* (pp. 45–61). Palgrave Macmillan.

Massau, P. (2013). La traducción inversa en el grado de traducción: ¿un mal necesario? [L1>L2 translation in the translation degree: A necessary evil]. In M. T. Tortosa Ybáñez, J. D. Alvarez Teruel, & N. Pellín Buades (Coords.), *XI Jornadas de Redes de Investigación en Docencia Universitaria: Retos de futuro en la enseñanza superior: docencia e investigación para alcanzar la excelencia académica* (pp. 282–295). Universidad de Alicante. http://hdl.handle.net/10045/31305

Newmark, P. (1988). Introduction. In *A textbook of translation.* Prentice Hall.

Neuhouser, J., Argüelles, A., Cruz, R., & Díaz, A. (2022). *Polarización y transfobia: Miradas críticas sobre el avance de los movimientos antitrans y antigénero en México [Polarization and transphobia: Critical views on the advance of the anti-trans and anti-gender movements in Mexico*]. Comun.al.

Paiz, J. M. (2016, August). A call to queer L2 writing. *SLW News.* http://newsmanager.commpartners.com/tesolslwis/issues/2016-10-14/3.html

Paiz, J. M. (2020). *Queering the English language classroom: A practical guide for teachers.* Equinox.

Pokorn, N. K. (2005). *Challenging the traditional axioms: Translation into a non-mother tongue.* John Benjamins.

Proceso de Adquisición de la Competencia Traductora y Evaluación. (2017). In A. Hurtado Albir (Ed.), *Researching translation competence.* John Benjamins.

Radi, B. (2019). Políticas del conocimiento: Hacia una epistemología trans* [Knowledge politics: Towards a trans* epistemology]. In D. Link & M. López Seoane (Eds.), *Los mil pequeños sexos: Intervenciones críticas sobre políticas de género y sexualidades.* EDUNTREF.

Rhodes, C. M., & Coda, J. (2017). It's not in the curriculum: Adult English language teachers and LGBQ topics. *Sage Journal, 28*(3), 99–106.

Rodríguez-Otero, L. M., & García-Andrés, A. (2022). Actitudes negativas e interiorización de mitos hacia las personas trans en estudiantes mexicanas de trabajo social [Negative attitudes and internalization of myths towards trans people in Mexican social work students]. *Interdisciplinaria Revista de Psicología y Ciencias Afines, 39*(2), 229–248.

Santoyo, J. C. (2005). Autotraducciones: Una perspectiva histórica [Self-translation: A historic perspective]. *Meta, 50*(3), 858–867. https://doi.org/10.7202/011601ar

Schleiermacher, F. (2000). *Sobre los diferentes métodos de traducir* [On the different methods of translating] (V. García Yebra, Trans.). Gredos. (Original work published 1813)

Schwarz, A. (2021). *Get to know you sheet 2.0.* https://www.teachingoutsidethebinary.com/classroom-resources

Shlasko, D. (2017). *Trans allyship workbook: Building skills to support trans people in our lives.* Think Again Training.

Spurlin, W. J. (2017). Queering translation: Rethinking gender and sexual politics in the spaces between languages and cultures. In B. J. Epstein & R. Gillet (Eds.), *Queer in translation* (pp. 172–183). Routledge.

Stewart, D. (2000). Poor relations and black sheep in translation studies. *Target, 12*(2), 205–228.

Tomozeiu, D., Koskinen, K., & D'Arcangelo, A. (2018). Introduction. In D. Tomozeiu, K. Koskinen, & A. D'Arcangelo (Eds.), *Intercultural competence for translators* (pp. 1–17). Routledge.

Tomozeiu, D., & Kumpulainen, M. (2018). Operationalising intercultural competence for translation pedagogy. In D. Tomozeiu, K. Koskinen, & A. D'Arcangelo (Eds.), *Intercultural competence for translators* (pp. 18–34). Routledge.

Trinh, E. (2021). Visibility. In K. K. Strunk & S. A. Shelton (Eds.), *Encyclopedia of queer studies in education* (pp. 756–757). Brill.

Trinh, E. (2022). Supporting queer SLIFE youth: Initial queer considerations. In L. J. Pentón Herrera (Ed.), *English and students with limited or interrupted formal education: Global perspectives on teacher preparation and classroom practices* (pp. 209–225). Springer International. https://doi.org/10.1007/978-3-030-86963-2_12

Trinh, E. (in press). Queer allyship in TESOL: We need to ACTS now! *TESOL Journal.*

Trinh, E., & Tinker Sachs, G. (2023). Thinking queer with Vietnamese EFL textbooks. *Critical Inquiry in Language Studies.* https://doi.org/10.1080/15427587.2023.2190524

Velázquez-Lora, L. A. (2022a). Including them and all the rest: Gender-neutral pronouns in EFL class. *Journal of Language and Sexuality, 11*(2), 240–250. https://doi.org/10.1075/jls.20025.vel

Velázquez Lora, L. A. (2022b). Los retos de traducir del inglés al español personajes de género no binario en textos literarios [The challenges of translating literary texts with nonbinary characters from English to Spanish]. *Hesperia: Anuario de filología hispánica, 24*(2), 31–50. https://doi.org/10.35869/hafh.v24i2.4107

Velázquez Lora, L. A. (2023). *Estrategias y alternativas para traducir al español la caracterización de personajes de género no binario en The Mirror Empire de Kameron Hurley* [Strategies and alternatives to translate to Spanish the characteristics of non-binary characters in The Mirror Empire by Kameron Hurley; Master's thesis, El Colegio de México]. https://repositorio.colmex.mx/concern/theses/12579v51v?locale=es

Venuti, L. (1995). *The translator's invisibility: A history of translation.* Routledge.

Vigo, F. (2019). Turning translation training into life training. In M. De Marco & P. Toto (Eds.), *Gender approaches in the translation classroom: Training the doers* (pp. 9–26). Palgrave Macmillan.

Yuste Frías, J. (2005). Didáctica de la traducción inversa español-francés: El fin justifica los medios [Didactics of L1>L1 translation Spanish-French: The end justifies the means]. In J. Yuste Frías & A. Álvarez Lugrís (Eds.), *Estudios sobre traducción: Teoría didáctica, profesión* (pp. 147–170). Servizo de Publicacións da Universidade de Vigo.

Yuste Frías, J. (2014). Realidad profesional de la industria de la traducción y falacia de la competencia nativa [The professional reality of the translation industry and the fallacy of native proficiency] (pp. 77–91). In X. Montero Domínguez (Ed.), *Traducción e industrias culturales: Nuevas perspectivas de análisis*. Peter Lang. https://doi.org/10.3726/978-3-653-04446-1

Educating English Language Teachers on LGBTQIA+S Language Variation and Play for Allyship in Language Courses

Vance Schaefer and Tamara Warhol

"We're all born naked. And the rest is drag" (Charles & Piane, 2014). Just as in the phrases "clothes make the person" and "dressing for the occasion," people adopt and switch between different speech styles and codes to perform identity (Butler, 2002). Speakers possess a linguistic repertoire of various codes and styles from different languages, regional dialects, politeness registers, and sociolects of gender, sexuality, and more. Speakers also alternate between these codes and styles when triggered by different social cues in specific contexts with specific people or for varying effects such as expressing multiple, fluid identities. The LGBTQIA+ community in its diversity also uses an array of codes and styles to express their identities and participate in their communities through enacting in-group membership.

Yet, though learners of English as an additional language (EAL) are often taught linguistic forms demonstrating linguistic competence, they may not be sufficiently taught when and how to use the forms, resulting in weak communicative competence (Canale & Swain, 1980). In particular, they are likely not to be taught LGBTQIA+ varieties of English (e.g., lexicon used in the LGBTQIA+ community, gay male speech patterns), thus impeding their expression of their identities and their participation in EAL classrooms and LGBTQIA+ communities. In response, we advocate a pedagogical framework inclusive of LGBTQIA+ varieties that centers on students' linguistic repertoire and translanguaging skills in the EAL classroom; within such a framework, students may not only use grammatically correct LGBTQIA+ forms but also use these forms appropriately (Canale & Swain, 1980). Instructors gauge learners' communicative repertoires as a starting point and design materials accordingly (3Ds of discovery, design, and doing discussed later in the chapter; Rymes et al., 2016). Through these designs, learners progress through stages from explicit instruction to exploring social issues related to language variation, known as the EXposure process (Schaefer & Warhol, 2020). We adopt an allyship approach where allies find common ground in working together to challenge and combat normative assumptions, including heteronormative assumptions of oneself (cf., Trinh, in press), which all speakers may experience when using marginalized speech styles. To promote allyship, we propose an LGBTQIA+S communicative repertoire framework that embraces all codes and styles and treats them equally, including S for straight, whether the styles are standard/nonstandard variants or straight/LGBTQIA+ variants. In learning about linguistic diversity, learners come to understand that everyone uses language that may not be accepted as "mainstream English" whether LGBTQIA+, gendered, nonnative, or other varieties. We further appeal to all EAL instructors and learners to acknowledge that each person expresses multiple, intersecting, fluid identities indexed by various codes and styles in a society where "it's not easy to be green" (as Kermit the frog sang about it being difficult to be different from others).

This chapter discusses how language teacher educators (LTEs) might introduce English language teachers (ELTs) to a pedagogical framework for teaching LGBTQIA+ English variants, which will improve EAL learners' translanguaging skills and allow for discussions of related social issues. The ultimate objective is to support EAL learners who identify as LGBTQIA+ in more faithfully expressing their identities and more fully participating in various LGBTQIA+ communities, including the EAL classroom, by augmenting their communicative repertoire.

Classroom Setting

We describe the promotion of allyship between ELTs and their students presented in the context of a semester-long course on teaching language variation for U.S. and international students in a master's program in applied linguistics and TESOL or a doctoral program in second language studies at a university in the southeastern United States. Students in this program aim for careers as English or foreign language teachers, researchers in second language acquisition/pedagogy, and/or university professors of English or other languages as an additional language (hereafter referred to as ELTs despite non-English foreign language careers). The majority of students are international, coming from the Middle East, Africa, Central and South America, East Asia, and South Asia. The mix of students with varying social, political, and religious backgrounds and career objectives posed a challenge in addressing LGBTQIA+ codes/styles, forms, translanguaging, and social issues; however, we addressed this potential challenge by encouraging allyship under an LGBTQIA+S communicative repertoire approach.

Student Learning Outcomes

We set the following student learning outcomes (SLOs) for ELTs in the course. By the end of the course, ELTs will be able to do the following:

1. Explain how every speaker employs various codes/styles (e.g., speaking straight is just one variety) presenting multiple intersecting identities.

2. Identify and list codes, styles, and their linguistic forms in the possible communicative repertoires used by some speakers who identify with the LGBTQIA+ community.
3. Identify and describe translanguaging in the LGBTQIA+ community.
4. Describe allyship and advocate for the LGBTQIA+ community in the EAL classroom through concrete teaching methods, lessons, and materials that promote diversity, equity, and inclusivity among all EAL learners.
5. Identify issues that LGBTQIA+ EAL learners may encounter in the English language classroom and in English-speaking communities (cf., Paiz, 2019), for example, linguistic profiling, passing, expressing identity, and participating in various communities.
6. Identify issues that ELTs face when teaching LGBTQIA+ EAL learners.
7. Adopt-adapt teaching approaches, methods, and techniques to create lessons to fulfill the language needs and wishes of LGBTQIA+ EAL learners.

To help LTEs prepare their ELTs in affirming learners' identities in and outside the classroom, this chapter covers the following topics:

- overview of LGBTQIA+S varieties and forms in English and translanguaging
- pedagogical framework for promoting LGBTQIA+S allyship
- sample activities

LGBTQIA+S English Varieties, Forms, and Translanguaging

To educate ELTs about allyship in an LGBTQIA+S communicative repertoire framework, we first discuss key concepts concerning styles, codes, translanguaging, and social issues in the course. We summarize these concepts here to guide LTEs in promoting LGBTQIA+S allyship among ELTs.

A speaker's communicative repertoire may include codes of various languages and speech styles in a language, such as regional dialects, (im)politeness registers of formality, and sociolects (i.e., social dialects) used by diverse social groups that may indicate their generation, neurodivergency, gender, sexuality, and more. Moreover, speakers translanguage among these varieties, adopting different forms in various manners as triggered by various cues (e.g., context, participants) and for various effects. For example, speakers may accommodate their interlocutor and converge toward common codes or styles (i.e., in-group status) or speakers may project an identity of difference by potentially diverging in speech from their interlocutor (i.e., out-group status). Additionally, when the relationship between the speakers is hierarchical, speech styles may diverge to show respect or dominance or converge to express solidarity (Giles et al., 2012). That is, speech styles may vary as shaped by the formality of the situation, calling for polite forms or casual forms. Also, speakers may alternate between styles and codes to express a particular stance (i.e., what they think about what is said, the topic, etc.). Furthermore, speakers may wish to project a particular identity through using a particular code or style or may adopt a particular identity in order to pass in society and enjoy the advantages that generally the most accepted style or code confers (e.g., approval, opportunities, safety).

In order not only to make themselves understood, but also to assert a particular identity and stance (i.e., how a speaker positions themselves to what other people may say), people draw on and use resources from their communicative repertoire (Rymes, 2014). These resources may include a "standard" language variety, which valorizes cisgender, heteronormative codes and styles (e.g., for male-identifying speakers: masculine, deep voice; male intonation patterns; certain facial expressions and gestures; particular lexicon). Yet a "standard" variety rarely is used alone. Instead, people select among and alternate between codes, styles, and other features, including those used by the LGBTQIA+ community. For example, gay males may present more masculine at the workplace and use more stereotypical gay male speech when among other gay men. Traditionally, such selection and alternation among communicative resources has been described as codeswitching (i.e., alternation between sentences), code mixing (i.e., alternation within a sentence), or style shifting, (i.e., alternating between varieties within a language; Ervin-Tripp, 2001); however, it is perhaps more appropriately conceptualized as translanguaging.

Translanguaging has been theorized as the way multilinguals use resources from a single communicative repertoire comprising multiple language varieties; multilinguals strategically select among these language varieties to make meaning appropriate to the sociolinguistic context (García & Li, 2014). Translanguaging as it was originally conceptualized focused on the use of distinct languages and not between styles within one language (e.g., dialects, registers, sociolects) and arose out of the field of multilingual education as a way of protecting the rights of language-minoritized students (García, 2009). Rather than considering multilingual language learners as having deficient language acquisition in a target language, a translanguaging approach affirms learners' practices of alternating between language varieties (Otheguy et al., 2015). Given this social justice agenda, translanguaging offers a lens for considering the intralanguage alternation of other traditionally minoritized groups, such as the LGBTQIA+ community.

Sociolects of sexuality index the identities in the rainbow of the LGBTQIA+S coalition, including S for straight speech, which is just one distinct sociolect that many LGBTQIA+ members also use. The other sociolects of the LGBTQIA+ community are those used by individuals who identify as lesbian, gay, bisexual, transgender, queer or questioning, intersex (physical variation beyond the male-female dichotomy of sexual anatomy), and asexual (i.e., complete or partial lack of sexual attraction or interest), where there may be mixtures and even more variation due to individuality and other factors (Human Rights Campaign, 2023). Additionally, just as speakers may consider general American or mainstream American English often used in news programs to be a White, middle-class midwestern English variety spoken with an accent without any regional dialectal features (Kretschmar, 2004; Wells, 1982, p. 470), some speakers might consider general American as "straight speech" or a cisgender male, heteronormative variety. Moreover, LGBTQIA+ speakers may not use language forms and patterns commonly associated with speakers of the same physical sex. LGBTQIA+ speakers may also not use linguistic forms and patterns commonly associated with speakers of the opposite physical sex (e.g., gay men do not outright imitate straight women in their speech styles; Munson & Babel, 2007), and there are many subvariants with LGBTQIA+ speech styles reflective of an array of subgroups (Podesva et al., 2000). Examination of the language usage of nonbinary speakers (i.e., identifying as neither male nor female), including transgender individuals, within the LGBTQIA+ community shows that stereotypical male and female language forms may be fused while novel linguistic innovations may also be created (see Smakman, 2018, pp. 139–141).

Moreover, speakers' multiple identities undeniably intersect. That is, speakers do not employ only one distinct style but in fact mix or overlap styles in expressing multiple identities simultaneously: a speaker expressing their three identities of being gay, Black, and male wielding African American language and gay male speech as shaped by topic and interlocutor (Cornelius, 2020). Triggered by various factors (e.g., context, participants, goals), LGBTQIA+ speakers may shift between different personas by manipulating linguistic features, as in the case of a gay man indexing a laid-back, fun partier image by switching to different vowels in speech (cf., California vowel shift, where vowels begin to sound like other vowels, e.g., the vowel in *bet* begins to sound like the vowel in *bat*), voice quality, and intonation when interacting with gay friends (Podesva, 2011). They may even try to pass as straight, adopting perceived masculine or neutral forms (Thorpe, 2014). As such, some members of the LGBTQIA+ community may use many gay speech features all the time or some of the time while other LGBTQIA+ members may never use these forms but will likely recognize them. In short, the intersectionality of identities shapes the degree, manner, and timing of the usage of gay speech features (Podesva, 2011). Also, speakers identifying as non-LGBTQIA+ may use or be perceived to use some of these features (e.g., some straight-identifying men having a lisp, high voices, or intonation patterns associated with female speech). Again, we reiterate the LGBTQIA+ communicative repertoires of codes and styles while acknowledging that some features are not monolithic but reflect the diversity of the LGBTQIA+ communities.

LGBTQIA+ Linguistic Features

LGBTQIA+ sociolects differ and may be characterized by variations in phonology, morphology, lexicon, syntax, discourse, pragmatics, and paralinguistics. The gay male accent may employ wider pitch ranges for intonational contours than straight male speech and/or H*L intonational contours (i.e., coarsely put, a fall from a high to low pitch on a syllable) and may hyperenunciate their pronunciation, resulting in nonreduced forms or hyperextended vowels as in *FAAABulous*. Barrett (1997, 2010) noted that such vowels rendered with an H*L intonational contour may cause listeners to perceive a lisp. Additionally, gay male speech may feature differences in vowel duration (Podesva et al., 2000) and pitch range (Smyth et al., 2003). Features of gay male speech may also include overarticulated segments (i.e., vowels, consonants) such as [p], [t], [k] (i.e., longer voice onset times, where the time is longer between the release of aspiration of the [p]/[t]/[k] and the beginning of vocal fold vibration of the following vowel); clearer vowels; and longer [s], clearer [l], nasalization, and s-fronting or the stereotypical archetype of gay male speech of lisping (Smyth, in Thorpe, 2014). Stereotypically, listeners associate perceived higher pitch and exaggerated intonational variation with gay male speech (Rogers & Smyth, 2003). By contrast, female gay speech seems to have more limited stereotyped and observed speech features. Lesbians are noted in comparison to gay men to use a lower voice and less pitch variation (Van Borsel et al., 2013) and are described as masculine being monotone (i.e., restricted pitch range), with variation in some vowels and less clearly produced speech (Munson et al., 2006).

Lexically, gay men may use female language forms such as hedges, boosters, richer or more precise color terms, and "empty" adjectives such as *marvelous* or *adorable* (cf., Barrett, 1997, 2010; Lakoff, 1975). LGBTQIA+ people may use community-specific language forms: *lesbian, gay, bisexual, transgender, queer, intersex, queer/questioning, asexual, butch, femme, bear, otter, top,* and more. Pronouns have been spotlighted more recently with LGBTQIA+ members using *they/them/their* or pronouns that match the gender they identify with and not necessarily their physical sex, or new forms such as *ze, zir,* and more. Gay men may use *bitch* as a loose first, second, and third person pronoun as in *this bitch*; *bitch, you*; and *that bitch,* respectively. *Bitch* along with *she* and *girl* may be used to address any gay male even if that male does not use gay male speech.

There also appear to be discursive, pragmatic, and other linguistic features that characterize LGBTQIA+ speech. For example, many members of the LGBTQIA+ community, such as transgender speakers, may employ particular linguistic strategies concerning gendered words (e.g., *handsome* vs. *beautiful*) and pronouns in the construction of identity (Zimman, 2017). There are also paralinguistic features such as gestures, facial expressions, voice qualities, and more that may be associated with gay male speech (cf., Gerrard et al., 2022). In sum, there are concrete, stereotyped, and observed gay speech features that may be addressed in the EAL classroom.

Pedagogical Framework for Promoting LGBTQIA+ Allyship

Both critical queer pedagogy and the explicit teaching of dialects are relatively new phenomena in English language classrooms (e.g., Paiz, 2019, regarding queer pedagogy; Schaefer & Warhol, 2020, regarding English language dialect instruction). Traditionally, ELTs have focused on using a communicative approach to teach a neutral variety of English, but that "variety" is in reality stereotypical of cisgender, heteronormative, middle-class, White communities (e.g., textbooks; Paiz, 2015; Trinh & Tinker Sachs, 2023). This approach to language teaching neglects how language users draw on communicative repertoires, comprising different languages, dialects, sociolects, paralinguistic cues, and other features to codemix, codeswitch, styleshift, and translanguage (Goodman & Tastanbek, 2021; Rymes, 2014) to present intersectional, fluid identities (Paiz & Coda, 2021). Moreover, it may position the instructor in opposition to their culturally and linguistically diverse students as opposed to building allyship with those students (Nelson, 2009). Thus, this chapter proposes instead teaching novice/future ELTs a communicative repertoire approach based on a framework of boosting awareness of language varieties in general and LGBTQIA+ varieties in particular through (a) explanation/comparison of varieties juxtaposed against "straight varieties" (i.e., LGBTQIA+S approach), (b) variety usage/alternations as pragmatic acts informed by pragmatics teaching (i.e., explicit instruction, raising awareness, discussion, modeling, sufficient input, natural context, practice, feedback; Félix-Brasdefer & Cohen, 2012), and (c) adoption of language variation teaching methods (5Cs [American Council on the Teaching of Foreign Languages, n.d.]; 3Ds [Rymes et al., 2016]; EXposure process [Schaefer & Warhol, 2020]).

Kaiser (2017) noted that sexuality is a reality that cannot be avoided in the EAL classroom and should in fact be acknowledged and met head on, embracing all learners: "A discourse inquiry approach asks students to investigate how linguistic and cultural practices define all sexualities and construct power relations among them" (Nelson, 2009, cited in Kaiser, 2017, p. 13). Sexuality may be considered a taboo discussion topic among students, but it should be explicitly discussed while respecting differences in viewpoints in order to accept LGBTQIA+ communities as a natural part of the larger community (Brown, 1997). Additionally, how and whether ELTs handle LGBTQIA+ language and issues in the EAL classroom impact learners in developing both their first language and second language identities. Language output may be minimized as learners avoid identifying their sexuality by not speaking or by using expected pronouns or referencing expected gendered partners or employing other strategies. Learners may not have the opportunities to practice being themselves in social interactions (Kaiser, 2017). Thus, learners who identify as LGBTQIA+ may need to learn "identity vocabulary" (e.g., *queer, gay, transgender*) and the language used in LGBTQIA+ communities to more faithfully express their identities and more fully participate in LGBTQIA+ communities and the EAL classroom. And if "LGBTQIA+ language" is not included in textbooks and courses, teachers could supplement the curricula to include it.

One approach to discussing language used in the LGBTQIA+ community and promoting allyship is to employ an LGBTQIA+S communicative repertoire approach where every code and style is on equal footing. That is, ELTs and EAL learners recognize that each person speaks several language codes and/or styles (i.e., various forms of one language such as regional dialects, registers, sociolects). Any so-called standard language is merely one such code or style, although likely the variant "authorized" to be used in the classroom and therefore the variant that all other styles and codes are compared to. Instructors and learners can be united and be allies when they negotiate meanings through many intersecting codes and styles to express multiple, fluid identities and stances and translanguage between these codes/styles for pragmatic reasons.

Various pedagogical theories and practices can support the approaches, methods, and techniques to teach the forms of LGBTQIA+S varieties, their functions, translanguaging, and associated issues. We believe modeling and putting theory and research findings into practice are the cornerstones of training ELTs and, as such, demonstrating lessons to ELTs. We now discuss in brief our pedagogical framework to guide LTEs.

The course adopts a three-pronged approach where ELTs examine (1) a particular variety of English, (2) specific sociolinguistic feature(s) and/or issue(s), and (3) pedagogical approaches, methods, techniques, and other topics during each week. To promote LGBTQIA+ allyship, LGBTQIA+S varieties are taught within a framework emphasizing diversity, equity, and inclusion among all language varieties, which informs the teaching/learning of not only LGTBQIA+ varieties but other varieties as well. Additionally, the framework stresses that speakers both mix and switch between varieties and, as such, LGBTQIA+S varieties might be brought up when discussing varieties of gender and ethnicity. The varieties covered in the course include standard, regional varieties, registers, sociolects (e.g., gender, sexuality), marginalized varieties (e.g., African American English), neurodivergent varieties (e.g., monotone, differing pragmatics), youth language, nonnative Englishes, and World Englishes. Additionally, sociolinguistic issues such as language ideology, linguistic profiling, crossing, racism, sexism, bias (cf., *no fats, no fems, no Asians*; BIPOC fetishism; transgender discrimination) are discussed in the course.

We adopt several approaches to facilitate training ELTs and in turn, promote these approaches in their teaching of EAL learners. We utilize a communicative repertoire approach using the 3Ds of discovery, design, and doing (Rymes et al., 2016). Instructors *discover* what linguistic resources of styles, codes, and translanguaging skills their students use (e.g., they learn their students' knowledge and/or usage of various speech styles in English and their awareness of styles, codes, and translanguaging cues/effects). In response, instructors then *design* student learning outcomes and lessons accessing learners' existing codes, styles, and translanguaging in order to augment their codes, styles, and translanguaging skills. Finally, students *do* activities and exercises using their current communicative resources and newly learned ones as part of their communicative repertoire. Under the discovery stage, instructors need to be reflective teachers, consider the efficacy of their lessons, and adopt a do-it-yourself approach in tailoring materials to their students' needs and in implementing lesson delivery approaches that meet students' learning styles and allow them to use their full communicative repertoire. These approaches include a flipped classroom (i.e., lectures or explicit instruction assigned as homework while traditional homework is done during class time) and blended learning (i.e., face-to-face interaction effectively combined with online learning).

As the choice of language variety and translanguaging are pragmatic acts, we reference pragmatics teaching suggesting the promotion of awareness, input, and production practice: explicit instruction, raising awareness, discussion, modeling, sufficient input, natural context, practice, and feedback (Bardovi-Harlig, 2020; Félix-Brasdefer & Cohen, 2012). Within such a pragmatics teaching approach, we employ an EXposure process of learning language varieties (Schaefer & Warhol, 2020), which aligns with the 3D communicative repertoire approach. An EXposure process involves the following steps:

1. ELTs *EXplain* forms and functions of varieties and translanguaging.
2. ELTs/learners then *EXamine* samples of varieties and translanguaging intensively (i.e., short samples).
3. ELTs/learners then *EXperience* these varieties and translanguaging by listening and reading samples extensively (i.e., longer samples).
4. ELTs/learners subsequently *EXperiment* with these varieties and translanguaging by doing activities (e.g., pragmatic-focused task-based learning; Schaefer et al., 2023).
5. Finally, ELTs/learners *EXplore* linguistic and social issues surrounding the use of these varieties and translanguaging.

The order of these steps is not necessarily linear, starting with or returning to steps as needed. For example, under an EXposure process, lessons could focus on the following:

- Exploration of identities with readings on language variation and identity. ELTs/ learners describe themselves and others: perceived/desired identities, language usage (varieties/forms/alternations).
- Examination of (stereotypical) features (lexicon, phonology, syntax, pragmatics, paralinguistics) and functions/styleshifting/translanguaging used by LGBTQIA+ characters in non-English-language (e.g., Japanese with English subtitles) versus English-language media (e.g., *POSE*, *Do I Sound Gay?*), including LGBTQIA+ varieties among World Englishes and marginalized varieties (e.g., African American English). ELTs/learners describe and compare varieties/forms/functions and participate in learning activities: shadowing, lip syncing, dubbing, storytelling, "translating," role-playing, and/or script writing.
- Experimentation with teaching LGBTQIA+ varieties/features/alternation in flipped, blended, do-it-yourself lessons. ELTs choose features/varieties; create materials/lessons; demonstrate lessons; and justify chosen features/varieties, teaching techniques, and materials.

Additionally, we mine entertainment media and social media as they both provide a rich range of materials to document and teach language styles, codes, and translanguaging, and are likely already an accessible and influential part of most learners' lives and perhaps their first exposure to LGBTQIA+ communicative repertoires. Entertainment media exploits LGBTQIA+ codes and styles to portray LGBTQIA+ speakers, perpetuating stereotypical speech patterns in both the LGBTQIA+ and non-LGBTQIA+ communities. However, ELTs and EAL learners must consider that though entertainment media seems to reflect actual language usage, it may at times do so incorrectly, exaggeratedly, or insufficiently. Instructors need to be selective when choosing materials in order to ensure representation of learners given that many EAL learners are not of European ancestry and therefore may not share similar viewpoints and issues with European American characters, for example. Given the diversity of the LGBTQIA+ communities and intersecting identities, instructors need to perhaps search for and use media representative of their EAL demographics. As such, ELTs might consider using scenes from a show like *POSE* (Murphy et al., 2018–2021), which focuses on marginalized BIPOC groups like African American and Latina/Latino LGBTQIA+ people and the intersectionality of identities (e.g., race, ethnicity, sexuality) reflected in language usage (e.g., words such as *y'all* and *ain't*; accents). Additionally, the show depicts racism, sexism, and bias against transgender persons, in addition to health issues (e.g., HIV), poverty, homelessness, drugs, and other issues that concern many in the LGBTQIA+ community.

Flexibility in learners' language is called for in developing the pragmatic competence to adapt "language to the situation and to changes of direction in conversation and discussion" (Council of Europe, 2020, p. 138), reflecting social relationships, stances, and identities. In response, the following measurable, concrete SLOs referencing Bloom's taxonomy guide ELTs in creating SLOs for teaching their EAL learners.

By the end of the course, EAL learners will be able to do the following:

1. Identify, differentiate, list, and describe the features of LGBTQIA+S varieties.
2. Identify (dis)similarities between LGBTQIA+S varieties and other varieties.
3. Identify, list, and describe the cues and effects of translanguaging.
4. Identify and describe issues surrounding the usage of LGBTQIA+ varieties and translanguaging.
5. Compare and contrast LGBTQIA+S varieties in Englishes with LGBTQIA+S varieties in other languages (e.g., first language of EAL learners).

To summarize, to educate ELTs and EAL learners as LGBTQIA+ allies, the objectives of lessons focus on the following:

- Students describe their identities and how they may express them in their native language and/or in their second language. Given the potential sensitivity of outing themselves as a member of the LGBTQIA+ community or other marginalized communities (e.g., nonvisible ethnicity, caste, religious affiliation, psychiatric disabilities, socioeconomic background), this activity can be done online anonymously as a group and/or privately though accounts between the LTE and ELTs.
- ELTs explore through readings and videos the forms and functions of English varieties, sociolinguistic issues, and pedagogical theory and practices informing their teaching of LGBTQIA+S varieties.
- ELTs examine stereotypical features of LGBTQIA+S varieties and translanguaging among the community. ELTs watch and analyze language usage in media. ELTs participate in activities that they would use with their EAL learners, such as shadowing, lip syncing, dubbing, storytelling, role playing, rescripting the dialogue in other varieties, and improvising.
- ELTs experiment with teaching LGBTQIA+S varieties, translanguaging, and social issues. They create SLOs, lesson plans, activities, and materials. They demonstrate lessons and share materials. They justify their chosen features/varieties/issues and their teaching approaches/methods/techniques. ELTs employ the 3Ds, EXposure process, pragmatics teaching approaches, as well as flipping, blending, pragmatics-focused task-based learning, scaffolding exercises, DIY materials, and/or adopt-adapt material approach.

Sample Activities

We offer the following sample activities as resources shaped by our pedagogical framework to be used by LTEs to teach ELTs and, in turn, by ELTs to teach EAL learners. These activities might also serve as templates to create similar activities for different varieties, linguistic features and/or forms, and issues. Additionally, these activities may serve as course assignments or a final project (e.g., a portfolio of teaching materials on a particular variety or issue, a final paper discussing a variety and/or issues and possible teaching approaches/methods/techniques, a research proposal, a project of the students' choosing).

We recommend that LTEs remind ELTs that variety exists among the LGBTQIA+ community and their language usage and that entertainment media may not necessarily accurately reflect LGBTQIA+ language usage. As such, LTEs and ELTs need to keep in mind that some forms and functions are stereotypes and to be careful about laughing at rather than laughing with some portrayals in media. To further create an open, relaxed atmosphere, we suggest LTEs focus on linguistic forms and functions and remind ELTs that the objective of doing these activities is not to judge LGBTQIA+ people or non-LGBTQIA+ people. Moreover, we teach within the framework of allyship where all speakers have particular speech styles that may not be part of the mainstream and where ELTs need to consider the needs of their EAL learners.

Activity: Survey

ELTs/EAL learners anonymously describe themselves and/or others in a survey. They discuss their perceived and desired identities and language usage to reflect those identities in terms of varieties/forms/alterations. This survey might be anonymous as respondents may not wish to share their identity, opinions, and so on. Questions might include: What are your identities? What varieties of your first language do you use? When, where, how, to whom, and why do you use these varieties? What varieties are you aware of in your native language that other people like friends, family, TV characters, and others might use? How might members of the LGBTQIA+ community speak in your native language?

Activity: LGBTQIA+ Paralinguistic Features, Voice

Please watch the following actors read the same script twice in different styles:

- "Video Combination 1" (www.youtube.com/watch?v=fWrBCOIDY-I)
- "Video Combination 2" (www.youtube.com/watch?v=rkbxKhntg-4)

Then, answer the following questions:

1. How do the two readings/performances differ for each actor?
2. Which reading/performance might appeal to consumers for this pretend Sydney tourism campaign ad? Why?
3. How do other groups talk? Women? Straight men? European Americans? U.S. Southerners? Others? How might this influence consumers depending on the product?

(Source: Gerrard et al., 2022)

Activity: Gay Voice/Accent

Please watch the documentary (or trailer) *Do I Sound Gay?* (Thorpe, 2014), and answer the following questions:

1. What are the features of a so-called gay voice that are discussed in the video or that you may have noticed?
2. Why do the men who appear in the video think they sound gay (i.e., cause, features)? What do they feel about sounding gay?
3. What do they do to try to change their "gay voice"?

Activity: LGBQIA+ Identity Terms

1. Read the descriptions for members of the LGBTQIA+ community as defined on the GLAAD website (https://www.glaad.org/reference/terms) or a similar website.
2. How familiar are you with these terms? Have you heard them before? Did you misunderstand them before reading the website?
3. How might LGBTQIA+ people use these terms? Which are derogatory words you are familiar with? What terms have LGBTQIA+ people reclaimed? Why do you think they reclaimed them?
4. How familiar are you with other terms used in the LGBTQIA+ community (e.g., *bear, otter, twink, rice queen, femme, butch*? Please create a lesson in a respectful manner to teach these terms and their associated culture concerning the LGBTQIA+ community as a whole and/or a particular subgroup within the LGBTQIA+ community (i.e., terms represented by the letters in the acronym, such as lesbian, gay, and bisexual). Instructors might do a Google search for terms and websites and/or assign students to do so.

Activity: Pronouns

English uses the pronouns *she* and *he* to refer to a person (and as an insult *it*). There are also newer pronouns such as *ze and zir*. Some languages also encode gender into other parts of speech (e.g., adjectives, as in the French *belle/beau*). Some languages like Mandarin Chinese use [ta] pronounced with tone one for *he, she,* and *it* in spoken speech although the characters differ in writing: 他, 她, 它, respectively. Some languages (e.g., Spanish, French) drop pronouns more often than English but may encode gender into other grammatical forms. English and other languages may use other terms that may or may not be gendered to stand in for third person pronouns (e.g., *older brother/sister, uncle/aunt,* job title, status) or other gender-binary relationships (e.g., *mother–father, uncle–aunt, sister–brother*). Instructors might use a scene from entertainment media such as the following; these scenes are sometimes publicly available as a short video on YouTube, or a few minutes could be shown via subscription streaming platforms if in line with copyright laws.

Please watch this scene from Season 4 Episode 1 of *Kim's Convenience* (Fecan et al., 2016–2021) concerning transgender pronouns used by the character Eva, and answer/discuss the following questions.

1. What pronouns were mentioned in the scene? How are these pronouns used? What pronouns might you or someone you know use in English or your first language? Why?
2. What has confused Mr. Kim about the usage of these pronouns?
3. What did Janet find politically incorrect about Mr. Kim's words and behavior? Are you more like Mr. Kim or Janet?
4. How might you use this scene to teach EAL learners?

Activity: BIPOC LGBTQIA+ Communities

Please watch scenes from *POSE* (Murphy et al., 2018–2021) and answer/discuss the following questions.

1. Describe the characters and the setting.
2. Observe the following features:
   a. Hyperarticulation
   b. Usage of the words *bitch, girl, she* among the characters
   c. African American English: *y'all, ain't,* double negatives, *be*-verb (absence or uninflected form), *done* (as a helping verb), intonation, and so on. Which forms are also used in other varieties of English?
   d. Translanguaging (situations, forms)
3. Try to use African American English forms as the language of the EAL classroom in order to understand imposing "standard" language onto speakers of marginalized varieties.
4. Work with a scene and listen, analyze, shadow, lip sync, dub, perform, and role-play/improv the lines and/or script the following scene. "Translate" the dialogue into another variety of English and examine the effect.
5. What social issues appear in the scenes (e.g., sexuality, gender, race, transgenderism)?
6. Which social issues may concern non-LGBTQIA+ EAL learners?

Activity: LGBTQIA+ Varieties in Other Languages

1. Listen to the following scene from the Japanese TV series *What Did You Eat Last Night?* (Abe, 2019). Without understanding Japanese, what possible features do you notice that may characterize LGBTQIA+ speakers (e.g., paralinguistic features such

as body language, facial expressions; suprasegmental features such as intonation)? Discuss other features that might not be noticed by non-Japanese speakers.

2. Look at the following terms potentially used by the LGBTQIA+ community in Japanese society. Japanese gay terms: *gai-sen* (preference for non-Japanese), *fuke-sen* (preference for "old" men), *nonke* (straight), *gei* (gay), *dooseiaisha* (homosexual), *neko* (passive role), *o-tachi* (active role), *tachi-neko* (masculine-acting passive role), and so on. What insights into the Japanese LGBTQIA+ community might these terms provide? How might these terms be translated into English (e.g., translated or untranslated terms in subtitles)? What LGBTQIA+ terms are you familiar with in other languages?

3. What kind of lesson might you create to teach LGBTQIA+ linguistic forms/usages and terms for L1 speakers of English learning Japanese or for L1 speakers of Japanese learning English as informed by the scene and/or Japanese gay terms?

Activity: Interview or Guest Speaker

1. Interview a member (perhaps an EAL learner) of the LGBTQIA+ community about LGBTQIA+ identity, speech patterns, issues, and so on. Instructors can determine questions with the class beforehand and guide discussion during the interview.

2. Interview a nonmember of the LGBTQIA+ community about LGBTQIA+ identity, speech patterns, issues, and so on. Again, instructors can determine questions with the class beforehand and guide discussion during the interview.

Activity: Cisgender, Heteronormative English as an Additional Language Lessons

Examine dialogues and units/lessons in EAL textbooks and consider the following questions.

1. How might the lessons exclude LGBTQIA+ EAL learners?

2. How might you revise the dialogues and lessons to be more inclusive?

3. How might you make the dialogues and lessons "homonormative"?

4. How might dialogues and lessons exclude EAL learners with other types of identities (e.g., religious, socioeconomic, rural/urban)? How might you remedy this situation?

You might consider situations and spaces relevant to LGBTQIA+ communities. You might consider the usage of gay speech (e.g., lexicon such as *gorgeous*, *lovely*; being camp).

Activity: Planning a Lesson on Language Variation

1. Plan a lesson on teaching LGBTQIA+ varieties, particularly linguistic form(s), translanguaging, and/or social issue(s).
2. What teaching approaches, methods, and/or techniques might best support your lesson on LGBTQIA+ varieties?
3. What linguistic forms and/or social issues might apply to non-LGBTQIA+ speakers (e.g., intersectionality of identities, race/ethnicity, bisexuality, sexism [*sissy, throw like a girl, butch*], linguistic profiling, passing)?
4. Referencing your lesson teaching LGBTQIA+ varieties, plan a lesson on teaching another variety of English, its particular linguistic form(s), translanguaging, and/or social issue(s) (e.g., African American English, women's language, men's language, language in religion).

Activity: Supporting LGBTQIA+ Students in the English as an Additional Language Classroom

1. Read Paiz (2019) and/or Kaiser (2017).
2. How might you incorporate Paiz's and/or Kaiser's observations and suggestions into your teaching to help EAL learners more fully, safely, and comfortably participate in the EAL classroom, mainstream society, and particular communities, including of course LGBTQIA+ communities.
3. How might these observations and suggestions about LGBTQIA+ EAL learners inform the learning experience of other types of non-LGBTQIA+ EAL learners, including other marginalized groups such as visible minorities?

Lastly, concerning student reactions to learning about LGBTQIA+ varieties, issues, and teaching ideas, responses to some of the activities were interestingly matter of fact. For example, students noted and described the contrasting facial features and gestures of gay male speakers and noted how they might be similar to those of women. They enjoyed watching TV scenes from *Kim's Convenience* on pronoun usage and expressed their own initial confusion and so could relate to Mr. Kim. They offered thoughts on how textbooks can be biased. In sum, they actively participated in these activities and responded to discussion questions just as they had for other varieties introduced in the course.

Overall, the students were respectful and did not show any resistance or negative pushback. This may have been influenced by an allyship approach of teaching LGBTQIA+ varieties as one type of English among many varieties (e.g., African American Englishes, gendered language, youth language, neurodivergent varieties, regional dialects, language in religious contexts) in a course on teaching language variation in English. Additionally, this adopted allyship approach juxtaposed "straight English" as just one variety reflecting heteronormative, cisgender speech styles against LGBTQIA+ varieties in an LGBTQIA+S approach. Students mentioned in general that they were happy to have learned about variation in language and felt it to be useful to them as speakers of English and teachers of English.

Conclusion

In conclusion, we advocate educating ELTs on LGBTQIA+ language variation within an allyship approach. This approach allies LGBTQIA+ varieties with other marginalized varieties in educating ELTs and then EAL learners about language in order to better express their many fluid and intersecting identities and communicate competently with a wide range of speakers in multiple communities. Furthermore, an allyship approach champions LGBTQIA+S varieties on an equal footing with straight variants being touted and examined as just one language style among many in the communicative repertoire of speakers. Lastly, an allyship approach accesses the potential richness of linguistic variation in order to better understand LGBTQIA+ varieties in English through contrast with other languages. Our suggested activities promote this allyship approach to better appeal to both LGBQIA+ and non-LGBTQIA+ ELTs and EAL learners. We hope LTEs and ELTs will adopt this allyship approach in teaching English and reach out to those teaching other foreign languages or language courses (e.g., linguistics, language arts). We further hope LTEs and ELTs will act to explore LGBTQIA+ varieties and experiment with teaching methods, techniques, and activities as suggested by an allyship approach.

Trinh (in press) challenges us to "ACTS" now, in other words, to become "**a**llies who work together to challenge **c**ommon heteronormative assumptions of oneself to **t**hink queer and provoke actions in relational **s**ystems of support." Implicit in ACTSing is creatively, or queerly, using language as a means to disrupt heteronormative systems and continually re-co-constructing these systems to be inclusive of all intersectional identities. In the English language classroom, ACTS also implies providing ELTs and EAL learners with the language to ACTS, that is to say, challenge heteronormative language ideologies and express their identities. This chapter specifically offers ELTs and EAL learners resources to ACTS. In adopting a communicative repertoire approach, instructors queer pedagogy by highlighting and promoting the use of different varieties to express multiple and intersectional identities.

Authors

Vance Schaefer (he, him, his), PhD in second language studies, Indiana University, is an associate professor of applied linguistics and TESOL in the Department of Modern Languages at the University of Mississippi. His work focuses on pronunciation pedagogy, teaching language variation, and translation pedagogy, informed by his experience as a language instructor (EFL/ESL, Japanese as a foreign language), learner, and translator in Japan, Thailand, Taiwan, Morocco, and the United States.

Tamara Warhol (she, her, hers) is an associate professor of applied linguistics and TESOL in the Department of Modern Languages at the University of Mississippi. A discourse analyst, her research explores professional discourse, language variation, language and linguistics pedagogy, and language teacher education.

References

Abe, M. (Executive Producer). (2019). *What did you eat yesterday?* [TV series]. Shochiku.

American Council on the Teaching of Foreign Languages. (n.d.). *World-readiness standards for learning language.*http://www.actfl.org/publications/all/national-standards-foreign-language-education

Bardovi-Harlig, K. (2020). Pedagogical linguistics: A view from L2 pragmatics. *Pedagogical Linguistics, 1*(1), 44–65. https://doi.org/10.1075/pl.19013.bar

Barrett, R. (1997). The "homo-genius" speech community. In A. Livia & K. Hall (Eds.), *Queerly phrased: Language, gender, and sexuality* (pp. 181–201). Oxford University Press.

Barrett, R. (2010). Markedness and styleshifting in performances by African American drag queens. In M. Meyerhoff & E. Schleef (Eds.), *The Routledge sociolinguistics reader* (pp. 514–531). Routledge.

Brown, H. D. (1997). The place of moral and political issues in language pedagogy. *Asian Journal of English Language Teaching*, 7, 21–33.

Butler, J. (2002). *Gender trouble*. Routledge.

Canale, M., & Swain, M. (1980). Theoretical bases of communicative approaches to second language teaching and testing. *Applied Linguistics, 1*(1), 1–47.

Charles, R., & Piane, L. (2014). Born naked [Song]. On *Born naked*. RuCo.

Cornelius, B. R. (2020). *Talkin' Black and sounding gay: An examination of the construction of a multiplex identity via intraspeaker variation* [Doctoral dissertation, University of South Carolina]. https://scholarcommons.sc.edu/etd/6147

Council of Europe. (2020). *Common European framework of reference for languages: Learning, teaching, assessment—Companion volume.*

Ervin-Tripp, S. M. (2001). Variety, style-shifting, and ideology. In P. Eckert & J. R. Rickford (Eds.), *Style and sociolinguistic variation* (pp. 44–56). Cambridge University Press.

Fecan, I., et al. (Executive Producers). (2016–2021). *Kim's convenience* [TV series]. Thunderbird Films.

Félix-Brasdefer, J. C., & Cohen, A. D. (2012). Teaching pragmatics in the foreign language classroom: Grammar as a communicative resource. *Hispania, 95*(4), 650–669. https://www.jstor.org/stable/41756418

García, O. (2009). *Bilingual education in the 21st century: A global perspective*. Wiley/Blackwell.

García, O., & Li, W. (2014). *Translanguaging: Language, bilingualism and education*. Palgrave Macmillan.

Gerrard, B., Morandini, J., & Dar-Nimrod, I. (2022). Gay and straight men prefer masculine-presenting gay men for a high-status role: Evidence from an ecologically valid experiment. *Sex Roles, 88*, 119–129. https://doi.org/10.1007/s11199-022-01332-y

Giles, H., Bonilla, D., & Speer, R. B. (2012). Acculturating intergroup vitalities, accommodation and contact. In J. Jackson (Ed.), *Routledge handbook of language and intercultural communication* (pp. 244–259). Routledge.

Goodman, B., & Tastanbek, S. (2021). Making the shift from a codeswitching to a translanguaging lens in English language teacher education. *TESOL Quarterly, 55*(1), 29–53. https://doi.org/10.1002/tesq.571

Human Rights Campaign. (2023). *Resources: Glossary of terms.* https://www.hrc.org/resources/glossary-of-terms

Kaiser, E. (2017). LGBTQ+ voices from the classroom: Insights for ESOL teachers. *CATESOL Journal, 29*(1), 1–21.

Kretschmar, W. A., Jr. (2004). Standard American English pronunciation. In E. W. Schneider, K. Burridge, B. Kortmann, R. Mesthrie, & C. Upton (Eds.), *A handbook of varieties of English: Vol. 1: Phonology* (pp. 257–269). Mouton de Gruyter.

Lakoff, R. (1975). *Language and woman's place.* Harper and Row.

Munson, B., & Babel, M. (2007). Loose lips and silver tongues, or, projecting sexual orientation through speech. *Language and Linguistics Compass, 1*(5), 416–449. https://doi.org/10.1111/j.1749-818X.2007.00028.x

Munson, B., McDonald, E. C., DeBoe, N. L., & White, A. R. (2006). The acoustic and perceptual bases of judgments of women and men's sexual orientation from read speech. *Journal of Phonetics, 34*(2), 202–240. https://doi.org/10.1016/j.wocn.2005.05.003

Murphy, R., et al. (Executive Producers). (2018–2021). *POSE* [TV series]. Brad Falchuk Teley-Vision, Ryan Murphy Television, 20th Television, FXP.

Nelson, C. D. (2009). *Sexual identities in English language education: Classroom conversations.* Routledge.

Otheguy, R., García, O., & Reid, W. (2015). Clarifying translanguaging and deconstructing named languages: A perspective from linguistics. *Applied Linguistics Review, 6*(3), 281–307. https://doi.org/10.1515/applirev-2015-0014

Paiz, J. M. (2015). Over the monochrome rainbow: Heteronormativity in ESL reading texts and textbooks. *Journal of Language and Sexuality, 4*(1), 77–101. https://doi.org/10.1075/jls.4.1.03pai

Paiz., J. M. (2019). Queering practice: LGBTQ+ diversity and inclusion in English language teaching. *Journal of Language, Identity, & Education, 18*(4), 266–275. https://doi.org/10.1080/15348458.2019.1629933

Paiz, J. M., & Coda, J. E. (2021). Reflections on intersectionality in applied linguistics and world languages education: Lessons learned and paths forward. In J. M. Paiz & J. E. Coda (Eds.), *Intersectional perspectives on LGBTQ+ issues in modern language teaching and learning* (pp. 261–277). Palgrave MacMillan.

Podesva, R. J. (2011). The California vowel shift and gay identity. *American Speech, 86*(1), 32–51. https://doi.org/10.1215/00031283-1277501

Podesva, R. J., Roberts, S. J., & Campbell-Kibler, K. (2000). Sharing resources and indexing meanings in the production of gay styles. In K. Campbell-Kibler, R. J. Podesva, S. J. Roberts, & A. Wong (Eds.), *Language and sexuality: Contesting meaning in theory and practice* (pp. 175–189). CSLI.

Rogers, H., & Smyth, R. (2003). Phonetic differences between gay- and straight-sounding male speakers of North American English. In M. J. Solé, D. Recasens, & J. Romero (Eds.), *Proceedings of the 15th International Conference of Phonetic Science* (pp. 1855–1858). Universitat Autònoma de Barcelona.

Rymes, B. (2014). *Communicating beyond language: Everyday encounters with diversity.* Routledge.

Rymes, B., Flores, N., & Pomerantz, A. (2016). The Common Core State Standards and English learners: Finding the silver lining. *Language, 92*(4), e257–e273. https://doi.org/10.1353/lan.2016.0080

Schaefer, V., Sedeek, Y., & Warhol, T. (2023). Developing the linguistic repertoire and translanguaging skills of learners of Arabic as an additional language. *Journal of the National Council of Less Commonly Taught Languages, 34*, 265–344.

Schaefer, V., & Warhol, T. (2020). There ain't no doubt about it: Teaching EALs to recognize variation and switch/shift between varieties and registers is crucial to communicative competence. *TESOL Journal, 11*(3), Article e504. https://doi.org/10.1002/tesj.504

Smakman, D. (2018). *Discovering sociolinguistics: From theory to practice*. Palgrave.

Smyth, R., Jacobs, G., & Rogers, H. (2003). Male voices and perceived sexual orientation: An experimental and theoretical approach. *Languages in Society, 32*(3), 329–350. https://doi.org/10.1017/S0047404503323024

Thorpe, D. (Director). (2014). *Do I sound gay?* Impact Partners, Little Punk, ThinkThorpe.

Trinh, E. (in press). Queer allyship in TESOL: We need to ACTS now! *TESOL Journal.*

Trinh, E., & Tinker Sachs, G. (2023). Thinking queer with Vietnamese EFL textbooks. *Critical Inquiry in Language Studies*. https://doi.org/10.1080/15427587.2023.2190524

Van Borsel, J., Vandaele, J., & Corthais, P. (2013). Pitch and pitch variation in lesbian women. *Journal of Voice, 27*(5), 656.E13–656.E16. https://doi.org/10.1016/j.jvoice.2013.04.008

Wells, J. C. (1982). *Accents of English: Vol. 3 Beyond the British Isles*. Cambridge University Press.

Zimman, L. (2017). Transgender language reform: Some challenges and strategies for promoting trans-affirming, gender-inclusive language. *Journal of Language and Discrimination, 1*(1), 8–105. https://doi.org/10.1558/jld.33139

Fostering Gender and Sexual Diversity in TESOL Educator Classrooms: A Teacher Educator's Allyship Through Classroom Interaction

Andrew Seibert

Being an ally of any oppressed group has been defined as "a person who is a member of the dominant or majority group who works to end oppression in his or her personal and professional life through support of, and as an advocate with and for, the oppressed population" (Washington & Evans, 1991, p. 195). Indeed, Reason and Davis (2005) agreed that an ally of any minority group is an individual who uses their privileged identities to challenge systems of oppression affecting the oppressed group. So being an ally to the queer community can be actively using one's privileged identities to challenge systems of oppression affecting LGBTQ+ individuals (DeTurk, 2011), working to create a more inclusive and equitable society for all. Additionally, a queer ally in educational spaces may be one whose role is constructed through daily school experiences and involves a conscious taking-up of an ally positionality/identity in specific moments and in specific encounters with others (Vicars & Toledo, 2021).

A language educator who is an ally to the queer (LGBTQ+) community may be primarily associated with adopting an inclusive lens (Smith, 2018), which involves incorporating LGBTQ+ literature, history, and perspectives into language teaching materials and lesson plans as part of an inclusive curriculum design. However, it is essential to recognize that being an ally goes beyond merely embracing inclusivity. It also entails combating heterosexism (Blackburn & Smith, 2010) and questioning norms surrounding gender and sexual identity and their complex intersections with racial, socioeconomic, age, and linguistic identities. This deeper level of allyship involves challenging existing power structures, advocating for marginalized voices, and dismantling discriminatory practices in educational settings. By confronting and questioning these normative boundaries, allies contribute to creating safer, more empowering, and truly inclusive learning environments for all students, regardless of their gender or sexual identities. Part of challenging the status quo regarding gender and sexual identities is emphasizing intersectionality, highlighting the interconnectedness of

LGBTQ+ identities with other aspects of students' lives, such as race, ethnicity, class, and ability. Furthermore, cultivating allyship is an ongoing, evolving process that involves constant reflection and action to combat cisgenderism and heteronormativity both within and beyond the confines of the classroom environment (Trinh, in press). This approach ensures that discussions about gender, sexual, and other identity norms are nuanced and comprehensive.

A teacher educator (TE) in particular may embody the same strategies of queer-inclusive pedagogies as a teacher ally, which may involve engaging their preservice teachers (PSTs) in an inclusive curriculum design that includes open and honest dialogue (Steck & Perry, 2016), addressing prejudice and discrimination (Goldstein & Davis, 2010), connecting theory to practice, introducing and modeling critical inquiry around gender and sexual identity matters (Case et al., 2020), modeling inclusive language (Linley et al., 2016), and engaging in active self-reflection (Blanchard et al., 2018). The TESOL TE in the study described in this chapter embodies many of these virtues that a strong LGBTQ+ ally possesses. By employing these strategies, the TE fosters an environment where his TESOL PSTs engage with him in challenging identity norms, ultimately becoming advocates for inclusive and affirming TESOL classrooms.

Literature Review

Despite the global advancements in social acceptance and legal recognition of LGBTQ individuals, deeply rooted homophobias and transphobias persist in U.S. society (Martin & Kitchen, 2020). Teacher education programs can be heteronormative, and LGBTQ+ issues are often marginalized in the education of preservice teachers (Dykes & Delport, 2018). However, scholars call for teacher education programs to prioritize LGBTQ issues as crucial and integral components of discussions on social justice education (Brant & Willox, 2022; Clark, 2010; Sherwin & Jennings, 2006), including language teacher education programs (Brochin, 2019). Though most preservice teachers will undoubtedly be cisgender and straight, it is important for TEs to prepare PSTs to become allies of queer students and colleagues. However, efforts to integrate discussions of gender and sexual diversity in teacher education programs have resulted in some preservice teachers' attempts to depoliticize ally work in education and distance themselves from addressing gender and sexuality issues (Shelton et al., 2019; Smith, 2018).

Research on the teaching and learning of gender and sexual diversity (GSD) pedagogies in teacher education is extensive and began in the early 1980s (Mitton-Kukner et al., 2016; Petrovic & Rosiek, 2003). Research focused on GSD teacher education comes in a variety of forms, from individual course sessions or modules devoted to GSD pedagogies (Mitton-Kukner et al., 2016; Petrovic & Rosiek, 2003) to research about whole GSD courses (Staley & Blackburn, 2023) to analysis of course materials (Benson et al., 2014; Cahnmann-Taylor et al., 2022; Clark, 2010). GSD pedagogies have been written about from courses that take it as their core topic (Staley & Leonardi, 2016) and as part of broader equity- and diversity-framed courses (Athanases & Larrabee, 2003; Butler, 1999; Schmidt et al., 2012), from planned instruction on GSD (Kitchen & Bellini, 2012) to organic moments where GSD is discussed on the spot (Kumashiro, 2004). However, research shows that teacher education programs that address GSD tend to overlook the topic of GSD in PSTs' student teaching or practicum experiences, while other types of diversity trainings are better integrated (e.g., race/ethnicity trainings; Sherwin & Jennings, 2006).

Language arts, literacy, and literature teacher education are the most common education contexts for GSD research. Other content areas include science, physical education, and social studies. The vast majority have taken place in U.S. contexts, and a few outside the United States have been in EFL contexts (e.g., Barozzi & Ojeda, 2014; Mojica & Castañeda-Peña, 2021), but no studies in a U.S. context were found to have investigated a TESOL teacher education context, which shows a need for research in such contexts.

A broad purpose of the empirical work included in GSD research in teacher education investigates what GSD-focused work looks like and/or how PSTs respond. The overwhelming majority of data collected across empirical qualitative classroom studies is oral (classroom, group discourse, and interviews) and written work mostly in the forms of reflective journaling (Cahnmann-Taylor et al., 2022; Hermann-Wilmarth, 2010; Hyland, 2010; Schmidt et al., 2012; Staley & Leonardi, 2016).

The studies focusing on oral discourse investigated what the structure of discourse did to PSTs in the space or how PSTs structured discourse to accomplish a stance toward GSD in education. For example, Hyland (2010) investigated through classroom dialogue how a group of PSTs expressed and challenged each other's contradictory discourses about teaching for social justice. Similarly, Shelton et al. (2019) worked to understand the ways that PST group interactions in a particularly volatile focus group worked to verbally define and categorize teaching and what it means to be a queer ally. Schmidt et al. (2012) examined the values and experiences PSTs bring to their university education that shape their interaction with queer curricula via classroom dialogue. Hermann-Wilmarth (2010) investigated whether the opportunity to practice dialogue around issues that have traditionally caused resistance or silence can inform how students approach those topics when they arise in their future classrooms. Though these studies show how PST classroom discourse is structured around GSD training, no studies show how TEs embody LGBTQ allyship with their PSTs. Therefore, this study explored how a TESOL TE engaged his PSTs through LGBTQ allyship.

The Study

In general, the findings from the GSD in teacher education literature show that dialogue between PSTs and their TEs has great potential to challenge thinking, evaluate contributions, and problematize taken-for-granted ideologies with respect to an individual's gender and/or sexual identity. Given the lack of such teacher education classroom studies in language education, particularly TESOL PST contexts, the study described here sought to answer the following research question: How does a TESOL TE show LGBTQ+ allyship in preparation of preservice TESOL teachers for GSD in the classroom?

Context and Participants

The context for this study was a TESOL PST seminar course that was held in conjunction with a field experience or student teaching internship in a K–12 TESOL setting. The goals of the one-credit seminar course were to process, reflect on, and enhance the benefits of TESOL

PST's K–12 field experiences. One of the explicit aims of the course was to create a collaborative professional development group of TESOL practitioners that focused on reflective practice concerning PSTs' experiences in their K–12 classroom field placements and their professional educator growth. Members supported each other by addressing professional concerns in preparation for student teaching (Crookes, 2003).

In his 2022–2023 seminar syllabus, the TE, Thomas, stated the following: "Using a sociocultural approach that views development as mediated through language and tools (Vygotsky, 1978), we will establish habits that promote verbal reflection, inquiry, and critical academic reflection in writing." Thomas characterized these habits of reflective practice as essential for PSTs' success on key program assessments and in dialogues with other educators. Indeed, every class session began with a community circle where TESOL PSTs were given a prompt related to that day's topic. Students shared their thoughts on the prompt or on exciting, new, or strange happenings in their placements. This type of discourse data in GSD PST contexts has been referred to as "fishbowl conversations" (Staley & Leonardi, 2016, p. 215). After obtaining informed consent from the TESOL PSTs and the TE, I collected classroom discourse and PSTs' weekly written exit tickets from the first session to the sixth session. The sixth session was devoted to the topic of queer inquiry and GSD in K–12 TESOL spaces and is the source of data for this chapter.

PSTs read Coda (2018) and watched Coghill-Behrends's (2010) webinar in preparation for the class session. These assigned sources of information examined the impact of incorporating queer perspectives, identities, and experiences into language teaching, emphasizing the importance of creating a safe and accepting space for LGBTQ+ students. Offering queer-inclusive pedagogies and GSD training as a separate, one-off course topic or module is a common way for TEs to integrate GSD-focused topics into their courses (e.g., Benson et al., 2014; Mitton-Kukner et al., 2016).

Thomas was a White, Catholic-raised, cisgender, heterosexual male who had been in his teacher educator role for over 8 years. In his role, he taught two seminar courses per semester for TESOL and world language educators, and he supervised groups in their K–12 field placements. The cohort of students in his undergraduate TESOL seminar course consisted of 15 students, with 13 cisfemales and 2 cismales who were all in their junior year at a large, public university in the midwestern United States. Though the cohort boasted a full classroom of people interacting with one another, only a select few students were included in the discourse data for this chapter. The main participants of this session were the main actors throughout the data corpus (the first five sessions + this sixth session).

Method

Using the audio recording of the class session, I manually transcribed the classroom data from the session into an Excel spreadsheet (see Table 1). When transcribing, I used capital letters and punctuation to aid me in better conveying how each utterance was said in context—especially when it came to false starts and word/grammatical mistakes in the online language processing/production that occurred in this classroom space. All speakers were multilingual, and fluent English speakers; yet, as the transcript reveals, nonstandard grammar and missing words were common in these participants' speech. I used a consistent formatting style, punctuation, and timestamps across the whole-class dialogue turned transcript. Transcription of the 1-hour-and-50-minute class session resulted in 221 turns at talk.

Table 1. Transcription Spreadsheet Column Headings

A	B	C	D	E	F
Turn at talk	Timestamp	Speaker	Text	TE-PST unit	Analysis

Note. TE = teacher educator; PST = preservice teacher.

I went through the transcript to identify segments of dialogue where the TE was meaningfully engaging with a PST or group of PSTs in classroom dialogue on matters related to gender and sexuality and identity more broadly. These TE-PST units resulted in 13 total meaningful interactions across the 221 turns at talk. For space purposes, four representative interactions are analyzed and discussed. The four classroom dialogue excerpts included in the following section show the TE engaging a PST in classroom talk about gender and sexual identity in TESOL spaces. The proceeding discussion section identifies the ways the TE forged LGBTQ+ allyship through these classroom dialogic encounters with his TESOL PSTs.

Findings

The findings presented here are based on excerpts from interactions between Thomas, the TESOL TE, and the PSTs engaged in discussions about curriculum design, cultural sensitivity, and the incorporation of GSD into language instruction. The excerpts provide valuable insights into the educators' perspectives, experiences, and approaches in promoting LGBTQ+ inclusivity in TESOL classrooms. "The authors" that Thomas references are Coda (2018) and Coghill-Behrends (2010). Many turns at talk are long and somewhat rambling. For space purposes, some of the turns have been pared down to just the essential dialogue (to the analysis) that was spoken. Clipped dialogue is signified by an ellipses (...) in the transcribed excerpts.

Excerpt 1

Excerpt 1 follows a short interaction between Thomas and a gay TESOL PST named Trent, where Trent exclaims that TESOL educators can be students' cultural ambassadors to tell/show sexually minoritized students that they can be who they want to be in the U.S. context: "We can be the person who is like, you know you're in America now. You can be who you want to be" (Trent, turn 151).

Excerpt 1: There are legal protections, there are choices, there's language now.		
Turn	**Speaking**	**Text**
158	Thomas	So the TESOL curriculum gives space for that as a part of understanding some of the cultural mores or norms of the U.S. ... there are legal protections, there are choices, there's language now.
159	Trent	Because if they are coming from anywhere that is not South Africa or Taiwan, every other country is gonna say uh no sorry. And we get a lot of kids from those continents and so we should talk about it.
160	Thomas	Yeah, it has implications for the curriculum. And as many of you have probably realized or have seen, we don't have textbooks so the curriculum is very much driven by what you or your mentor decide or are given freedom to do. Or whatever they feel that they can add to whatever the mainstream teachers do.

In Turn 158, Thomas affirms that the PSTs all agree that teaching culture is part of what TESOL curriculum is. He then lists positive aspects of being in the United States as a sexual or gender minority. By remarking on these considerations in the classroom dialogue, Thomas shows ways of promoting inclusivity and understanding for students from different cultural backgrounds. When Trent brings up the issue of students coming from countries other than South Africa or Taiwan facing potential obstacles or rejections (Turn 159), Thomas responds by agreeing that inserting instruction on cultural norms around gender and sexuality has implications for the TESOL curriculum. By acknowledging and discussing this concern raised by Trent, Thomas is encouraging in Turn 160, saying that because most PSTs in their placements do not have textbooks, creative inclusion of content is an important tool that TESOL educators have in their pedagogical repertoire.

Excerpt 2

Excerpt 2 directly follows Excerpt 1. Margo brings up the topic of gender equality in the curriculum, saying that from her perspective, issues of gender equality are more explicitly discussed in the classroom compared to LGBTQ+ issues. She shares her experience in a high school with a large population of Somalian students, teaching them about differences in gender roles in Somalia compared to the United States, which may be a "more accepted way in curriculum." Margo expresses concern that there is less explicit discussion about LGBTQ+ issues, and she wonders how students from different countries might perceive this kind of instruction.

Excerpt 2: Let's go deeper.		
Turn	**Speaking**	**Text**
161	Margo	… I feel like that we already kind of do that in a different way in a kind of more accepted way in curriculum with issues of gender equality. I feel that that is something highlighted a lot more than LGBT issues. I was in a high school last semester and we had a large population of Somalian students and the gender roles in Somalia for women are a lot different but my
162	Thomas	Than what you would expect in
163	Margo	Than what we would expect here like the equality and stuff. Like how Trent was saying oh you can have a lesson and be like hey in America, this is ok this is ok.… And I feel like it like that conversation happens a lot less than the way we so explicitly talk about equality of genders in the United States. In my class, we had explicit discussions like men and women are equal. You can get jobs you have equal this like that was a lot more explicitly stated and instructed and like those young girls like in the classroom I'm not like sure what they were thinking but I think they might see it as being different from the country where they are from and I know there are countries where students come from where there is a disparity between equality of genders …
164	Thomas	… Another way to think of it is well let's go deeper. What educational opportunities were available in Somalia? Let's say for your father and your mother, and you could be like there could be many for both they may not be the same or they may not be positioned equally. So it's not that there is or there isn't it could be having students investigate well what do I see in these opportunities even with gender itself thinking the United States context …
165	Margo	But I feel like the inclusivity that is talked about like LGBT issues still aren't as present because for example in like every ESL Pinterest classroom and also in my own mentor's classroom, it's decorate the room with tons of flags of different countries and let them know that we are all like loved here because we all come from different places … But let's kind of back away or ignore the identity aspect or maybe not outwardly say yes I agree or no I don't by placing a Pride flag or something in the room …

Turn	Speaking	Text
166	Thomas	So, a central question our director asks is who is excluded? And so like can students themselves, are they able to understand and define or investigate well who's not here? Um and the flags might be able to give a start. Like well who is represented? And how do you see that? Oh students from Somalia because of the flag. Well what about a student who was born in the United States? How are they represented? And then you go into gender. We have what we know but for most of us there could be something beyond our immediate experience that can be added to do that. And for our students, it's very possible to have them either explain to us because they are quite knowledgeable or they are the ones who can do the inquiring and learn for themselves

Thomas engages with Margo's observations and tries to encourage her to think deeper about the issue. In Turn 164, he suggests considering the educational opportunities available to individuals based on their gender in different contexts, such as Somalia and the United States. By asking Margo to investigate what her students see in these opportunities, Thomas encourages Margo to explore the complexities of gender issues with her students and their impact on TESOL education. Furthermore, in Turn 166, Thomas uses Margo's contribution in Turn 165 about ESL classrooms being decorated in the world's flags to remark how such a classroom decor practice might allow students to critically examine what sort of representation might be missing. He suggests that his PSTs engage their students in learning about individuals not in their immediate experience, which may include in some cases students teaching teachers or teachers learning alongside their students by developing sensitivity to gender and sexually diverse individuals.

Excerpt 3

In Excerpt 3, Trent, the only out queer person in the 15-person cohort, reveals his experience of encountering a derogatory remark by an ESL student.

Excerpt 3: I'm not gonna let it go.		
Turn	**Speaking**	**Text**
104	Trent	I had a kid and in a different past placement too say we were teaching him something and he said "dude, that's gay" and I literally looked at him ... like I never I'm never gonna go and be like "No, no, ehh wrong!" I didn't do that. I looked at him and said "If you can tell me why that's gay, I'll let it slide" and then I said "What do you think? Why is this—why is this lesson gay?" And he goes "I don't know." And I said "Exactly, but I need you to tell me why you said that." And he goes "It's just cause it's what people say." I'm like "Ok well maybe we don't say that anymore because it's not a nice thing to say when gay people are around you."
184	Thomas	How do you make space to disrupt the practice when an elementary school student says something and that's not the norm of our school or our classroom? And I'm not gonna let it go, and I'm not gonna punish the child, so what do I do?

In this interaction, Trent shares a challenging experience he had with a student using the phrase "that's gay" to express displeasure. Instead of directly reprimanding the student, Trent took a different approach. He engaged the student in a conversation, asking him to explain why he used that phrase, challenging the student's understanding of its meaning. Trent emphasized to the ESL student the importance of being mindful of using hurtful language, especially when it may impact others negatively, such as gay people who could be present in the classroom.

Later in the class session, Thomas reflected on Trent's experience, seizing this teaching moment and asking a reflective question about how to handle such situations when elementary school students use inappropriate language that goes against the inclusive norms of the school or classroom. Thomas's question implies the need to create a space to address such behaviors in a way that promotes learning and understanding rather than punishment.

Excerpt 4

In this excerpt, the initial conversation (Turns 187–195) revolves around a global perspective of LGBTQ+ inclusion in ELT with an English class in Taiwan that incorporates LGBTQ+ themes using the book *Love Simon* as part of the curriculum. Favua shares information about how the class discusses the book, its themes, and the gay couple in the story, which allows for open-ended discussions. Then, Thomas (in Turn 190) draws PSTs' attention to a handout asking them pointed questions about incorporating gender and sexual diversity into language instruction and brings up questions about how teachers teach aspects of grammar, vocabulary, and culture in the class. This seems like an attempt to connect the topic of LGBTQ+ content to broader language instruction and its benefits in teaching language and culture.

Excerpt 4: Something very real.		
Turn	**Speaking**	**Text**
187	Favua	I recently read about an English class in Taiwan an EFL class, since 2019 the gender equity education act was passed in Taiwan so we can talk about LGBTQ stuff in Taiwan now in class and the English teacher used the book *Love Simon*
188	Qi	Mmhhmm mmhhmm
189	Favua	Yeah there's a movie about the book. In the English class, they used the book to read and learn English and asked comprehension questions, but they also have open-ended discussions about the theme and the gay couple in the book.
190	Thomas	So can I have you look at numbers 6, 7 and 8? Describe how teachers teach aspects of grammar, describe how teachers teach vocabulary, describe how teachers teach culture. What I'm hearing is that by reading that book as part of the curriculum that was actually a means for teaching English language, the grammar, vocabulary, the culture of this
191	Favua	Right.
192	Thomas	Social context.
193	Favua	mmhhmm
194	Thomas	And these functions of language and being human.
195	Favua	I know that they learn the grammar and the vocabulary in the first class and in the second class they have discussions about the content. The first make sense of the words then the second class, they have discussion about the novel and the plot.
196	Thomas	It's content-embedded language instruction except the content here is not some decontextualized social studies topic of like American Reconstruction, which are valid, but here it's something very real.
197	Favua	Mmhhmm yeah
198	Thomas	Um that students can add information to and it is sanctioned by the government. They are actually giving teachers creative space to do content-based instruction given these themes and topics.
199	Favua	Mmhhmm
200	Thomas	Thank you for sharing that. It sounds like this is something other people recognize and would say yeah this is great literature great content.

In Turn 196, Thomas recognizes Favua's contribution as content-embedded language instruction. He recalls other pedagogical examples of content instruction that, although possibly relevant to English learners in the United States, would be less relatable content to English learners in Taiwan ("decontextualized social studies topic"). Here, Thomas calls discussions around same-sex relationships in the wake of Taiwan's gender equity education act "something very real," meaning more relatable to students because it is a reality closer to their lives, and so a topic to which students themselves can add knowledge and insight. Thomas again points his TESOL PSTs toward the freedom of content inclusion in TESOL spaces. Thomas concludes the interaction by showing gratitude to Favua for mentioning this important approach of including LGBTQ+ perspectives in ELT.

Discussion

Thomas emerges as a passionate and committed LGBTQ+ ally, evident through various characteristics he embodies in his role as a TESOL TE. First, his decision to include a module of GSD in language education spaces shows him using his privileged identity as a straight TE to expose the TESOL PSTs to social justice training that he saw as missing during their TESOL practicum. His inclusive curriculum design is a testament to his dedication to promoting LGBTQ+ inclusivity in language education. In Excerpt 1, Thomas recognizes the importance of cultural sensitivity and legal rights for individuals from diverse backgrounds, showcasing his efforts to create a curriculum that embraces and respects the sexual identities and genders of all learners. By incorporating these considerations into the TESOL curriculum, Thomas fosters an environment where students from sexually minoritized backgrounds feel seen and affirmed, empowering them to be their authentic selves in the U.S. context. This finding also reaffirms that teachers need to build a safe or positive space to explore the complexities of GSD with their students (Kearns et al., 2014).

Engaging in open and honest dialogue and introducing and modeling critical inquiry around gender and sexual identity matters are other hallmarks of allyship (Case et al., 2020; Steck & Perry, 2016), and Thomas demonstrates this open, honest, critical dialogue in Excerpt 2. When Margo raises concerns about the limited discussion of LGBTQ+ issues compared to gender equality in local TESOL curriculum, calling into question the perceived appropriateness of the topic in K–12 TESOL classrooms, Thomas engages with her observations in a supportive and encouraging manner. He urges her to explore the complexities of gender roles in different cultural contexts, fostering her critical thinking and empathy. By inviting such conversations, Thomas shows allyship by creating a space for constructive dialogue about gender matters, thus challenging preconceived notions and encouraging his PSTs to approach gender and sexual identity matters with sensitivity and understanding. Engaging in such open discussions encourages exploration through discourses of difference, as advocated by previous scholars (Britzman, 1995; Trinh, 2022) in the context of classroom discourse.

Reducing sexual prejudice and discrimination is a core aspect of what it means to be an ally (Goldstein & Davis, 2010). In Excerpt 3, Thomas addresses how a teacher may confront LGBTQ+ prejudice and discrimination in a K–12 setting in an effort to reduce offensive comments and promote understanding for ESL students. When Trent shares his experience with a student using derogatory language, Thomas seizes the teaching moment to reflect on how to disrupt harmful practices without resorting to punishment. By encouraging PSTs to engage in a compassionate conversation with such a student, Thomas models an approach that addresses discriminatory behavior with empathy and educational intent. This not only empowers Trent as an educator but also sends a strong message to the PSTs about the importance of advocating for inclusivity and understanding in the face of prejudice. By enacting allyship with his teaching practice, Thomas reflects advocacy (Tompkins et al., 2017) in the teacher education classroom in order to address hate speech in the K–12 TESOL classroom.

Thomas further demonstrates his allyship as an educator by connecting theoretical or hypothetical instances of GSD to classroom practice, as seen in Excerpt 4. By referencing authors Coda (2018) and Coghill-Behrends (2010), he encourages his PSTs to engage in a deeper exploration of LGBTQ+ topics in the curriculum. Thomas's emphasis on content-embedded language instruction and GSD's relevance to students' real-life experiences reflects his commitment to making language education more meaningful and inclusive for learners. By connecting theory to practice, Thomas equips the PSTs with the tools to be effective advocates for LGBTQ+ inclusivity in their future classrooms.

Thomas's active self-reflection is a driving force behind his allyship. Active self-reflection provides a mechanism by which TEs and PSTs "provide candid and real-time responses as they begin to look within themselves to determine which of their own practices may or may not be culturally or ethically responsive" (Blanchard et al., 2018, p. 349). In interviews with me, Thomas consistently evaluated his own positionality and how his identities were implicated in his teaching, as he sought new critical methods to improve and better support the PSTs. In his reflections on Trent's experience with a student's derogatory language, Thomas demonstrates his willingness to critically assess his responses and explore alternative approaches. This commitment to continuous growth and learning empowers the PSTs to be more effective allies, adapting and refining his approach to promote LGBTQ+ inclusivity in TESOL education.

In conclusion, Thomas exemplifies the characteristics of an LGBTQ+ ally through his inclusive curriculum design, open and honest dialogue, efforts to address prejudice and discrimination, introduction of critical inquiry, modeling of inclusive language, connection of theory to practice, and active self-reflection. As a TESOL TE, Thomas's commitment to promoting LGBTQ+ inclusivity empowers his PSTs to become compassionate and effective educators who will strive to create affirming and supportive learning environments for all students, regardless of their gender or sexual identity. His dedication to allyship sets a powerful example for the broader TESOL community, encouraging educators to embrace diversity and actively work toward fostering inclusive classrooms.

Recommendations for Teacher Educators and Researchers Working in Gender and Sexual Diversity Language Education Contexts

TEs play a vital role in advancing LGBTQ+ allyship among preservice teachers. Therefore, it is important for them to promote open dialogue on gender and sexual identity matters in language education, encouraging critical inquiry about gender and sexual identities (Nelson, 2006). Addressing prejudice and discrimination with empathy, they can model inclusive approaches that avoid punitive measures and promote critical thinking. To ensure cultural and ethical responsiveness, continuous self-reflection is crucial for adapting and refining teaching methods, ultimately fostering LGBTQ+ inclusivity in the classroom. By connecting theoretical concepts of GSD to practical classroom instruction and integrating LGBTQ+ topics in the curriculum, TEs can create a more inclusive learning environment reflecting students' real-life experiences.

Researchers also contribute significantly to LGBTQ+ allyship in language teacher education. It is significant for future researchers to conduct further research on the impact of LGBTQ+ allyship, exploring how it influences PSTs' attitudes and practices. Investigating the long-term effects of inclusive curriculum design and critical inquiry on pedagogical approaches is essential to understand how the effects of social justice training persist in language teachers' classroom practices. Understanding how active self-reflection develops effective LGBTQ+ allies among TEs is vital for promoting cultural and ethical responsiveness in language education. Additionally, researchers should identify best practices for integrating critical language awareness and queer theory/pedagogy into language teacher education. By designing studies that investigate the implementation of transformative pedagogies such as these into language teacher education, researchers can identify strategies to help teachers and TEs foster social justice and equity in diverse language classrooms. These collaborative efforts between TEs and researchers will create more inclusive and supportive learning environments for LGBTQ+ students, promoting positive change and queer allyship in future language education.

Author

Andrew Seibert is a PhD candidate in multilingual language education at The Ohio State University, where he teaches preservice teachers. His dissertation project explores TESOL and world language education preservice teachers learning critical pedagogies, including queer theory.

References

Athanases, S. Z., & Larrabee, T. G. (2003). Toward a consistent stance in teaching for equity: Learning to advocate for lesbian-and gay-identified youth. *Teaching and Teacher Education, 19*(2), 237–261. https://doi.org/10.1016/S0742-051X(02)00098-7

Barozzi, S., & Ojeda, J. R. G. (2014). Discussing sexual identities with pre-service primary school English-language teachers from a Spanish context. *Perspectives in Education, 32*(3), 131–145.

Benson, F. J., Smith, N. G., & Flanagan, T. (2014). Easing the transition for queer student teachers from program to field: Implications for teacher education. *Journal of Homosexuality, 61*(3), 382–398. https://doi.org/10.1080/00918369.2013.842429

Blackburn, M. V., & Smith, J. M. (2010). Moving beyond the inclusion of LGBT-themed literature in English language arts classrooms: Interrogating heteronormativity and exploring intersectionality. *Journal of Adolescent & Adult Literacy, 53*(8), 625–634. https://doi.org/10.1598/JAAL.53.8.1

Blanchard, S. B., King, E., Van Schagen, A., Scott, M. R., Crosby, D., & Beasley, J. (2018). Diversity, inclusion, equity, and social justice: How antibias content and self-reflection support early childhood preservice teacher consciousness. *Journal of Early Childhood Teacher Education, 39*(4), 346–363. https://doi.org/10.1080/10901027.2017.1408722

Brant, C. A., & Willox, L. (2022). Are we all doing it? Addressing LGBTQIA+ topics in teacher education. *Teaching and Teacher Education, 116*, Article 103746. https://doi.org/10.1016/j.tate.2022.103746

Britzman, D. P. (1995). Is there a queer pedagogy? Or, stop reading straight. *Educational Theory, 45*, 151–165. https://doi.org/10.1111/j.1741-5446.1995.00151.x

Brochin, C. (2019). Queering bilingual teaching in elementary schools and in bilingual teacher education. *Theory Into Practice, 58*(1), 80–88. https://doi.org/10.1080/00405841.2018.1536917

Butler, K. L. (1999). Preservice teachers' knowledge and attitudes regarding gay men and lesbians: The impact of a cognitive educational intervention. *American Journal of Health Education, 30*(2), 126.

Cahnmann-Taylor, M., Coda, J., & Jiang, L. (2022). Queer is as queer does: Queer L2 pedagogy in teacher education. *TESOL Quarterly, 56*(1), 130–153. https://doi.org/10.1002/tesq.3044

Case, K. A., Rios, D., Lucas, A., Braun, K., & Enriquez, C. (2020). Intersectional patterns of prejudice confrontation by White, heterosexual, and cisgender allies. *Journal of Social Issues, 76*(4), 899–920. https://doi.org/10.1111/josi.12408

Clark, C. T. (2010). Preparing LGBTQ-allies and combating homophobia in a US teacher education program. *Teaching and Teacher Education, 26*(3), 704–713. https://doi.org/10.1016/j.tate.2009.10.006

Coda, J. (2018). Disrupting standard practice: Queering the world language classroom. *Dimension*, pp. 74–89.

Coghill-Behrends, W. (2010, November 10). Willkommen, bienvenido, bienvenue, you are welcome here. *YouTube*. https://www.youtube.com/watch?v=UPw49EM8nHo

Crookes, G. (2003). *A practicum in TESOL: Professional development through teaching practice.* Cambridge University Press.

DeTurk, S. (2011). Allies in action: The communicative experiences of people who challenge social injustice on behalf of others. *Communication Quarterly, 59*(5), 569–590. https://doi.org/10.1080/01463373.2011.614209

Dykes, F. O., & Delport, J. L. (2018). Our voices count: The lived experiences of LGBTQ educators and its impact on teacher education preparation programs. *Teaching Education, 29*(2), 135–146. https://doi.org/10.1080/10476210.2017.1366976

Goldstein, S. B., & Davis, D. S. (2010). Heterosexual allies: A descriptive profile. *Equity & Excellence in Education, 43*(4), 478–494. https://doi.org/10.1080/10665684.2010.505464

Hermann-Wilmarth, J. M. (2010). More than book talks: Preservice teacher dialogue after reading gay and lesbian children's literature. *Language Arts, 87*(3), 188–198.

Hyland, N. E. (2010). Intersections of race and sexuality in a teacher education course. *Teaching Education, 21*(4), 385–401. https://doi.org/10.1080/10476210.2010.495769

Kearns, L. L., Mitton-Kukner, J., & Tompkins, J. (2014). LGBTQ awareness and allies: Building capacity in a bachelor of education program. *Canadian Journal of Education/Revue canadienne de l'éducation, 37*(4), 1–26.

Kitchen, J., & Bellini, C. (2012). Addressing lesbian, gay, bisexual, transgender, and queer (LGBTQ) issues in teacher education: Teacher candidates' perceptions. *Alberta Journal of Educational Research, 58*(3), 444–460.

Kumashiro, K. K. (2004). Uncertain beginnings: Learning to teach paradoxically. *Theory Into Practice, 43*(2), 111–115.

Linley, J. L., Nguyen, D., Brazelton, G. B., Becker, B., Renn, K., & Woodford, M. (2016). Faculty as sources of support for LGBTQ college students. *College Teaching, 64*(2), 55–63. https://doi.org/10.1080/87567555.2015.1078275

Martin, A. D., & Kitchen, J. (2020). LGBTQ themes in the self-study of teacher educators: A queer review of the literature. In J. Kitchen, A. Berry, S. M. Bullock, A. R. Crowe, M. Taylor, H. Guðjónsdóttir, & L. Thomas (Eds.), *International handbook of self-study of teaching and teacher education practices* (pp. 589–610). Springer.

Mitton-Kukner, J., Kearns, L. L., & Tompkins, J. (2016). Pre-service educators and anti-oppressive pedagogy: Interrupting and challenging LGBTQ oppression in schools. *Asia-Pacific Journal of Teacher Education, 44*(1), 20–34. https://doi.org/10.1080/1359866X.2015.1020047

Mojica, C. P., & Castañeda-Peña, H. (2021). Helping English language teachers become gender aware. *ELT Journal, 75*(2), 203–212. https://doi.org/10.1093/elt/ccaa076

Nelson, C. D. (2006). Queer inquiry in language education. *Journal of Language, Identity & Education, 5*(1), 1–9.

Petrovic, J. E., & Rosiek, J. (2003). Disrupting the heteronormative subjectivities of Christian pre-service teachers: A Deweyan prolegomenon. *Equity & Excellence in Education, 36*(2), 161–169.

Reason, R. D., & Davis, T. L. (2005). Antecedents, precursors, and concurrent concepts in the development of social justice attitudes and actions. *New Directions for Student Services, 110*, 5–15.

Schmidt, S. J., Chang, S. P., Carolan-Silva, A., Lockhart, J., & Anagnostopoulos, D. (2012). Recognition, responsibility, and risk: Pre-service teachers' framing and reframing of lesbian, gay, and bisexual social justice issues. *Teaching and Teacher Education, 28*(8), 1175–1184. https://doi.org/10.1016/j.tate.2012.07.002

Shelton, S. A., Barnes, M. E., & Flint, M. A. (2019). "You stick up for all kids": (De)politicizing the enactment of LGBTQ+ teacher ally work. *Teaching and Teacher Education, 82*, 14–23. https://doi.org/10.1016/j.tate.2019.03.001

Sherwin, G., & Jennings, T. (2006). Feared, forgotten, or forbidden: Sexual orientation topics in secondary teacher preparation programs in the USA. *Teaching Education, 17*(3), 207–223.

Smith, M. J. (2018). "I accept all students": Tolerance discourse and LGBTQ ally work in US public schools. *Equity & Excellence in Education, 51*(3–4), 301–315. https://doi.org/10.1080/10665684.2019.1582376

Staley, S., & Blackburn, M. V. (2023). Troubling emotional discomfort: Teaching and learning queerly in teacher education. *Teaching and Teacher Education, 124*, Article 104030. https://doi.org/10.1016/j.tate.2023.104030

Staley, S., & Leonardi, B. (2016). Leaning in to discomfort: Preparing literacy teachers for gender and sexual diversity. *Research in the Teaching of English, 51*(2), 209–229.

Steck, A. K., & Perry, D. R. (2016). Fostering safe and inclusive spaces for LGBTQ students: Phenomenographic exploration of high school administrators' perceptions about GSAs. *Journal of LGBT youth, 13*(4), 352–377. https://doi.org/10.1080/19361653.2016.1185759

Tompkins, J., Kearns, L. L., & Mitton-Kükner, J. (2017). Teacher candidates as LGBTQ and social justice advocates through curricular action. *McGill Journal of Education, 52*(3), 677–697.

Trinh, E. (2022). Supporting queer SLIFE youth: Initial queer considerations. In L. P. Herrera (Ed.), *English and students with limited or interrupted formal education: Global perspectives on teacher preparation and classroom practices* (pp. 209–225). Springer International.

Trinh, E. (in press). Queer allyship in TESOL: We need to ACTS now! *TESOL Journal.*

Vicars, M., & Van Toledo, S. (2021). Walking the talk: LGBTQ allies in Australian secondary schools. *Frontiers in Sociology, 6*, Article 611001. https://doi.org/10.3389/fsoc.2021.611001

Vygotsky, L. (1978). Interaction between learning and development. *Readings on the Development of Children, 23*(3), 34–41.

Washington, J., & Evans, N. J. (1991). Becoming an ally. In N. J. Evans & V. A. Wall (Eds.), *Beyond tolerance: Gays, lesbians, and bisexuals on campus* (pp. 195–204). American Association for Counseling and Development.

Cultivating Critical Love in Professional Organizations: A Queering Approach for English Language Teaching Leaders

Ethan Trinh, Luciana de Oliveira, and Bruno Andrade

Sexuality is both absent and present in schools (Epstein et al., 2003). Sexualities that deviate from the norm are—often tacitly rather than overtly—repressed in educational spaces such as schools, classrooms, professional organizations, conferences, and online. Sexuality is not given; it is a product of negotiation and struggles (Weeks, 1986). Sexuality, thus, is the result of diverse social practices that give meaning to human activities and to "struggles between those who have the power to define, and those who resist" (Weeks, 1986, p. 26). Therefore, the study of (hetero)normalization of sexuality needs to take on a critical perspective toward fundamental normative frameworks of professional organizations as "a dynamic set of social relations" (Butler, 2009, p. 162).

Further, language classrooms have been deemed dominated by a heteronormative framing of identities (Liddicoat, 2009). Heteronormativity in the language classroom is the (re)affirmation and (re)presentation of heterosexuality as the only acceptable sexual identity in life and society, while homosexuality is deemed othered and unaccepted (L. Nelson, 1999). Stuck, inspired, and determined to explore in what ways professional organizations could disrupt this heteronormative frame in English language teaching (ELT), we write this chapter to (re)introduce the concept of critical love with hope to guide professional organizations to build allyship with queer individuals in their own spaces. The purpose of this chapter is not to ask queer individuals to *come out* to colleagues and administrators in professional organizations; instead, it asks how the administrators and colleagues *come in* to break the circle of normality (Trinh, 2019, 2020b), to become insiders, allies, huggers, listeners, and advocates with queer individuals who are always outsiders in heteronormative conversations.

The term *queerness* could be understood in multiple ways. Queer, an inclusive term embracing lesbian, gay, bisexual, transgender, and questioning, among other sexualities that are emerging (LGBTQ+), is used to describe abuse (Halperin, 1997), othering and ostracization (Paiz, 2019), and objectification to dehumanize a person (Nussbaum, 1995). Though it is a contested term, queerness invites openness and possibilities to disrupt cisheteronormativity[1] and categories deemed "normal versus abnormal," "good versus bad," or binary ways of doing, thinking, and being in the world, which is a product of social (re)creation and (re)regulation of sexual identity (Rubin, 1984). As such, queerness in queer theory offers a resistance to normalcy (Halperin, 2003) and confronts dichotomies between gay/straight, homosexuality/heterosexuality, and heteronormativity/homonormativity[2] that perpetuate injustices in personal and professional lives.

The three of us (two who identify as queer and one a cisgender female) working in different contexts (Vietnam, Brazil, United States) come to this space together to think together about ways to disrupt the dichotomies and ontological assumptions (i.e., sexuality and queerness) produced and perpetuated by professional organizations in ELT. We aim to resist and contest cisheteronormativity in professional spaces, especially in ELT, by introducing the idea of critical love to advocate for marginalized populations in schools and research (i.e., queer students and teachers in language classrooms; C. D. Nelson, 2009; Paiz, 2019, 2020; Trinh, 2019, 2020a, 2020b, 2021, 2022a), for queer selves and others who are stuck in the normative frameworks that remain "uncontested and incontestable" (Butler, 2009, p. 149), and for critical inquiry to challenge heteronormativity through critical storytelling (Coda et al., 2021; Pentón Herrera & Trinh, 2021). One important aspect is that critical love not only aims to support queer individuals but also creates a bridge of mutual understanding, empathy, and respect for those who are nonqueer to enter the circle of conversation to build allyship together. Queer allyship "describes allies who work together to challenge common heteronormative assumptions of oneself to think queer and provoke actions in relational systems of support" (Trinh, in press). We thus contend that incorporating critical love is another way of queer imagining (Talburt, 2008) to rehumanize and regain justice for queerness and sexuality in professional organizations in ELT. As hooks (2000) emphasized, there can be no love without justice. In this chapter, we posit that there can be no justice without love.

A guiding question of this chapter is: How can ELT leaders incorporate notions of critical love in professional organizations? This chapter proposes a queering and intersectional approach to support professional organizations that particularly connect with multilingual learners, teachers, and leaders. In this chapter, we reintroduce the concept of *critical love* as an analytical queering approach for educational leaders to engage in the discourse of difference (Britzman, 1995; Trinh, 2022a), ultimately pushing members in ELT to become allies and create a safe space for all identities to be included in professional spaces such as classrooms, schools, and policy, among others. "Safe space" for us starts with a critical awareness of hidden identities in these spaces (Vandrick, 1997) while putting identities of queerness and sexuality front and center to challenge power, boundaries, and ideologies of cisheteronormativity and normative frameworks in the policymaking process. "Safe space" for us starts with bringing critical love that challenges systems of domination, oppression, biases, and assumptions toward queer individuals whose voices and representations have been neglected and silenced due to political, cultural, religious, and social restrictions and ideologies. As

1. Cisheteronormativity refers to the discourse based on the assumption that heterosexuality is the norm and privileges this over any other form of sexual orientation and that cisgender is the norm and privileges this over any other form of gender identities.

2. Homonormativity refers to the discourse based on the assumption that homosexuality is the norm and privileges this over any other form of sexual orientation.

such, critical love is a transformational queering approach that provides a crucial route for professional communities, including queer and nonqueer leaders, to resist the imperialist, white supremacist, capitalist, heterosexist, heteronormative, and heteropatriarchal systems of oppression in ELT.

In the next section, we identify the aspects of critical love drawing from queer, decolonizing, feminist, antiracist, and intersectional approaches (Butler, 2009; Crenshaw, 1989; hooks, 2000; Jimenez-Luque, 2021; Motha, 2020). Then, we present incidents that happened in different schooling contexts and cultures (i.e., microaggressions, bullying, exclusion, and discrimination) and use the critical love approach to unpack these incidents. We close the chapter by making policy suggestions for ELT leaders to adapt to their own institutions in order to embrace all identities in professional spaces.

Thinking With Different Approaches

In this section, we share a snippet of different theories from queer theory, decolonization, feminism, antiracism, and intersectionality and bring them together to build a foundation for our critical love approach.

Queer Theory and Feminism

Queer theory in critical theory emerged in an attempt to examine, challenge, and problematize the ways in which society constructs and understands gender and sexuality. Building on Giroux's (1985) critical pedagogy, which sees education as a means of creating a less oppressive society, queer theory examines the history of sexuality by analyzing how society constructs, regulates, controls, and understands sexuality and how this construction is linked to power and knowledge (Foucault, 1976/1984; Sedgwick, 1990). In addition, queer theory explores the notion of gender performativity and how the concepts of "grievability" and critical love are constructed (Butler, 1990) and inquires about the intersection of race, sexuality, and gender (Muñoz, 2009). Thus, queer theory aims to understand the numerous intersecting layers of dominance and oppression by reinforcing philosophies that share a radical vision of education as the way to achieving a truly equitable and just society (Meyer, 2007).

Additionally, there is a connection between queer theory and feminism. Specifically, hooks (2000) has written extensively on the concept of love as an analytical tool for understanding power dynamics and social justice issues. hooks argued that love should be understood as a praxis. She suggested that using love as an analytical approach can help us examine how power and oppression operate in our relationships with others. hooks also argued that love can be a powerful tool for personal and collective healing. In her work, she emphasized the importance of self-love and loving relationships in overcoming the trauma caused by systemic racism and oppression. She encouraged individuals to engage in practices of self-love and self-care as a way to build resilience and resistance to oppressive systems and advocated for creating loving communities as a way to build collective power and work toward social change.

As such, we want to bring queer theory and feminism together in the context of English language teaching and learning. Applying these theories to ELT professional associations will offer a critical, loving, empathetic, and dialogic space so that teachers and leaders will codesign a more inclusive and representative curriculum, which includes queer perspectives and the representation of diverse identities aimed to challenge heteronormativity, misogyny, sexism, and other gender- and sexuality-related discriminatory acts. Additionally, these theories create a safe space for teaching associations to invite all teachers and leaders *in* to critically analyze their pedagogies to raise awareness and challenge biases they may hold that can negatively impact queer students and teachers in their own spaces. Therefore, incorporating queer theory and feminism creates transformational social change by touching on the lives of those who are outsiders of the heteronormative circle, asking for a justice plea for their pain, grief, wounds, and other traumatic events that happen in their lives due to biases, assumptions, judgment, discrimination, and other ostracizations that would/could lead to someone's death.

Antiracism and Decolonization

Antiracism includes the identification and opposition of racism by challenging and changing values, structures, and attitudes that perpetuate systemic racism (de Oliveira, 2022). In addition, it includes the implementation of policies and practices that actively oppose oppression in its many forms. Antiracist practices include consideration of various forms of oppression, including discrimination based on language, gender, sexual orientation, ability, and class, for example. An antiracist leadership approach recognizes the role of institutions, professional associations, practices, and people in producing and reproducing racial inequality.

Decolonization is the process of confronting, challenging, and undoing colonizing practices. In education, schools have been sites of colonization through forced assimilation. Colonialism is often perpetuated through curriculum, educational practices, and institutional structures. Decolonizing the curriculum involves a process of identification of whose knowledge and ways of knowing are given priority in educational contexts. Establishing links to the community to deepen understanding and encouraging community involvement are essential parts of decolonizing education. It is vital that teachers build and reframe teaching spaces that seek to produce knowledge, discussions, and problematizations that, in an intersectional way, aim to alleviate the effects of the marks of racism, homophobia, and colonial thinking (Andrade, 2023). Reflection and change play a major role in decolonizing practices, or as Asher (2009) put it: "The work of decolonization entails not only our self-reflexive efforts to work through mind-numbing alienation and essentializing divides but also the commitment to transformation in social and educational contexts" (p. 75).

As such, both decolonization and antiracism have been helpful in creating a safe space for leaders to challenge the colonized and racist practices in professional organizations and to respond to Motha's (2020) question, "Is an antiracist and decolonizing applied linguistics possible?" We concur with Motha's statement that "there is no space of not-racist" (p. 132). In order to challenge colonialism, capitalism, and racism in the context of ELT, we are doing the work of queer imagination in this chapter to respond to disrupting the space of racism and colonialism in professional organizations and offer an agency for both queer and nonqueer leaders to come together to build a bridge of inclusivity and belonging for all.

Intersectionality

Intersectionality (Crenshaw, 1989) helps us understand that it is impossible to explore one dimension of identity without including other dimensions. Certain identities make individuals more vulnerable to various modes of oppression in social contexts (Crenshaw, 1989).

Intersectionality is a theory to understand and analyze complex issues in the world, in people, and in human experiences. As Bilge and Hill Collins (2016) pointed out: "The events and conditions of social and political life and the self can seldom be understood as shaped by one factor" (p. 2). Using an intersectional approach requires an exploration of how the different dimensions actually interconnect and relate to the need to use inclusive thinking with an emphasis on a multitude of positions, moving away from dichotomous thinking that emphasizes opposites (Hill Collins, 1993). Therefore, we connect various identities as a collection of positions, narratives, and discourses constructed from relationships and experiences to propose a collaborative work and thinking to challenge binarism and delve deeper into the complexity of each individual situated in their own cultural and social contexts.

Critical Love as a Queering Approach

The concept of critical love is built on queer theory, feminism, antiracism, decolonization, and intersectionality. Love is not just an individual and subjective feeling, but is also shaped and influenced by familial, social, cultural, and political norms. Therefore, critical love is an act of inviting all identities *in* to critically examine our own biases and judgments, which are often rooted in White colonial thinking. It involves having honest and sometimes difficult conversations about issues such as racism, homophobia, and binarism, with the goal of embracing diversity and empathy toward others' intersecting identities. Critical love is a queering approach that creates a more inclusive, equitable, and safe space for all identities to speak up and share their stories in a respectful and deep-listening manner. From this perspective, we believe that critical love is the stigma of a hibiscus flower with five petals (see Figure 1) that embrace beauty, a sense of guard, protection, nurture, kindness, respect, belonging, resistance, and rebellion, with its anther representing queer theory, feminism, antiracism, decolonization, and intersectionality.

Figure 1. Hibiscus flower, a goddess of critical love.

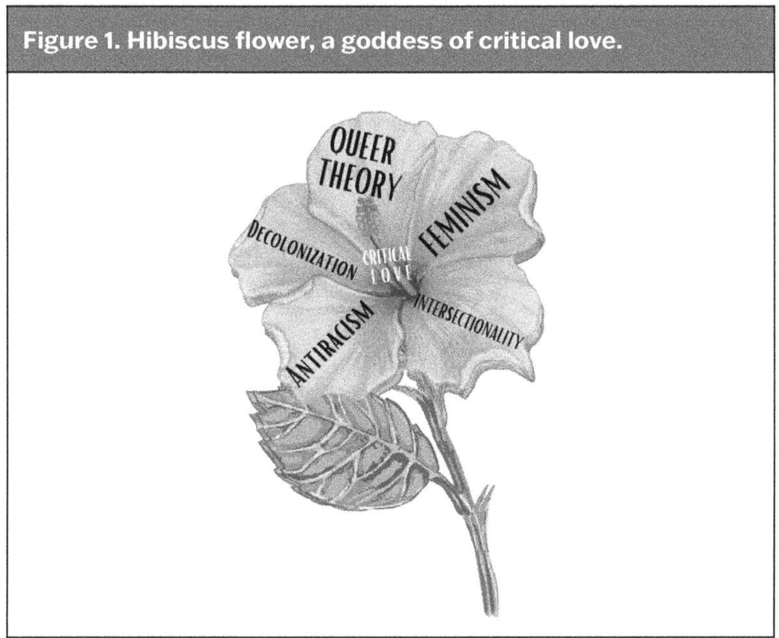

We envision that critical love is an analytical queering approach to promoting a culture of belonging and inclusivity for all identities in professional spaces in ELT. Specifically, leaders can incorporate critical love through a welcoming, empathetic, nonjudgmental, antiracist, compassionate, and inclusive environment with/for all, especially in the policymaking process. A specific example of critical love is how members of professional organizations are open to listening to the perspectives and experiences of all members of the school community and are willing to learn from and adapt to their needs and stories (e.g., gender pronouns, bathrooms, support for emotional labors). Another example is how leaders approach conflicts and challenges with a focus on finding common ground and building connections and seeing the intersectional identities of each person, rather than simply trying to impose their own views or priorities. In addition, critical love asks practitioners and leaders to challenge the doings of colonization and racism in both personal and professional spaces to build allyship for/with one another, expanding and disrupting the notion of binary ways of thinking in schools, cultures, and societies. The ultimate goal of critical love is to create a safe space where those belonging to minoritized populations such as queer individuals could feel seen, heard, appreciated, and valued as equitably as other people in their spaces.

Incidents

In this section, we present three incidents that occurred in our workplaces. By sharing and analyzing them through the lens of critical love, we hope readers will be able to co-reimagine possibilities of dealing with such issues by promoting understanding and empathy. Or, more appropriately, loving critically.

Incident 1

Linh identifies as an Asian American Pacific Islander, Vietnamese immigrant, cat parent, and nonbinary English language teacher at a college in the southern United States. As a teacher, Linh complies with the dress code to adhere to the heteronormative rules of the workplace. As a person using they/them as a gender-neutral pronoun, Linh has encountered inquiries from students for their pronouns as well as resistance to introducing pronouns and queer-related topics into the classroom. Linh was asked to talk to their manager because of their outfit as well as the content of their curriculum, which was not approved by the school administrator. Linh asked their manager when they would be able to introduce the concepts of queerness and gender pronouns because they have found students expressing interest and curiosity, in addition to pushing the students to question the norms in the English textbook. Despite students' excitement to learn, Linh was asked to "think carefully" about the content as well as the "school mission." Linh explained to their manager that incorporating queer-related topics into the discussion is a way to create a trusting and safe space for all of their students to engage in the conversation and understand queer lives from different perspectives. By building mutual understanding and empathy, students would be able to build queer allyship in and beyond the classroom. Unfortunately, the manager was not in favor of this idea and Linh resigned after that.

Incident 2

During a professional development at a bilingual school in Brazil, Paulo Pita was one of the psychologists responsible for running a free-to-all support group for queer people in the city of São Paulo, and he shared the case of one of his patients, Luana, a trans woman who started her trans experience at the age of 14 in school. During her school years, she missed being taken care of, especially by her parents, who would send her to school on her own, even though she knew the path was dangerous. She claimed to have been robbed once on the way to school. Moreover, Luana shared that at school she felt teachers and staff cared about trans people through a number of initiatives but she still felt invisible. She shared that at school there was a lot of talk about transness, but people never talked to her. Paulo's report helped teachers understand how trans people can be invisibilized through simple actions at school even when there is an effort to minimize these issues.

Incident 3

In her role, Lu works with department chairs on various issues related to academic affairs. This incident happened the first year she joined her current institution. One department chair came to her for guidance on how to work with an adjunct faculty member who was misusing pronouns to refer to a gender-nonconforming student. The school and university offer resources for instructors to work with students to understand where students are coming from. Lu referred the department chair to these and other resources she knew of from her previous work as a department chair before her current role. The department chair and Lu worked together on an email to the adjunct faculty member to help her understand that it is a form of violence to misgender a student because it connects to their emotions and well-being, and impacts their academic performance.

Incorporating Critical Love to Build Queer Allyship

In this section, we bring critical love to see through and see double (Anzaldúa, 1987) about the incidents mentioned in the previous section and argue that critical love is an analytical approach to critique, inquire, and transform our actions to build allyship with one another. To begin with, critical love is a way to queer, question, and challenge norms to create inclusivity and equity in professional spaces. As a queering approach to promoting a culture of belonging for all identities at all places, critical love needs to be thought of as a disruption to various forms of oppression and the cisheteronormativity that is present in societies. Misgendering a person, as Incidents 1 and 3 show, creates an oppressive and violent environment for the people being misgendered. What we mean by "oppressive and violent environment" connects with the idea of the erasure of someone's identity and existence. The consequence of this toxic environment is that the well-being and emotions of the misgendered people will be detrimentally damaged, which will affect their academic and personal performances tremendously. Therefore, we contend that allies, especially leaders in professional organizations in ELT, can address these forms of oppression explicitly and visibly to create a safe and trusting space for all. By incorporating critical love, leaders take care of the well-being of their members ecologically (Pentón Herrera et al., 2023), where the space they create serves as a potential site of pedagogical intervention and implication to represent inclusivity and belonging for all. A visible demonstration of critical love may take many forms, and Incidents 1 and 3 show

how we can act together to empower each and every individual and humanize leadership (de Oliveira, 2023).

Additionally, critical love enacts the embodiment of care, empathy, and compassion for others while also critically examining the systems and structures that perpetuate discrimination and oppression. Incident 1 connects to the idea of critical love by highlighting the difficulties faced by an "out" queer teacher in the classroom and the fact that their sexual orientation and gender identity are often neither recognized nor addressed. This lack of recognition contributes to their marginalization and discrimination, "conflating or ignoring intragroup differences" (Crenshaw, 1989, p. 1242), which goes against the idea of critical love in this chapter. Thus, it is important to critically examine and challenge the systems and structures that contribute to such discrimination and work toward creating a more inclusive and loving society that recognizes and embraces the diversity of sexual orientation and gender identity instead of "politicizing violence" (Crenshaw, 1989, p. 1242) against other minoritized groups. Therefore, it is impossible to explore one dimension of identity without including other dimensions to understand the challenges they have gone through due to the multiple oppressions of their intersectional identities. Identifying as queer and multilingual, for example, makes individuals more vulnerable, often falling into "a minority within a minority" (Trinh, 2020a), to various modes of oppression in educational, social, and political contexts.

Further, critical love pushes the leaders to ask: How can we make queerness visible, acceptable, and thinkable for leaders? The visibility of queerness is extremely complex because "visibility is not a fixed binary state of visible/invisible; rather, it always embeds and attaches with invisibility and hypervisibility simultaneously" (Trinh, 2022b, p. 756). Critical love pushes leaders to think critically about the complexity of queerness in professional organizations by looking at the systems, structures, attitudes, and White, colonized, cisheteronormative ideologies that contribute to the marginalization and discrimination of human beings who dwell at the borders of society, including queer people and people of color.

In the context of professional ELT organizations, critical love means acknowledging the systemic barriers and prejudices that make it tremendously difficult for queer people to be open about themselves and be accepted. By examining how these systems are used to justify and maintain oppression, ELT leaders can come up with critical ways to design more equitable and just organizations and communities, aimed to "co-create and co-construct a space of togetherness to learn about ourselves and others in order to challenge the socio-cultural-political-gender-sexual norms from/with all parties (i.e., students, teachers, families, administrators, textbook publishers, policymakers, among others)" (Trinh, in press).

Finally, critical love is an approach to self-inquiry. This approach emphasizes the importance of self-reflection and the examination of one's own biases and privileges in order to actively work toward abolishing exclusionary institutions and systems. It also involves actively listening to and valuing the perspectives and experiences of marginalized communities and taking action to address and challenge discrimination and injustice.

Moving Forward

Building queer allyship through critical love is a significant step to acknowledging, validating, and co-constructing a community of unlearning to relearn with one another. Allyship comes not only from visible markers such as safe zone signs in the school space but also from the validation of adults and those who are in power positions such as teachers, administrators, district coordinators, and policymakers. As Trinh (2022a) suggested, adults (i.e., school leaders, instructional coaches, and policymakers) should drop their knowledge and reposition themselves and their positionalities to listen to the students critically. Therefore, we propose a list of actions for teachers and professional organizations to consider and think queerly about building queer allyship in professional organizations in ELT:

1. **Calling out:** Leaders, along with staff and teaching associations, name, address, and confront homophobic, ableist, xenophobic, and White privilege in public spaces such as meetings, conferences, and events, calling out these discriminatory acts in public and emphasizing that these actions are not accepted and allowed in professional spaces.
2. **Inviting in:** Leaders, along with staff, create a culture of belonging for all identities at school by promoting inclusivity and respect for all students, regardless of their race, ethnicity, gender, sexual orientation, religion, shape, or ability. This can be done through various means, such as providing diversity and sensitivity training for staff, implementing inclusive curriculum and policies, and fostering a positive school climate where everyone feels safe and valued. Additionally, actively seeking input and feedback from students and families from diverse backgrounds can help ensure that the school is meeting the needs of all community members.
3. **Using critical storytelling:** Leaders and staff use critical storytelling in professional spaces by inviting local queer communities to discuss challenges faced by queer individuals and suggest how to support their communities. Queer performance is another activity that shows cultural, social, pedagogical, and political validation to queer individuals.
4. **Inquiring one's self:** Critical love involves self-reflection and examination of one's own biases and privileges, which ask ELT organizations and leaders to identify and address the ways in which they may inadvertently perpetuate homophobia, transphobia, and biphobia. Leaders and staff actively listen to and value the perspectives and experiences of queer individuals and take action to address and challenge discrimination and injustice.
5. **Amplifying minoritized voices:** Professional organizations encourage and amplify the voices of minoritized individuals within their organizations, particularly those from the queer community.
6. **Using inclusive language:** Leaders in ELT organizations advocate for the use of inclusive language in their professional organizations, such as using gender-neutral terms and avoiding language that is offensive or harmful to the queer community.
7. **Hiring:** Leaders in ELT professional communities ensure that their organization's hiring practices are inclusive and diverse and that the workplace is free from discrimination based on sexual orientation and gender identity.

8. **Providing professional development:** Organization leaders offer professional development opportunities for employees to learn about queer issues and to develop their skills in working with and supporting the queer community.

9. **Creating a safe space:** Teachers, leaders, and associations create a culture of allyship in their professional organization, where everyone feels comfortable and supported in bringing their authentic selves to work.

10. **Working collaboratively:** As leaders, we must act and work collaboratively with others to explain the importance of using correct pronouns and knowing about the identities of our students, staff, and faculty. This is a form of love for the people we work with and an example of a humanizing approach to leadership.

In essence, homophobia, like all forms of discrimination, is rooted in societal prejudices and power imbalances. It is perpetuated through societal norms, institutions, and structures that invisibilize, marginalize, exclude, and eliminate queer individuals. Also, the intersection of race, gender, and sexuality reveals how the intersectional subordination system is shaped through a hierarchy of oppressions. This is even more relevant when we discuss bodies that are historically colonized, subalternized, and understood as oppressed (Andrade & Nicolaides, 2021). Therefore, we want to reiterate the message to readers, especially ELT leaders in professional organizations, that *there can be no justice without love.* By incorporating critical love as an analytical, queering approach, educational leaders in ELT can actively work toward challenging and dismantling these oppressive, racist, homophobic, colonized, sexist, and heteronormative systems and creating a more inclusive and equitable learning environment for all.

Authors

Ethan Trinh, PhD, is an associate director of the Atlanta Global Studies Center. As a Vietnamese queer immigrant, Ethan enjoys thinking with emotions, gender, and language and explores how to embrace queerness as healing and meditative teaching and research practices.

Luciana C. de Oliveira, PhD, is associate dean for academic affairs and graduate studies in the School of Education and a professor in the Department of Teaching and Learning at Virginia Commonwealth University. Her research focuses on the teaching and learning of multilingual learners in K-12.

Bruno Andrade, PhD candidate at the Federal University of Rio de Janeiro, is an English teacher at international schools in Brazil. As a queer brown Brazilian, he focuses his studies on bilingualism; diversity, equity, and inclusion; queer studies; and raciolinguistics.

References

Andrade, B. C. N. (2023). *Decolonial practices in bilingual education: Breaking paradigms, destabilizing hierarchies and transcending language boundaries 1,* 71–76. Editora Boc, São Paulo.

Andrade, B. C. N., & Nicolaides, C. S. (2021). Multiple and complex discursive constructions of a black and gay teacher at a bilingual school: An ethnography in a socio-historical and cultural perspective. *Revista Brasileira da Pesquisa Sócio-Histórico-Cultural e da Atividade,* 3(1), 23–23.

Anzaldúa, G. (1987). *Borderlands/la frontera: The new mestiza*. Aunt Lute Books.

Asher, N. (2009). Decolonization and education: Locating pedagogy and self at the interstices in global times. *Counterpoints, 369*, 67–77.

Bilge, S., & Hill Collins, P. (2016). *Intersectionality*. Polity.

Britzman, D. (1995). Is there a queer pedagogy? Or, stop reading straight. *Educational Theory, 45*(2), 151–165.

Butler, J. (1990). *Gender trouble: Feminism and the subversion of identity*. Routledge.

Butler, J. (2009). *Frames of war: When is life grievable?* Verso.

Coda, J., Cahnmann-Taylor, M., & Jiang, L. (2021). "It takes time for language to change": Challenging classroom heteronormativity through teaching proficiency through reading and storytelling (TPRS). *Journal of Language, Identity & Education, 20*(2), 90–102. https://doi.org/10.1080/15348458.2020.1726755

Crenshaw, K. W. (1989). Mapping the margins: Intersectionality, identity politics, and violence against women of color. *Stanford Law Review, 43*(6), 1241–1299. https://doi.org/10.2307/1229039

de Oliveira, L. C. (2022). Principles and practices for the preparation of antiracist ESOL teachers. *CATESOL Journal, 33*(1), 1–9.

de Oliveira, L. C. (2023). Antiracist leadership in TESOL: Principles and practices. *European Journal of Applied Linguistics and TEFL, 12*(2), 41–45.

Epstein, D., O'Flynn, S., & Telford, D. (2003). *Silenced sexualities in schools and universities*. Trentham Books.

Foucault, M. (1984). *The history of sexuality* [Translated from French by Robert Hurley]. Pantheon Books. (Original work published 1976)

Giroux, H. A. (1985). Critical pedagogy, cultural politics and the discourse of experience. *Journal of Education, 167*(2), 22–41.

Halperin, D. M. (1997). *Saint Foucault: Towards a gay hagiography*. Oxford Paperbacks.

Halperin, D. M. (2003). The normalization of queer theory. *Journal of Homosexuality, 45*(2–4), 339–343.

Hill Collins, P. (1993). Toward a new vision: race, class and gender as categories of analysis and connection. *Race, Sex and Class, 1*(1), 25–45.

hooks, b. (2000). *All above love: New visions*. HarperCollins.

Jimenez-Luque, A. (2021). Reframing the past to legitimate the future: Building collective agency for social change through a process of decolonizing memory. *Leadership, 17*(5), 586–605. https://doi.org/10.1177/1742715021999892

Liddicoat, A. (2009). Sexual identity as linguistic failure: Trajectories of interaction in the heteronormative language classroom. *Journal of Language, Identity and Education, 8*(3), 191–202.

Meyer, E. J. (2007). "But I'm not gay": What straight teachers need to know about queer theory. In N. Rodriguez & W. F. Pinar (Eds.), *Queering straight teachers* (pp. 1–17). Peter Lang.

Motha, S. (2020). Is an antiracist and decolonizing applied linguistics possible? *Annual Review of Applied Linguistics, 40*, 128–133. https://doi.org/10.1017/S0267190520000100

Muñoz, J. E. (2009). *Cruising utopia: The then and there of queer futurity*. New York University Press.

Nelson, C. D. (2009). *Sexual identities in English language education: Classroom conversations*. Routledge.

Nelson, L. (1999). Bodies (and spaces) do matter: The limits of performativity. *Gender, Place and Culture: A Journal of Feminist Geography, 6*(4), 331–353.

Nussbaum, M. (1995). Objectification. *Philosophy and Public Affairs, 24*, 249–291.

Paiz, J. M. (2019). Queering practice: LGBTQ+ diversity and inclusion in English language teaching. *Journal of Language, Identity & Education, 18*(4), 266–275. https://doi.org/10.1080/15348458.2019.1629933

Paiz, J. M. (2020). *Queering the English language classroom: A practical guide for teachers*. Equinox.

Pentón Herrera, L. J., Martínez-Alba, G., & Trinh, E. (Eds.). (2023). *Teacher well-being in English language teaching: An ecological approach*. Routledge.

Pentón Herrera, L. J., & Trinh, E. (Eds.). (2021). *Critical storytelling: Multilingual immigrants in the United States*. Brill/Sense. https://doi.org/10.1163/9789004446182

Rubin, G. (1984). Thinking sex: Notes for a radical theory of the politics of sexuality. In C. Vance (Ed.), *Pleasure and danger: Exploring female sexuality* (pp. 267–319). Routledge.

Sedgwick, E. K. (1990). *Epistemology of the closet: Updated with a new preface*. University of California Press.

Talburt, S. (2008). Queer imaginings. *Journal of LGBT Youth, 5*(3), 99–103.

Trinh, E. (2019). Breaking down the Coatlicue state to see a self: Queer voices within a circle. *The Assembly: A Journal for Public Scholarship on Education, 2*(1), 28–32. https://doi.org/10.33011/assembly.v2i1.487

Trinh, E. (2020a). "Still you resist": An autohistoria-teoria of a Vietnamese queer teacher to meditate, teach, and love in the Coatlicue state. *International Journal of Qualitative Studies in Education, 33*(6), 621–633. https://doi.org/10.1080/09518398.2020.1747662

Trinh, E. (2020b). Suicide and nepantla: Writing in in-between space to crave policy change. *LGBTQ Policy Journal, 10*, 31–37.

Trinh, E. (2021). Crossing the split in nepantla: (Un)successful attempts to dismantle a TESOL teacher candidate in after-queer research. *Journal of Homosexuality, 69*(12), 2027–2048. https://doi.org/10.1080/00918369.2021.1987749

Trinh, E. (2022a). Supporting queer SLIFE youth: Initial queer considerations. In L. J. Pentón Herrera (Ed.), *English and students with limited or interrupted formal education: Global perspectives on teacher preparation and classroom practices* (pp. 209–225). Springer International. https://doi.org/10.1007/978-3-030-86963-2_12

Trinh, E. (2022b). Visibility. In K. K. Strunk & S. A. Shelton (Eds.), *Encyclopedia of queer studies in education* (pp. 756–757). Brill.

Trinh, E. (in press). Queer allyship in TESOL: We need to ACTS now! *TESOL Journal*.

Vandrick, S. (1997). The role of hidden identities in the postsecondary ESL classroom. *TESOL Quarterly, 31*(1), 153–157. https://doi.org/10.2307/3587980

Weeks, J. (1986). *Sexuality*. Tavistock.

PART 4

MOVING FORWARD

Demonstrative Allyship: Taking a Stand, Being Present, and Teaching Pride Forward

Ethan Trinh, Kate Mastruserio Reynolds, and James Coda

Demonstrating Our Allyship

In the last months as we have worked on this volume, we have had numerous situations in which we have had opportunities to take a stand in support of the LGBTQ+ community, colleagues, students, and even this volume. These opportunities have emerged from surprising corners. Colleagues who live and work in more conservative or religious cultures are concerned about losing their jobs or experiencing backlash because of any association with the LGBTQ+ community. Other colleagues would only speak about supporting the community in hushed tones for fear of political ramifications. And these are the colleagues who support the LGBTQ+ community. This is not to mention the colleagues in the field who are not supportive of the community due to personal, social, political, or religious views.

However, despite the increasing global challenges that queer and transgender identities are facing in English language teaching (ELT; e.g., Andrade & Trinh, in press; Banegas & Govender, 2022; Knisely & Paiz, 2021; Lander, 2018; Le et al., 2023; Lin et al., 2020; Tarrayo & Potestades, 2023; Tran-Thanh, 2020; Trinh et al., 2022), we have observed brave colleagues willing to take a stand and demonstratively support the LGBTQ+ community in their teaching, research, professional engagements, and personal lives. These colleagues also risk their jobs as well as their personal and professional standing and prestige. They advocate persuasively for their students and peers, gently steering others by painting a picture of LGBTQ+ individuals' personal and professional life experiences while they appeal to their interlocutors' sense of morality, individuals' rights and freedoms, and sense of fair play and equity. We can learn from their rhetorical moves and their advocacy strategies.

In the field of ELT, we, the editors, would like to encourage colleagues to reflect on the world we hope to create, and teach explicitly about and model implicitly open-mindedness, acceptance of others just as they are, and peace. Therefore, this conclusion chapter reviews the literature on effective allyship and advocacy efforts in social movements. In this section, we note strategies and approaches that individuals in the LGBTQ+ community and in other social movements prefer allies to avoid in their support of the community. Finally, this chapter concludes with future directions for research, practice, and activism regarding LGBTQ+ allyship.

What Can Allies Do?

Allies can support marginalized groups and social movements, in this case LGBTQ+ individuals and the LGBTQ+ equity movement, by emphasizing a common group identity during efforts for social change. Some organizations that promote a shared group identity are the Sexuality and Gender Alliance (SAGA), GLSEN, and gay straight alliances. Through sharing a group identity that includes all individuals, social movements are strengthened. Moreover, when a group shares a common identity, they can "frame movement demands as shared goals" (Selvanathan et al., 2020, pp. 1347–1348).

In addition to the common group identity, allies can express empathy with marginalized group members by offering emotional support, providing hope, and prioritizing relationship-building efforts (Radke et al., 2020; Rattan, & Ambady, 2014; Selvanathan et al., 2020). This type of strategy communicates the emotional support necessary to sustain individuals and help them withstand the barrage of negative messages received in their daily interactions that may make them question themselves and/or engage in self-loathing, for instance. Thus, marginalized groups tend to feel more respected and empowered when they can collaborate with allies to create social environments that validate their experiences (Selvanathan et al., 2020, p. 1354).

Allies will make mistakes and errors. A common example is making mistakes with pronouns even when the pronoun is known and the ally does respect the individual. Therefore, allies need to be willing to accept criticism (Droogendyk et al., 2016) and make amends when necessary. Moreover, assuming the best intention is an important part of accepting allies into the movement as well as providing grace when a mistake or error occurs. We agree with Trinh's (in press) discussion of acknowledging allies' mistakes, and that it is part of becoming an ally:

> Instead of calling people out, allyship invites people in by setting the ground rules for the conversation, sitting in discomfort, listening to one another's perspectives and rationales deeply, contributing and sharing ideas respectfully despite differences, aimed to build a mutually understanding relationship and create a collective human-oriented system of support with one another.

Therefore, in our understanding of allyship, we approach it not as an act that is static, but rather as a process of becoming in which one will make mistakes. As Trinh (in press) notes, "Building queer allyship, then, is an in-the-making, incomplete, contested, and situated process." As allies, our performative, linguistic, and embodied actions are always becoming in this process, which invites critical reflection so that we can continually revisit and reimagine our allyship efforts. To cultivate critical reflection as allies, we can draw on the insights of queer theories and pedagogies, which have been paramount in destabilizing cisheteronormativity and its harmful effects on LGBTQ+ individuals and beyond.

Future Directions

This book brings together queer research and pedagogy, ELT, and allyship. We recognize this is the first time these areas have been brought together and that we are only just beginning to understand allyship in ELT. This book is one example to respond to Trinh's (in press) question about the lack of allyship in teaching and research: "Who has been listening to us? Who has been standing with us? Who has been acting with us?" The studies and pedagogical enACTSment[1] in this book have exemplified the beauty of allyship across the world in different cultures, societies, and schooling and how teachers, educators, and researchers are ACTSing together. However, there is a dearth of evidence demonstrating what administrators and policymakers are doing in creating allyship in and beyond their workplaces.

Some questions remain after this edited volume: Who is the voice of authority when it comes to the discourse of queer allyship? Or should the voice of authority be put aside to allow the *space of togetherness* (Trinh, in press) to come? Can an ally have insights and strategies that further the cause of diversity, equity, respect, inclusion, and access for members of the LGBTQ+ community? How do we have challenging conversations while honoring diverse voices and perspectives? Further, how do we have constructive, authentic conversations about difficult topics together in safe spaces and listen with compassion to what the other has to say? How can we learn how to listen with compassion and forgive the mistakes or errors made during conversations? When we have conflict, how do we mediate it in a manner that refocuses on the essentials of our work?

In order to continue this allyship work, we want to challenge future readers, researchers, teachers, educators, administrators, and policymakers to ACTS with us by investigating, implementing, thinking, and incorporating allyship in your own spaces despite challenges and contexts that may not be welcoming for LGBTQ+ individuals. We advocate that allies play an important role in promoting equity, inclusion, and access for the LGBTQ+ community without whom fewer voices would advocate. This book is thus cocreated by wonderful scholars around the world who reflect equity, inclusion, accessibility, and diversity, but also we continuously need allies and allyship beyond this book to sustain, expand, and empower each other to move forward with this important work.

With the ascendance of what have been termed "parental rights bills" in the United States and other places that seek to limit discussions related to gender and sexuality as well as transgender rights (Mayo, 2021), contexts such as the United States, from which we write, are what Paiz (2019) described as frigid in relation to LGBTQ+ issues. Moreover, educators who engage in inclusive and representative practices in contexts such as Florida, in the United States (Peele, 2023), may potentially face reprisal. We do, however, recognize the valuable role of contributions, such as this edited volume and other queer-related scholastic

---

1. ACTS "describes allies who work together to challenge common heteronormative and cisgender assumptions of oneself to think queer and provoke actions in relational systems of support" (Trinh, in press).

and pedagogical endeavors, that trouble normative assumptions related to LGBTQ+ issues. We hope that the pedagogical and research approaches from this work will continue making positive impacts for students and teachers, lowering suicide risks (Trevor Project, 2023), and supporting queer students and teachers in and beyond school despite challenges (Kosciw et al., 2022).

The following is a list of suggestions that we challenge you to enACTS in allyship in your context to make a positive impact with each other. This list is not exhaustive. We welcome other future research studies and pedagogical enACTSment and policymaking to complicate, multiply, and build allyship with us. This work is created by trust, understanding, patience, and, most importantly, love with and by everyone.

Research

- Call for more research in language teaching and learning related to LGBTQ+ experiences, focusing on intersectionality and allyship.
- Call for research on intersectional perspectives related to interactions among LGBTQ+ and allies' multiple identities and enactment of prosocial behaviors and advocacy. For example, how do the multiple identities of participants in an interactional moment negotiate their identities and roles, assess pros/cons, and make determinations of whether to act up or remain silent?
- Call for allyship and intersectionality in challenging contexts for LGBTQ+ individuals. For example, how can we extend our allyship efforts in contexts that may not be amenable to LGBTQ+ identities coupled with our knowledge of the intersectional nature of identities?
- Call for research on the discourse of allies when advocating in ELT. What is said? How? How effective/productive was the advocacy in that situation and context?
- Call for research on the discourse of advocacy and allyship in ELT in non-Western communities that are accepting of LGBTQ+ identities. For example, what do advocacy and allyship with/for LGBTQ+ communities in non-Western contexts look like? What do activities and discourse look like? Who is involved? What are the outcomes? What are the challenges? How could the community challenge and inquire about the non-Western LGBTQ+ discourse in and beyond school?
- Call for personal projects from both queer and nonqueer students and teachers to explore their identities and emotions to become allies themselves. For example, how can we use queer walking meditation (Trinh, 2020), auto-/duo-/collaborative ethnography (Pentón Herrera et al., 2024; Yazan et al., 2023), or action research (Banegas & Villacañas de Castro, 2019; Barabas & Jiang, 2022; Uştuk, 2023) in ELT with students and teachers?

Practices

- Situated strategies for how to protect, support, and stand with LGBTQ+ students in our classrooms and schools. These strategies include but are not limited to discourse, classroom norms, and instructional practices.
- Situated strategies for contesting cisheteronormativity and being subversive with norms in contexts that may not be amenable to LGBTQ+ identities and experiences.

- Situated strategies for analyzing materials and instructional practices to eliminate biases and cisheteronormativity.
- Situated strategies for making room for diverse perspectives from members of the LGBTQ+ community in our workspaces.

Activism

- Movement toward informed community projects in and beyond the classrooms that provoke students' and teachers' allyship and advocacy with the LGBTQ+ community, especially in challenging contexts.
- Movement toward advocacy for diversity, equity, inclusion, and access for LGBTQ+ people in workspaces and communities. Consortia of members of the community and allies need to advocate for policies on local, national, and regional levels.
- Movement toward demonstrations of understanding and connections with people excluded and marginalized within the LGBTQ+ community, such as LGBTQ+ preteens and teens and queer homeless youths.
- Movement toward activities that discuss and take care of the emotions and well-being of queer teachers and students in challenging contexts.

Teaching Pride Forward

We—Ethan Trinh, Kate Mastruserio Reynolds, and James Coda—sincerely appreciate your trust in us, the authors, and our work in this book. We want to continue moving this work forward by wholeheartedly inviting healthy, loving, supportive conversations about allyship with (and perhaps beyond) members of the LGBTQ+ community. This book is a symbol of freedom, liberation, nourishment, inspiration, trust, and love shared among allies across the globe. Therefore, we would like to have you take a stand, stay present, and continue cultivating allyship in your work—with us and each other—in teaching pride forward.

Authors

Ethan Trinh, PhD, is an associate director of the Atlanta Global Studies Center. As a Vietnamese queer immigrant, Ethan enjoys thinking with emotions, gender, and language and explores how to embrace queerness as healing and meditative teaching and research practices.

Kate Mastruserio Reynolds, EdD, is a professor of TESOL/literacy at Central Washington University and a licensed K–12 educator who has taught teachers in several countries and multilingual learners of English in public school districts at elementary schools, middle schools, and universities in various contexts. In 2022, she was inducted onto TESOL International Association's Board of Directors (2022–2025).

James Coda, PhD, is assistant professor of ESL and world language education at the University of Tennessee Knoxville. His research interests include LGBTQIA+ issues in language teaching and learning, queer theories and pedagogies, and identity.

References

Andrade, B., & Trinh, E. (in press). "My body is a political stance": Critical love as a trans-formation in the Brazilian ELT context. In R. Jain, J. Chen, & E. Trinh (Eds.), *Humanizing language pedagogies and teacher education research: Critical perspectives on identities, pedagogy, and research.* Bloomsbury.

Banegas, D. L., & Govender, N. (Eds.). (2022). *Gender diversity and sexuality in English language education: New transnational voices.* Bloomsbury.

Banegas, D. L., & Villacañas de Castro, L. S. (2019). Action research. In S. Mann & S. Walsh (Eds.), *The Routledge handbook of English language teacher education* (pp. 570–582). Routledge.

Barabas, C. D., & Jiang, Q. (2022). Queering a high school EFL literature class in China: Teacher's and student's reflections. *TESOL Journal, 13,* Article e671. https://doi.org/10.1002/tesj.671

Droogendyk, L., Wright, S. C., Lubensky, M., & Louis, W. R. (2016). Acting in solidarity: Cross-group contact between disadvantaged group members and advantaged group allies. *Journal of Social Issues, 72*(2), 315–334. https://doi.org/10.1111/josi.12168

Knisely, K., & Paiz, J. M. (2021). Bringing trans, non-binary, and queer understandings to bear in language education. *Critical Multilingualism Studies, 9*(1), 23–45.

Kosciw, J. G., Clark, C. M., & Menard, L. (2022). *The 2021 National School Climate Survey: The experiences of LGBTQ+ youth in our nation's schools.* GLSEN.

Lander, R. (2018). Queer English language teacher identity: A narrative exploration in Colombia. *Profile: Issues in Teachers' Professional Development, 20*(1), 89–101.

Le, G. N. H., Dong, H. B., Tran, V., & Vu, L. H. (2023). "She is not a normal teacher of English": Photovoice as a decolonial method to study queer teacher identity in Vietnam's English language teaching. In A. Sahlane & R. Pritchard (Eds.), *English as an international language education: Critical intercultural literacy perspectives* (pp. 443–462). Springer.

Lin, H., Trakulkasemsuk, W., & Zilli, P. J. (2020). When queer meets teacher: A narrative inquiry of the lived experience of a teacher of English as a foreign language. *Sexuality & Culture, 24,* 1064–1081.

Mayo, C. (2021). Distractions and defractions: Using parental rights to fight against the educational rights of transgender, nonbinary, and gender diverse students. *Educational Policy, 35*(2), 368–382. https://doi.org/10.1177/0895904820983033

Paiz, J. M. (2019). Queering practice: LGBTQ+ diversity and inclusion in English language teaching. *Journal of Language, Identity, and Education, 18*(4), 266–275. https://doi.org/10.1080/15348458.2019.1629933

Peele, C. (2023, July 20). *Florida State Board of Education proposes new rules targeted LGBTQ+ students, parents, and educators.* Human Rights Campaign. https://www.hrc.org/press-releases/florida-state-board-of-education-proposes-new-rules-targeted-lgbtq-students-parents-and-educators

Pentón Herrera, L. J., Trinh, E., & Yazan, B. (Eds.). (2024). *Curating the self and embracing the community: Autoethnographic evocations of U.S. doctoral students in the fields of social sciences and humanities.* Brill.

Radke, H. R. M., Kutlaca, M., Siem, B., Wright, S. C., & Becker, J. C. (2020). Beyond allyship: Motivations for advantaged group members to engage in action for disadvantaged groups. *Personality and Social Psychology Review, 24*(4), 291–315. https://doi.org/10.1177/1088868320918698

Rattan, A., & Ambady, N. (2014). How "It gets better": Effectively communicating support to targets of prejudice. *Personality and Social Psychology Bulletin, 40*(5), 555–566. https://doi.org/10.1177/0146167213519480

Selvanathan, H. P., Lickel, B., & Dasgupta, N. (2020). An integrative framework on the impact of allies: How identity-based needs influence intergroup solidarity and social movements. *European Journal of Social Psychology, 50*(6), 1344–1361. https://doi.org/10.1002/ejsp.2697

Tarrayo, V. N., & Potestades, R. R. (2023). Understanding queer Filipino university teachers' queering efforts in the English Classroom. *TESOL Quarterly*. Advance online publication. https://doi.org/10.1002/tesq.3256

Tran-Thanh, V. (2020). Queer identity inclusion in the EFL classroom: Vietnamese teachers' perspectives. *TESOL Journal, 11*(3), Article e00512. https://doi.org/10.1002/tesj.512

Trevor Project. (2023). *2023 U.S. national survey on the mental health of LGBTQ young people.*

Trinh, E. (2020). "Still you resist": An autohistoria-teoria of a Vietnamese queer teacher to meditate, teach, and love in the Coatlicue state. *International Journal of Qualitative Studies in Education, 33*(6), 621–633. https://doi.org/10.1080/09518398.2020.1747662

Trinh, E. (in press). Queer allyship in TESOL: We need to ACTS now! *TESOL Journal.*

Trinh, E., Le, N. H. G., Dong, H. B., Tran, T., & Tran, V. (2022). Memory rewriting as a method of inquiry: When returning becomes collective healing. *The Qualitative Report, 27*(3), 824–841. https://doi.org/10.46743/2160-3715/2022.5245

Uştuk, Ö. (2023). "This made me feel honoured": A participatory action research on using process drama in English language education with ethics of care. *Research in Drama Education: The Journal of Applied Theatre and Performance, 28*(2), 279–294. https://doi.org/10.1080/13569783.2022.2106127

Yazan, B., Trinh, E. T., & Pentón Herrera, L. J. (Eds.). (2023). *Doctoral students' identities and emotional wellbeing in applied linguistics: Autoethnographic accounts.* Routledge.

Afterword: On Queer Allyship in English Language Teaching

Stephanie Vandrick

I remember well the excitement, starting about three decades ago, of seeing early publications in English language teaching (ELT) journals and conference sessions regarding queer faculty, students, and issues. We all owe a debt to the pioneering ELT scholars writing on LGBTQ+ theory and issues in those early years (and in some cases, still!). These scholars should be remembered not only for their research and advocacy, but also for their courage in writing about these matters when such topics were rarely addressed and when scholars were sometimes criticized for doing so. I also want to acknowledge the perhaps less remembered activists who, through the years, have done the arduous organizational work of forming and maintaining LGBTQ+-related interest sections, advocacy groups, and other official and unofficial groups within ELT/TESOL/applied linguistics–related professional bodies.

More recently, queer theory and practice have been addressed in new ways by an increasing number of ELT scholars, including by the editors of this book: Ethan Trinh, Kate Mastruserio Reynolds, and James Coda. The work of these more recent scholars is also pioneering in that it dramatically furthers and takes in new directions queer theory, scholarship, awareness, activism, and pedagogy. This book is a prominent example of this new phase in scholarly literature, providing a very valuable introduction and opening-up of a topic formerly seldom discussed in our ELT scholarship: queer allyship.

As soon as I eagerly started reading this book, I felt welcomed into it. Starting with the preface and the introduction, it was evident to me that the editors are very reader-aware and that along with (or rather as part of) their scholarship, they share their personal views and feelings with us and are willing to be vulnerable themselves. They approach the topic of allyship with passion and compassion. They are not judgmental of allies who are still learning and who may make mistakes. Along with the editors sharing their own research and expertise, they respectfully and caringly treat readers as if we are all open to learning, are all learning together, and all have something to contribute. Trinh, Reynolds, and Coda understand how complex and fraught allyship can be and how we all need to be reflective and figure out the best ways to practice allyship. Their preface and introduction create a foundation of trust and generosity for the rest of the book and thus feel like a gift to readers. The authors of the other chapters are also generous in sharing both their scholarship and their personal feelings. For example, some chapter authors are candid about times they have felt discomfort and even fear when doing the work of allyship; these feelings are familiar to me as well. Similar instances of personal reflection and of autoethnography are found throughout the rich and varied chapters of this book.

Some of the many themes addressed in the book are the need for allies to acknowledge their/our own privilege; the fact that allyship is never static, but always fluid; and the concept that allyship is not individual but collective. Other themes addressed are the importance of allies continuing to critique our own allyship, interrogating ourselves, and keeping ourselves honest; we should not oversimplify, be superficial, be co-opted, or be performative rather than substantive in our allyship practices.

Enhancing the value and interest of this book is its intentionally truly international scope. The educational sites of research, including several age levels of students and types of schools and institutions, also are varied. In addition, the chapters deal with aspects of queer allyship related to both students and educators. Further, throughout the book there is awareness and frequent discussion of the importance of recognizing the essential element of intersectionality in queer allyship.

Further enhancing the book's value and appeal is the scholarly yet accessible quality of the writing (not always the case in scholarly publications!), clearly a goal of the editors and authors. Accessibility is, after all, a way of respecting and caring for readers. There is also a welcome specificity and granularity to the descriptions of the various sites and conditions addressed by the chapter authors. An example of other specific ways in which the editors and authors support accessibility is through defining terms that may be unfamiliar to some readers, thus meeting readers where they are.

Yet another admirable attribute of this book is the way that the editors and authors intentionally worked hard to create a sense of community among the contributors. By extension, this sense of community is evident to, and embraces, readers as well. Just one specific example of this sense of community is the editors sharing, in their introduction, their personal responses to the individual chapters, in a very supportive and interactive way. The editors even use a word that is not common in academic writing: *love*. This is notable and welcome, in that it is quite seldom in academic writing that authors' emotions are openly acknowledged, especially the emotion of love. In the introduction, the editors' responses to the chapters intentionally employ sentences beginning with "I love..." and followed by specific mentions of aspects of those chapters. Love is also mentioned elsewhere in the book. Appreciating this focus, I in turn love the book's sense of community and, yes, of love!

I applaud and thank the editors of, and contributors to, this significant book, which offers readers a thoughtful combination of theory, on-the-ground research, advocacy, and attention to practice/pedagogy. I believe it will inspire and empower other ELT scholars and educators to explore and address queer allyship, and in fact, as the book's title advocates, to "teach pride forward."

About the Editors

Ethan Trinh, PhD, is an associate director of the Atlanta Global Studies Center. As a Vietnamese queer immigrant, Ethan enjoys thinking with emotions, gender, and language and explores how to embrace queerness as healing and meditative teaching and research practices. Ethan has published four edited volumes that focus on critical storytelling, teachers' well-being, and doctoral students' emotions, identities, and community. Ethan is the recipient of the 2022 Leadership Mentoring Program Award by TESOL International Association. Originally from Vietnam, Ethan enjoys creative writing, Vietnamese iced coffee, and playing with their doggie Shiba in their free time.

Kate Mastruserio Reynolds, EdD, is a professor of TESOL/literacy at Central Washington University. A licensed K–12 educator, she has taught teachers in several countries and multilingual learners of English in public school districts at elementary schools, middle schools, and universities in various contexts. Dr. Reynolds's publications include *Introduction to TESOL: Becoming a Language Teaching Professional*, *Research Methods in Language Teaching and Learning: A Practical Guide*, and *Approaches to Inclusive English Classrooms: A Teacher's Handbook for Content-Based Instruction*. In 2022, she was inducted onto TESOL International Association's Board of Directors (2022–2025).

James Coda, PhD, is assistant professor of ESL and world language education and of theory and practice in teacher education in the College of Education, Health, and Human Sciences at the University of Tennessee-Knoxville. He earned a doctorate in language and literacy education with an emphasis in TESOL and world language education from the University of Georgia. His professional experience spans K–12 as well as adult and higher education world language and ESOL contexts. His research interests include LGBTQ+ issues in language teaching and learning, gender and sexuality in education, queer theories and pedagogies, and the role of identities in the classroom.

Definitions of Terms in This Book

Allyship: A process of becoming that is never finished so that we can unlearn our assumptions, challenge cisheteronormativity, and cultivate inclusivity for LGBTQ+ individuals.

Cisheteronormativity: Oppression that is due to cisnormativity and heteronormativity.

Cisnormativity: The assumption that cisgenderism is the norm and causes exclusion for those who cannot or do not align with the normative ideals of cisgenderism.

Critical pedagogy: This pedagogy underscores the necessity of troubling normative assumptions and inclusivity of all individuals.

Gender: Different from sex, it is socially constructed terms such as male, female, and non-binary that individuals may use to describe themselves.

Heteronormativity: The presumed naturalness of heterosexuality and its ideals of monogamy, marriage, and reproduction.

Homonormativity: Like heteronormativity, for those who are LGBTQ-identified, it is the presumed naturalness of ideals such as monogamy, marriage, and reproduction.

Homophobia: Disdain, fear, and/or hatred of those who identify as lesbian, gay, bisexual, transgender, queer (LGBTQ).

Identity: In contrast to prior essentialist notions of identities as immutable characteristics of the self, a poststructuralist perspective approaches identities as multiple and discursively and performatively (re)produced.

Intersectionality: An approach that underscores how identities can intersect to produce multiple forms of oppression, exclusion, and discrimination encompassing identities related to race, class, gender, gender identity, sexuality, socioeconomic status, ethnicity, ability/(dis) ability, and beyond.

LGBTQQIP2SAA: lesbian, gay, bisexual, transgender, questioning, queer, intersex, pansexual, two-spirit (2S), androgynous, and asexual; often abbreviated to LGBTQ+.

Norm: A social rule that produces exclusion for those who do not adhere.

Out: This term refers to a person who has disclosed their sexual and/or gender identity with family members, friends, colleagues, and acquaintances.

Queer: Influenced by poststructuralism, queer is a way of troubling normal so as to upend normative assumptions that have produced what is permissible and thinkable. Also, *queer* can be employed to describe one's gender and sexual identities.

Queer linguistics: Utilizes the insights of queer theory and its notion of deconstruction to trouble cisheteronormativity linguistically.

Queer pedagogy: Drawing on the insights of queer theory, queer pedagogy asks us to destabilize our knowledges and to cultivate spaces in which knowledges can be co-constructed to make space for all identities to be included.

Queer theory: A disruption to essentialist understandings of gender and sexuality. In queer theory, gender and sexual identities are not an innate part of the self, but rather, are historical and cultural productions.

Sex: This term is utilized in relation to physiological and anatomical features that can be categorized in dichotomous terms such as male and female as well as intersex.

Sexuality: Refers to one's attraction to others of the same sex, different sex, or both.

www.ingramcontent.com/pod-product-compliance
Ingram Content Group UK Ltd.
Pitfield, Milton Keynes, MK11 3LW, UK
UKHW060611180726
13836UKWH00011B/2500